Learn Microservices with Spring Boot

A Practical Approach to RESTful Services using RabbitMQ, Eureka, Ribbon, Zuul and Cucumber

Moises Macero

Apress®

Learn Microservices with Spring Boot: A Practical Approach to RESTful Services using RabbitMQ, Eureka, Ribbon, Zuul and Cucumber

Moises Macero
New York, USA

ISBN-13 (pbk): 978-1-4842-3164-7   ISBN-13 (electronic): 978-1-4842-3165-4
https://doi.org/10.1007/978-1-4842-3165-4

Library of Congress Control Number: 2017962334

Cover image by Freepik (www.freepik.com)

Managing Director: Welmoed Spahr
Editorial Director: Todd Green
Acquisitions Editor: Steve Anglin
Development Editor: Matthew Moodie
Technical Reviewer: Manuel Jordan Elera
Coordinating Editor: Mark Powers
Copy Editor: Kezia Endsley

Distributed to the book trade worldwide by Springer Science+Business Media New York, 233 Spring Street, 6th Floor, New York, NY 10013. Phone 1-800-SPRINGER, fax (201) 348-4505, e-mail orders-ny@springer-sbm.com, or visit www.springeronline.com. Apress Media, LLC is a California LLC and the sole member (owner) is Springer Science + Business Media Finance Inc (SSBM Finance Inc). SSBM Finance Inc is a **Delaware** corporation.

For information on translations, please e-mail rights@apress.com, or visit http://www.apress.com/rights-permissions.

Apress titles may be purchased in bulk for academic, corporate, or promotional use. eBook versions and licenses are also available for most titles. For more information, reference our Print and eBook Bulk Sales web page at http://www.apress.com/bulk-sales.

Any source code or other supplementary material referenced by the author in this book is available to readers on GitHub via the book's product page, located at www.apress.com/9781484231647. For more detailed information, please visit http://www.apress.com/source-code.

Table of Contents

About the Author

Moises Macero has been a software developer since he was a kid. He has worked at big companies and also at startups, where being a full-stack developer was essential. During his career, Moises has most often worked in development, design, and architecture, for small and large projects, and in both Agile and waterfall environments. He likes working in teams where he can not only coach others but also learn from them.

Moises is also the author of the blog *thepracticaldeveloper.com*, where he shares with others solutions for technical challenges, guides and his view on ways of working in IT companies. In his free time, he enjoys traveling and hiking.

You can follow Moisés on his twitter account @moises_macero.

About the Technical Reviewer

Manuel Jordan Elera is an autodidactic developer and researcher who enjoys learning new technologies for his own experiments, which focus on finding new ways to integrate them.

Manuel won the 2010 Springy Award – Community Champion and Spring Champion 2013. In his little free time, he reads the Bible and composes music on his bass and guitar.

Manuel believes that constant education and training is essential for all developers. You can reach him mostly through his twitter account @dr_pompeii.

CHAPTER 1

Introduction

Setting the Scene

Microservices are getting very popular these days. It's not a surprise; this software architecture style has a lot of advantages, like flexibility and ease of scale. Mapping them into small teams in an organization also gives you a lot of efficiency in development. However, going on the adventure of microservices knowing only the benefits is a wrong call: you need to know what you are facing and be prepared for that in advance. You can get a lot of knowledge from many books and articles on the Internet but, when you get hands-on code, the story changes.

This book covers some of the most important concepts of microservices in a practical way, but not without explaining the concepts. First, we define a use case: an application to build. Then we start with a small monolith, based on some sound reasoning. Once we have the minimal application in place, we evaluate if it's worthy to move to microservices, and what would be a good way to do so. How should we communicate these different pieces? Then we can describe and introduce the event-driven architecture pattern to reach loose coupling by informing other parts of the system about *what happened* in your part of the process, instead of explicitly calling others to action. Once you have the microservices in place, you see in practice how the surrounding tools work: *service discovery, routing, etc.* We don't cover all of them at once but include them one by one, explaining the benefits of each for the application. Also, we analyze what would be a good way to test the distributed system, end-to-end.

© Moises Macero 2017
M. Macero, *Learn Microservices with Spring Boot*,
https://doi.org/10.1007/978-1-4842-3165-4_1

The advantage of going step-by-step, pausing when it's needed to settle down the concepts, is that *you will understand which problem each tool is trying to solve.* That's why the evolving example is an essential part of this book. You can also grasp the concepts without coding one single line: most of the source code is included so you can read it if you prefer.

The source code included in this book is available on the GitHub repository `https://github.com/microservices-practical`. It's divided into different versions, which makes it easier for you to see how the application evolves along the chapters. The book includes notes with the version that is being covered in that section.

Who Are You?

Let's first start with this: how interesting is this book going to be for you? This book is practical, so let's play this game. If you identify with any of these statements, this book might be good for you.

- I would like to learn how to build microservices with Spring Boot and how to use the related tools.

- Everybody is talking about microservices but I have no clue what a microservice is yet: either I read theoretical explanations or just hype-enforcing articles. I can't understand the advantages, even though I work in IT…

- I would like to learn how to design and develop Spring Boot applications, but people are recommending Don-Quixote-sized books,[1] sometimes even several of them. Is there any single source from which I can get a quick, practical grip on microservices without reading 1,000 pages?

---

[1]Don Quixote. Even though it is a long book, it is still a masterpiece.

- I got a new job, and they're using a microservices architecture. I've been working mainly in big, monolithic projects, so I'd like to have some knowledge and guidance to learn how everything works there.

- Every time I go to the cafeteria developers are talking about microservices... I can't socialize anymore with my colleagues if I don't get what they're saying. *Okay, this is a joke; don't read this book because of that, especially if you're not interested in programming.*

Regarding the knowledge required to read this book, the following topics should be familiar to you:

- Java (some code parts use Java 8 in this book)

- Spring (you don't need strong experience but you should know, at least, how dependency injection works)

- Maven (if you know Gradle, you'll be fine as well)

How Is This Book Different from Other Books and Guides?

Reasoning Behind the Techniques

Software developers and architects read many technical books and guides, either because we're interested in learning new technologies or just because we need it for our work. We need to do that anyway since it's a constantly-changing world. We can find all kinds of books and guides out there. Good ones are usually those from which you learn quickly, and ones that teach you not only how to do stuff, but also why you should do it that way. Using new techniques just because they're new is the wrong way to go about it; you need to understand the reasoning behind them so you use them in the best way possible.

This book uses that philosophy: it navigates through the code and design patterns, explaining the reasons to follow one way and not others.

Learning: An Incremental Process

If you look at the guides available on the Internet, you'll notice quickly that they are not real-life examples. Usually, when you apply those cases to more complex scenarios, they don't fit. Guides are too shallow to help you building something real.

Books, on the other hand, are much better at that. There are plenty of good books explaining concepts around an example; they are good because applying theoretical concepts to code is not always easy if you don't see the code. The problem with some of these books is that they're not as practical as guides. You need to read them first to understand the concepts, then code (or see) the example, which is frequently given as a whole piece. It's difficult to put into practice concepts when you see the final version directly. This book stays on the practical side and starts with code that evolves through refactoring, so the concepts are understood step-by-step. We cover the problem before exposing the solutions.

Because of this incremental way of presenting concepts, this book also allows you to code as you learn and to reflect on the challenges by yourself.

Is This a Guide or a Book?

The pages you have in front of you can't be called a guide: it won't take you 15 or 30 minutes to finish them. But this is not the typical book either, in which you go through concepts illustrated with some code fragments. Instead, you start with a version of the code that is not yet optimal, and you learn how to evolve it, after learning about the benefits you can extract from that process.

That does not mean that you can't just sit down and read it, but it's better if you code at the same time and play with the options and alternatives presented. That's the part of the book that makes it similar to a guide.

In any case, to keep it simple, from here onward we call this a book.

Contents
From the Basics to Advanced Topics

This book focuses first on some basics about how to design and implement a production-ready Spring Boot application using well-known architecture patterns (Chapters 2 and 3). From there, it takes you through the journey of tools and frameworks related to microservices with the introduction of a second piece of functionality in a different Spring Boot app (Chapters 4 and 5). It also shows you how to support such a distributed system with end-to-end integration tests (Chapter 6).

If you already know how to design Spring Boot applications, you can go quickly through Chapters 2 and 3 and focus more on the second part of the book. There, we cover topics like service discovery, routing, event-driven design, testing with Cucumber, etc. However, pay attention to the strategy we set up in the first part—test-driven development, the focus on the minimum viable product (MVP), and monolith-first.

Skeleton with Spring Boot, the Professional Way

First, the book guides you through the creation of an application using Spring Boot. It's mainly focused on the backend side, but you will create a simple web page to demonstrate how to expose functionality as a REST API.

It's important to point out that we don't create "shortcut code" just to see Spring Boot running: that's not the objective of this book. We use Spring Boot as a vehicle to teach concepts, but we could use any other technique, and the ideas of this book would still be valid.

You learn how to design and implement the application following the well-known three-tier, three-layer pattern. You do this supported by an incremental example, with hands-on code. The result will be more than enough for you to understand the professional way of writing applications.

5

Test-Driven Development

We use TDD to map the prerequisites presented to technical features (like you should do in real life). TDD is a technique that sometimes can't be used at work (for many different reasons, none technical). But this book tries to show it in a way that you can see the benefits from the beginning: why it's always a good idea to think about the test cases before writing your code. *AssertJ* and *Mockito* will serve us to build useful tests efficiently.

The plan is the following: you'll learn how to create the tests first, then make them fail, and finally implement the logic to make them work.

Connecting Microservices

Once you have your first application ready, we introduce a second one that will interact with the existing functionality. From that moment on, you'll have a *microservices architecture*. It doesn't make any sense to try to understand the advantages of microservices if you only have one of them. The real-life scenarios are always distributed systems with functionality split into different services. As usual, to keep it practical, you'll see how moving to microservices fits your needs.

The book covers not only the reasons to split the system but also what the disadvantages are that come with that choice. And once you make the decision, you'll learn which tools you should use to make the system work as a whole, and not as isolated services: service discovery, API gateway, load balancing, and some other supporting tools.

Event-Driven System

An additional concept that does not always accompany microservices is an *event-driven architecture*. This book uses it since it's a pattern that fits very well into a microservice architecture, and you'll make your choice based on good examples.

This asynchronous way of thinking introduces new ways of designing code; you'll look at it while coding your project, using RabbitMQ to support it.

End-to-End Testing

If you want to code your project the professional way, you need to have a production-ready mindset, so we'll cover this functionality with tests. We explain how to tackle the trickiest ones in a microservices architecture: the end-to-end tests. We'll use Cucumber since it's a framework that fits perfectly in many projects, filling the gap between the business requirements and the test development. Even though nobody should need reasons here to be convinced of why it is a good idea to have a proper test base, we explain them to keep the testing skeptics happy.

Summary

This chapter introduced the main goals of this book: to teach you the main aspects of a microservices architecture, by starting simple and then growing your knowledge through the development of a sample project.

We also covered briefly the main contents of the book: from monolith-first to microservices with Spring Boot, Test-Driven Development, Event-Driven Systems and End-to-End testing with Cucumber.

Next chapter will start with the first step of our learning path: a basic Spring Boot application.

CHAPTER 2

The Basic Spring Boot Application

Business Requirements

We could start writing code directly but that, even being pragmatic, would be far from being a real case. Software should have a goal: in this case, we do it purely for the fact of learning but, anyway, we'll give it a reason (a fictional one). This requirements-oriented approach is used throughout the book to make it more practical.

We want to write an application to encourage users to train their math skills every day. To begin with, we will have two-digit multiplications presented to users, one every time they access the page. They will type their alias (a short name) and the result of the operation, and for that they should use only mental calculation. After they send the data, a success or failure result will be presented.

In order to motivate the users, we will also introduce some simple gamification techniques: a ranking of users based on points they get when they try the calculation every day, and also when they succeed. We will show this on the results page.

This is the main idea of the whole application we will build (our *vision*) and this book will emulate an Agile way of working in which requirements come in the form of user stories. Agile, in spite of being criticized by many software developers, has become the standard methodology applied in

© Moises Macero 2017
M. Macero, *Learn Microservices with Spring Boot*,
https://doi.org/10.1007/978-1-4842-3165-4_2

a vast majority of IT companies. The reality is that, when implemented properly, it's a way of working that allows teams to deliver software that can be used as early as possible and to get a valuable feedback out of it.

Supported by Agile, we start simple, and then we build on top of that. Consider the first user story here.

USER STORY 1

As a user of the application, I want to be presented with a random multiplication that I can solve online—not too easy, so I can use mental calculation and make my brain work every day.

To make this work, we'll split the user story into several sub-tasks:

1. Create a basic service with the business logic.

2. Create a basic API endpoint to access this service (REST API).

3. Create a basic web page to ask the users to solve that calculation.

The Skeleton App

Skinny vs. Real-Life Apps

The first thing you'll find if you search *Spring Boot tutorial* on Google is the *Getting Started* guide from Pivotal (see https://spring.io/guides/gs/spring-boot/). Following the guide, you can build a Hello World (or *Greetings*) app, but that's not exciting when you already have some experience in software development. If you look for something more challenging, you'll find yourself diving into many other official *Getting Started* guides that, despite being really useful, are totally disconnected and don't provide real-life code examples. They help you build *skinny apps*.

Don't take this wrong: these guides are very useful for daily work. For example, you may not remember how to set up a RabbitMQ listener, and in that case, you can scan these guides for a quick answer. The main goal of such guides is to provide you with a quick example (that normally might take around 15 minutes) that covers the basics you need to set up the different functionalities of Spring Boot. Because of that, the applications are sometimes built with shortcuts, like having all the code in the same class or inserting data through command-line runners.

As you already know, the objective of this book is to help go further, using Spring Boot to build applications that are closer to real-life cases. You learn how to combine the different technologies together and set up a code with no shortcuts, following good practices and including a proper testing coverage.

Creating the Skeleton

Hands-on code! The first thing you do is create a Spring Boot application skeleton that will serve as the reference during the book. There are several ways to do this. Navigate to the *Spring Initializr* web site at `http://start.spring.io/` and generate a project from there (see Figure 2-1).

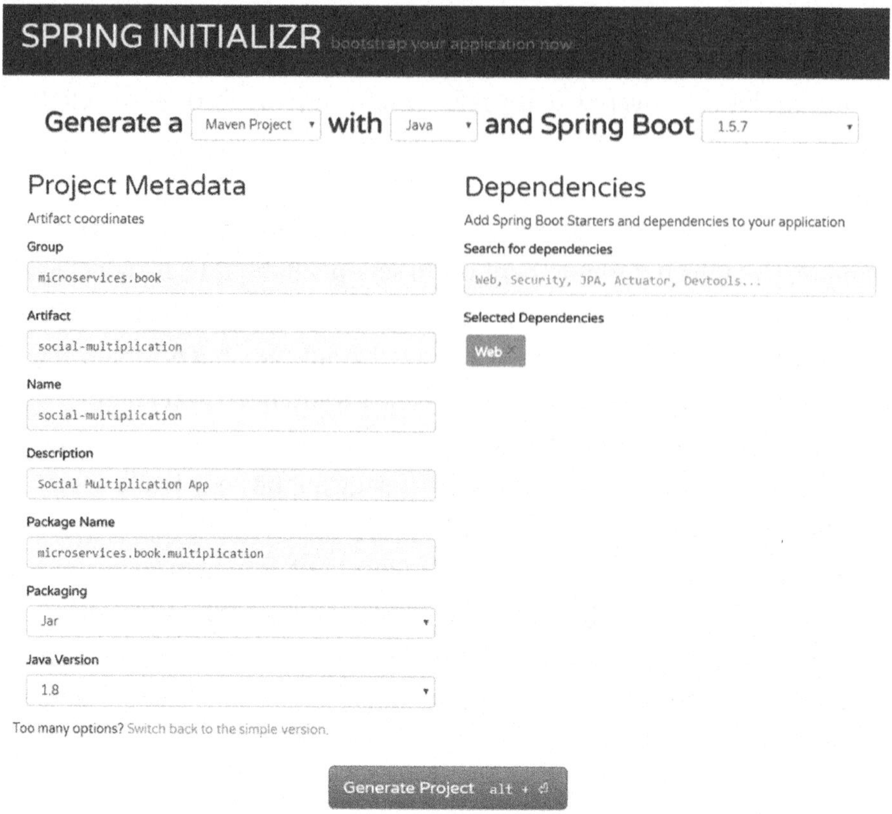

Figure 2-1. *The Spring Initializr web site helps you create a basic application*

Let's give some values to the Group (`microservices.book`) and to the Artifact (`social-multiplication`). Now click on Switch to the Full Version and change the package name to `microservices.book.multiplication`. Enter a custom description if you want. Then, under dependencies, select Web. The last step is to select the Spring Boot version, 1.5.7 in this case. That's all you need for now. Leave the other settings as they are, as you'll work with Maven and Java.

Generate the project and extract the ZIP contents. The `social-multiplication-v1` folder contains everything you need to run your app, including a Maven wrapper (mvnw) that you can execute from the source folder. If you prefer, you can use your own Maven installation instead.

Now you can use your favorite shell to run the application with this command:

```
$ mvnw spring-boot:run
```

Your application will start. The last line you should see there is something like this:

```
m.book.SocialMultiplicationApplication   : Started
SocialMultiplicationApplication in 2.385 seconds
(JVM running for 6.07)
```

This app, as you might have guessed, is not practical yet. There is no functionality in there, even though it's *occupying* a port at 8080. But it's useful to generate the skeleton project this way, having the Maven configuration in place and the root packages.

RUNNING THE SPRING BOOT APP

From here onward, it will be assumed that you know how to run the Spring Boot application. It's also recommended that you use your preferred IDE to work with the code or import the Maven projects (Eclipse, IntelliJ, Spring Tool Suite, etc.). The most popular IDEs have good integration with Spring Boot and Maven and allow you to run it directly without typing anything in the command line. If you need more help with this, just visit the official guides for these integrated development environments.

Warming Up: Some TDD in Action

Test-driven development is based on writing the application tests before the main code logic, making these tests fail first, and then writing the code to make them pass.

WHY IS TDD GOOD FOR DEVELOPERS?

There are many reasons why, but the most important one is that TDD forces you and the business person to think about the prerequisites in a *deeper way*. This includes thinking about what the code should do under certain situations or use cases. It will help you clarify vague prerequisites and reject invalid ones.

However, there is one idea usually associated with TDD that sometimes is taken to the extreme: continuous refactoring of code in several iterations. You should find a balance—it's not a good idea to write poor quality, unmaintainable code just to make the tests pass and then later refactor them.

Let's start thinking about what we need. We'll start with `MultiplicationServiceTest`, in which we want to check that a `Multiplication` has been generated. The `Multiplication` class is shown in Listing 2-1.

SOURCE CODE AVAILABLE WITH THE BOOK

You can find the code in this chapter in the `v1` repository on GitHub at `https://github.com/microservices-practical`.

Listing 2-1. Multiplication.java (social-multiplication v1)

```java
package microservices.book.multiplication.domain;

/**
 * This class represents a Multiplication in our application.
 */
public class Multiplication {
```

```java
// Both factors
private int factorA;
private int factorB;

// The result of the operation A * B
private int result;

public Multiplication(int factorA, int factorB) {
    this.factorA = factorA;
    this.factorB = factorB;
    this.result = factorA * factorB;
}

public int getFactorA() {
    return factorA;
}

public int getFactorB() {
    return factorB;
}

public int getResult() {
    return result;
}

@Override
public String toString() {
    return "Multiplication{" +
            "factorA=" + factorA +
            ", factorB=" + factorB +
            ", result(A*B)=" + result +
            '}';
}
}
```

Simple. It's a basic class, and it contains the result as well. There is no need to calculate it all the time across the application.

We define also the service interface, as shown in Listing 2-2.

Listing 2-2. MultiplicationService.java (social-multiplication v1)

```
package microservices.book.multiplication.service;

import microservices.book.multiplication.domain.Multiplication;

public interface MultiplicationService {

    /**
      * Creates a Multiplication object with two randomly-
      generated factors
      * between 11 and 99.
      *
      * @return a Multiplication object with random factors
      */
    Multiplication createRandomMultiplication();

}
```

Also, because we want to *generate random multiplications*, we create a service to provide random factors (see Listing 2-3). That will help us write proper tests; it would be much more difficult if we use Random inside the service implementation.

Listing 2-3. RandomGeneratorService.java (social-multiplication v1)

```
package microservices.book.multiplication.service;

public interface RandomGeneratorService {
```

```
/**
 * @return a randomly-generated factor. It's always a
 number between 11 and 99.
 */
int generateRandomFactor();
```

}

Once you have the interfaces you need, you can write the first test version, as shown in Listing 2-4.

Listing 2-4. MultiplicationServiceTest.java (social-multiplication v1)

```
package microservices.book.multiplication.service;

import microservices.book.multiplication.domain.Multiplication;
import org.junit.Test;
import org.junit.runner.RunWith;
import org.springframework.beans.factory.annotation.Autowired;
import org.springframework.boot.test.context.SpringBootTest;
import org.springframework.boot.test.mock.mockito.MockBean;
import org.springframework.test.context.junit4.SpringRunner;

import static org.assertj.core.api.Assertions.assertThat;
import static org.mockito.BDDMockito.given;

@RunWith(SpringRunner.class)
@SpringBootTest
public class MultiplicationServiceTest {

    @MockBean
    private RandomGeneratorService randomGeneratorService;

    @Autowired
    private MultiplicationService multiplicationService;
```

```java
@Test
public void createRandomMultiplicationTest() {
    // given (our mocked Random Generator service will
    return first 50, then 30)
    given(randomGeneratorService.generateRandomFactor()).
    willReturn(50, 30);

    // when
    Multiplication multiplication = multiplicationService.
    createRandomMultiplication();

    // then
    assertThat(multiplication.getFactorA()).isEqualTo(50);
    assertThat(multiplication.getFactorB()).isEqualTo(30);
    assertThat(multiplication.getResult()).isEqualTo(1500);
    }
}
```

The @MockBean annotation is important in this test: it tells Spring to inject a mock of the RandomGeneratorService bean, instead of letting it search for a suitable implementation of the interface (which doesn't exist yet).

We're using some benefits of both Mockito and Spring Boot to make a simple, concise unit test. We're also using behavior-driven development (BDD, supported by MockitoBDD) to define what should happen when RandomGeneratorService is called. That makes the test even easier to read, which is great for the goal we have: getting help from the person defining our requirements to build the use cases.

If we only write these three classes and execute the test, it will obviously fail, since there is no implementation of MultiplicationService to test. Again, that's exactly the point of TDD—we wrote the specs first, then validate those with a business analyst (like a Product Owner in Scrum; see https://tpd.io/prd-own), and then list which other cases should be covered. All of this with no implementation of the solution.

Once the test (requirement) is clear, we write the solution, as shown in Listing 2-5.

Listing 2-5. MultiplicationServiceImpl.java (social-multiplication v1)

```java
package microservices.book.multiplication.service;

import microservices.book.multiplication.domain.Multiplication;
import org.springframework.beans.factory.annotation.Autowired;
import org.springframework.stereotype.Service;

@Service
class MultiplicationServiceImpl implements
MultiplicationService {

    private RandomGeneratorService randomGeneratorService;

    @Autowired
    public MultiplicationServiceImpl(RandomGeneratorService
    randomGeneratorService) {
        this.randomGeneratorService = randomGeneratorService;
    }

    @Override
    public Multiplication createRandomMultiplication() {
        int factorA = randomGeneratorService.
        generateRandomFactor();
        int factorB = randomGeneratorService.
        generateRandomFactor();
        return new Multiplication(factorA, factorB);
    }
}
```

No surprises here either; it's simple. Now you can run the test successfully with the following command line (or you can also use your preferred IDE):

```
$ mvnw -Dtest=MultiplicationServiceTest test
```

YOU COWBOY! THE APPLICATION FAILS...

If you try to run all the tests instead of just `MultiplicationServiceTest`, you'll get an error (`No qualifying bean of type 'microservices.book.multiplication.service.RandomGeneratorService' available`). The reason is that, by default when you create the app from Spring Initializr, the package includes an empty `SocialMultiplicationApplicationTests` that tries to load the full application context. The same thing happens if you try to run the application. When loading the context, Spring will try to find an implementation of `RandomGeneratorService` to inject, but there is none. This doesn't mean you're doing cowboy development, you're just using an advantage of TDD—you test as you develop, even if you don't have the full application up and running yet.

Let's review the advantages of the TDD approach:

- We translate the requirements to code (by creating our test), and that forces us to think about what we need and what we don't need. So far we only need to generate a random multiplication; it's our first business requirement.

- We build testable code. Imagine that we would have started coding without having the test. It would have been easier to include the random generation logic directly inside the `MultiplicationService` implementation, making it really difficult to test afterward since the test would use random numbers, thus being unpredictable. By having to write the test in advance, we force ourselves to think of a good way to verify the functionality, coming up with the separate logic in `RandomGeneratorService`.

- Note that we didn't need to write the implementation of `RandomGeneratorService`. We can focus first on what's most important and later implement the helper services. We leave the `RandomGeneratorService` implementation for the next chapter.

Summary

The main goal of this chapter was to introduce the requirements and the test-driven development approach you'll follow in this book. You created a Spring Boot application by developing some basic functionality using TDD.

The chapter also set the stage for you to think in an *Agile* way, which is used more and more in software companies because of its benefits. You took some time to refine your first business requirement, split it into sub-tasks, and thought about a first *unit test*.

The next chapter goes much more into practical work: you'll create the first complete version of this application, including a simple UI. You'll do that using good design practices from the beginning: a three-tier, layered software that will give you the flexibility to evolve your application.

CHAPTER 3

A Real Three-Tier Spring Boot Application

Introduction

A multitier architecture will provide our application with a more production-ready look. Most of the real-world applications follow this architecture pattern and, to be more specific, the three-tier design is the most popular one and widely extended among web applications. The three tiers are:

- *Client tier*: Responsible for the user interface. Typically what we call the frontend.

- *Application tier*: It contains all the business logic together with the interfaces to interact with it and the data interfaces for persistence. This maps with what we call the backend.

- *Data Store tier*: It's the database, file system, etc., that persists the application's data.

© Moises Macero 2017
M. Macero, *Learn Microservices with Spring Boot*,
https://doi.org/10.1007/978-1-4842-3165-4_3

In this book we're mainly focused on the application tier, although we'll use the other two as well. If now we zoom in, that application tier is commonly designed using three layers:

- *Business layer*: The classes that model our domain and the business specifics. It's where the intelligence of the application resides. Normally, it will be composed of entities (our `Multiplication`) and Services providing business logic (like our `MultiplicationService`). Sometimes this layer is divided in two parts: domains (entities) and applications (services).

- *Presentation layer*: In our case, it will be represented by the `Controller` classes, which will provide functionality to the Web client. Our REST API implementation will reside here.

- *Data layer*: It will be responsible for persisting our entities in a data storage, usually a database. It can typically include Data Access Object (DAO) classes, which work with direct representation of the database model, or `Repository` classes, which are domain-centric and translate from domains down to the database layer (so they could use DAOs whenever they don't match).

The architecture pattern shown in Figure 3-1 is used in our application while we develop the required functionalities.

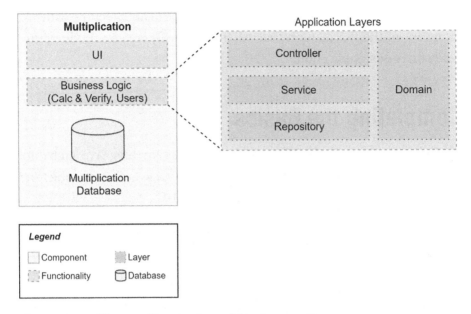

Figure 3-1. *The application's architecture pattern*

The advantages of using this software architecture are intrinsically related to the fact of decoupling layers. Let's summarize three important advantages:

- The domain part is isolated and independent from the solution, instead of mixed with interface or database specifics.

- Non-business layers are interchangeable (like for instance changing the database for a file storage solution, or changing from REST to any other interface).

- There is a clear separation of responsibilities: a class to handle database storage of the objects, a separate class for the REST API implementation, and another class for the business logic.

Spring is an excellent option to build this type of architecture, with many out-of-the-box features that will help us easily create a production-ready three-tier application.

Completing the Basics

Before continuing with the layering... did we miss anything? We left behind the implementation of our RandomGeneratorService. Let's create the test for it since we know what to expect. See Listing 3-1.

SOURCE CODE AVAILABLE WITH THE BOOK: V2

You can find the chapter's code in the v2 repository on GitHub:
https://github.com/microservices-practical.

Listing 3-1. RandomGeneratorServiceTest.java (social-multiplication v2)

```java
package microservices.book.multiplication.service;

import org.junit.Test;
import org.junit.runner.RunWith;
import org.springframework.beans.factory.annotation.Autowired;
import org.springframework.boot.test.context.SpringBootTest;
import org.springframework.test.context.junit4.SpringRunner;

import java.util.List;
import java.util.stream.Collectors;
import java.util.stream.IntStream;
```

```
import static org.assertj.core.api.Assertions.assertThat;

@RunWith(SpringRunner.class)
@SpringBootTest
public class RandomGeneratorServiceTest {

    @Autowired
    private RandomGeneratorService randomGeneratorService;

    @Test
    public void generateRandomFactorIsBetweenExpectedLimits()
    throws Exception {
        // when a good sample of randomly generated factors is
        generated
        List<Integer> randomFactors = IntStream.range(0, 1000)
                .map(i -> randomGeneratorService.
                generateRandomFactor())
                .boxed().collect(Collectors.toList());

        // then all of them should be between 11 and 100
        // because we want a middle-complexity calculation
        assertThat(randomFactors).containsOnlyElementsOf
        (IntStream.range(11, 100)
                .boxed().collect(Collectors.toList()));
    }

}
```

We use a Java 8 Stream of the first 1000 numbers to mimic a for loop. Then, we transform each number with map to a random int factor, we box each one to an Integer object, and finally we collect them into a list. The test checks that all of them are within the expected range that we define using a similar approach.

```
PRODUCTION READINESS: DON'T OVERUSE SPRINGBOOT TESTS
```

We've created both tests as @SpringBoot tests, running with
SpringRunner, which causes the application context to be initialized,
therefore having the beans injected. Luckily, context is being cached and
reused by Spring, so it's loaded only once per suite.[1]

This is an example of how Internet guides can be confusing sometimes. We don't
need dependency injection nor the application context to test the functionalities
of these classes; in these situations, it's better not to use @SpringBoot and just
test the implementation classes: build *real* unit tests that verify only one class.
We use tests with a Spring context for a different type of testing—integration
tests, which are intended to verify interactions between more than a class.
Even with context reuse, if we use @SpringBootTest, we're wasting time
loading resources and we have to make sure we roll back transactions and clean
the Spring application context to avoid side-effects.

Keeping that in mind, let's create an extra class for a real unit test
that doesn't need a Spring context to be executed (note the name change
since we're testing directly the implementation). We can safely remove
RandomGeneratorServiceTest since it's covering the same test (although you
can see them both in the v2 folder for educational purposes). See Listing 3-2.

Listing 3-2. RandomGeneratorServiceImplTest.java (social-
multiplication v2)

```
package microservices.book.multiplication.service;

import org.junit.Before;
import org.junit.Test;
```

---

[1]https://docs.spring.io/spring/docs/current/spring-framework-
reference/testing.html#testing-ctx-management

```
import java.util.List;
import java.util.stream.Collectors;
import java.util.stream.IntStream;

import static org.assertj.core.api.Assertions.assertThat;

public class RandomGeneratorServiceImplTest {

    private RandomGeneratorServiceImpl
randomGeneratorServiceImpl;

    @Before
    public void setUp() {
        randomGeneratorServiceImpl = new
        RandomGeneratorServiceImpl();
    }

    @Test
    public void generateRandomFactorIsBetweenExpectedLimits()
    throws Exception {
        // when a good sample of randomly generated factors is
        generated
        List<Integer> randomFactors = IntStream.range(0, 1000)
                .map(i -> randomGeneratorServiceImpl.
                generateRandomFactor())
                .boxed().collect(Collectors.toList());

        // then all of them should be between 11 and 100
        // because we want a middle-complexity calculation
        assertThat(randomFactors).containsOnlyElementsOf(IntStr
        eam.range(11, 100)
                .boxed().collect(Collectors.toList()));
    }

}
```

Do you see any disadvantage? Well, there is a small one: now we can't avoid generating the RandomGeneratorServiceImpl class, but the implementation of our method can return 0 to start with. See Listing 3-3.

Listing 3-3. RandomGeneratorServiceImpl.java: Temporary Solution (social-multiplication v2)

```
package microservices.book.multiplication.service;

import org.springframework.stereotype.Service;
import java.util.Random;

@Service
class RandomGeneratorServiceImpl implements
RandomGeneratorService {
    @Override
    public int generateRandomFactor() {
        return 0;
    }
}
```

Then we have our failing test compiling and waiting for us to write a proper implementation, as shown in Listing 3-4.

Listing 3-4. Console: Running RandomGeneratorServiceImplTest (social-multiplication v2)

```
$ mvnw test -Dtest=RandomGeneratorServiceImplTest
[...]
-------------------------------------------------
 T E S T S
-------------------------------------------------
Running microservices.book.multiplication.service.
RandomGeneratorServiceImplTest
```

```
Tests run: 1, Failures: 1, Errors: 0, Skipped: 0, Time elapsed:
0.109 sec <<< FAILURE! - in microservices.book.multiplication.
service.RandomGeneratorServiceImplTest
generateRandomFactorIsBetweenExpectedLimits(microservices.book.
multiplication.service.RandomGeneratorServiceImplTest)  Time
elapsed: 0.108 sec  <<< FAILURE!
java.lang.AssertionError: [...]
```

Let's make it pass! We need to give it a little bit more logic than just returning zero, as shown in Listing 3-5.

Listing 3-5. RandomGeneratorServiceImpl.java (social-multiplication v2)

```java
package microservices.book.multiplication.service;

import org.springframework.stereotype.Service;
import java.util.Random;

@Service
class RandomGeneratorServiceImpl implements
RandomGeneratorService {

    final static int MINIMUM_FACTOR = 11;
    final static int MAXIMUM_FACTOR = 99;

    @Override
    public int generateRandomFactor() {
        return new Random().nextInt((MAXIMUM_FACTOR - MINIMUM_
        FACTOR) + 1) + MINIMUM_FACTOR;
    }
}
```

Now, if we execute mvnw test -Dtest=RandomGeneratorServiceImpl
Test again, the test will pass. Great! And, since we have a better approach
to do unit testing, we need to do the same with MultiplicationService.
Let's create MultiplicationServiceImplTest and apply this knowledge
there as well, as shown in Listing 3-6.

Listing 3-6. MultiplicationServiceImplTest.java
(social-multiplication v2)

```java
package microservices.book.multiplication.service;

import microservices.book.multiplication.domain.Multiplication;
import org.junit.Before;
import org.junit.Test;
import org.mockito.Mock;
import org.mockito.MockitoAnnotations;

import static org.assertj.core.api.Assertions.assertThat;
import static org.mockito.BDDMockito.given;

public class MultiplicationServiceImplTest {

    private MultiplicationServiceImpl
multiplicationServiceImpl;

    @Mock
    private RandomGeneratorService randomGeneratorService;

    @Before
    public void setUp() {
        // With this call to initMocks we tell Mockito to
        process the annotations
        MockitoAnnotations.initMocks(this);
        multiplicationServiceImpl = new MultiplicationServiceImpl
        (randomGeneratorService);
    }
```

```java
@Test
public void createRandomMultiplicationTest() {
    // given (our mocked Random Generator service will
    return first 50, then 30)
    given(randomGeneratorService.generateRandomFactor()).
    willReturn(50, 30);

    // when
    Multiplication multiplication =
    multiplicationServiceImpl.createRandomMultiplication();

    // assert
    assertThat(multiplication.getFactorA()).isEqualTo(50);
    assertThat(multiplication.getFactorB()).isEqualTo(30);
    assertThat(multiplication.getResult()).isEqualTo(1500);
    }
}
```

Note that we don't inject a mock bean with @MockBean but just use the plain @Mock annotation to create a mock service, which we then programmatically use to construct the MultiplicationServiceImpl object.

At this point, we can also run the full suite of tests in the application with mvnw test, and see how all of them pass.

Designing the Domain

Prior to starting the development process, it's important to have a clear picture of the business domain, including the different *objects* (in the most generic sense of the word) you can identify in your system and how they relate. This exercise must be done as soon as possible when you're designing software. It will be the heart of your system and therefore the most difficult part to change.

Given our requirements, we can identify the following business objects:

- Multiplication: Contains the factors of the operation.

- User: Identifies the user who will try to solve a Multiplication.

- MultiplicationResultAttempt: Contains a reference to the Multiplication and a reference to the User, together with the value submitted (the attempt to solve the operation) and the actual result.

SOURCE CODE AVAILABLE WITH THE BOOK: V3

You can find these domain entities modeled in the v3 repository on GitHub: https://github.com/microservices-practical.

Immutability and Lombok

We'll see in a moment that the Multiplication class is final, and so are its fields, which are accessible only with *getters*. That makes our class immutable. Immutability comes with a lot of benefits, the most important being that it saves you a lot of potential problems when working with a multi-threaded system. If you want to know more about the advantages of immutability, visit https://en.wikipedia.org/wiki/Immutable_object.

We also include Lombok in our code, by adding an extra dependency in the pom.xml file (see https://projectlombok.org/). It's an annotation processor that will generate code before the compiler runs. What are the advantages of that? You can keep your classes small, removing all the boilerplate parts: getters, constructors, toString, hashCode, equals, etc. They are all replaced with annotations. There are even some shortcuts for grouping several of them (like @Data). The main disadvantage is that if your IDE doesn't have a plugin that supports Lombok, the code assistant won't work and the IDE integrated compiler will complain. However, there are plugins for the most important ones. (From the home page, use the menu to navigate to Install ➤ IDEs ➤ your preferred IDE.)

We'll use Lombok from here onward since it's also more convenient when looking at the code inside these pages, but it's up to you to keep your POJOs with all the rest of the code if you want to do so.

Adding Lombok to the project is as easy as including a new dependency in the pom.xml file, as shown in Listing 3-7.

Listing 3-7. pom.xml: Adding Lombok (social-multiplication v3)

```
<dependency>
  <groupId>org.projectlombok</groupId>
  <artifactId>lombok</artifactId>
  <version>1.16.12</version>
</dependency>
```

Listings 3-8 through 3-10 show how to implement the domain entities in Java using Lombok.

Listing 3-8. Multiplication.java (social-multiplication v3)

```
package microservices.book.multiplication.domain;

import lombok.EqualsAndHashCode;
import lombok.Getter;
import lombok.RequiredArgsConstructor;
import lombok.ToString;

/**
 * This represents a Multiplication (a * b).
 */
@RequiredArgsConstructor
@Getter
@ToString
```

```java
@EqualsAndHashCode
public final class Multiplication {

    // Both factors
    private final int factorA;
    private final int factorB;

    // Empty constructor for JSON (de)serialization
    Multiplication() {
        this(0, 0);
    }
}
```

Listing 3-9. User.java (social-multiplication v3)

```java
package microservices.book.multiplication.domain;

import lombok.EqualsAndHashCode;
import lombok.Getter;
import lombok.RequiredArgsConstructor;
import lombok.ToString;

/**
 * Stores information to identify the user.
 */
@RequiredArgsConstructor
@Getter
@ToString
@EqualsAndHashCode
public final class User {

    private final String alias;

    // Empty constructor for JSON (de)serialization
    protected User() {
```

```
        alias = null;
    }
}
```

Listing 3-10. MultiplicationResultAttempt.java (social-multiplication v3)

```java
package microservices.book.multiplication.domain;

import lombok.EqualsAndHashCode;
import lombok.Getter;
import lombok.RequiredArgsConstructor;
import lombok.ToString;

/**
 * Identifies the attempt from a {@link User} to solve a
 * {@link Multiplication}.
 */
@RequiredArgsConstructor
@Getter
@ToString
@EqualsAndHashCode
public final class MultiplicationResultAttempt {

    private final User user;
    private final Multiplication multiplication;
    private final int resultAttempt;

    // Empty constructor for JSON (de)serialization
    MultiplicationResultAttempt() {
        user = null;
        multiplication = null;
        resultAttempt = -1;
    }

}
```

- @RequiredArgsConstructor generates a constructor taking all the final fields.

- @Getter generates all the getters for our fields.

- @ToString includes a human-friendly toString() method in our class.

- @EqualsAndHashCode creates the equals() and hashCode() methods.

The Business Logic Layer

Once you have the domain model defined, it's time think about the other part of the business logic: the *application services*. Having a look at our requirements, we need:

- Some functionality to check if an attempt is correct or not

- A way of generating a mid-complexity multiplication

We'll include this new logic in the existing service layer. We already did the part to generate multiplications in the previous chapter (located in the service layer package), so Listing 3-11 shows how to implement the logic to verify the attempts (the checkAttempt method).

Listing 3-11. MultiplicationService.java (social-multiplication v3)

```
package microservices.book.multiplication.service;

import microservices.book.multiplication.domain.Multiplication;
import microservices.book.multiplication.domain.
MultiplicationResultAttempt;
```

```java
public interface MultiplicationService {

    /**
     * Generates a random {@link Multiplication} object.
     *
     * @return a multiplication of randomly generated numbers
     */
    Multiplication createRandomMultiplication();

    /**
     * @return true if the attempt matches the result of the
     *          multiplication, false otherwise.
     */
    boolean checkAttempt(final MultiplicationResultAttempt
    resultAttempt);
}
```

Since we're doing TDD, we'll create a dummy implementation that will always result in a wrong attempt, as shown in Listing 3-12.

Listing 3-12. MultiplicationServiceImpl.java Temporary Solution (social-multiplication v3)

```java
@Override
public boolean checkAttempt(final MultiplicationResultAttempt
resultAttempt) {
    return false;
}
```

Then we code our new test methods, knowing that one of them (checking a successful result) will fail, so we need to go back to the implementation and make it pass according to the use cases (see Listing 3-13). Again TDD in practice!

Listing 3-13. MultiplicationServiceImplTest.java
(social-multiplication v3)

```java
@Test
public void checkCorrectAttemptTest() {
    // given
    Multiplication multiplication = new Multiplication(50, 60);
    User user = new User("john_doe");
    MultiplicationResultAttempt attempt = new Multiplication
    ResultAttempt(user, multiplication, 3000);

    // when
    boolean attemptResult = multiplicationServiceImpl.check
    Attempt(attempt);

    // assert
    assertThat(attemptResult).isTrue();
}

@Test
public void checkWrongAttemptTest() {
    // given
    Multiplication multiplication = new Multiplication(50, 60);
    User user = new User("john_doe");
    MultiplicationResultAttempt attempt = new Multiplication
    ResultAttempt(user, multiplication, 3010);

    // when
    boolean attemptResult = multiplicationServiceImpl.check
    Attempt(attempt);

    // assert
    assertThat(attemptResult).isFalse();
}
```

Tests are done and ready, so let's go back and build the real stuff. As you probably imagined, this is the real implementation of the method that provides the real logic. See Listing 3-14.

Listing 3-14. MultiplicationServiceImpl.java New Method (social-multiplication v3)

```
@Override
public boolean checkAttempt(final MultiplicationResultAttempt
resultAttempt) {
    return resultAttempt.getResultAttempt() ==
            resultAttempt.getMultiplication().getFactorA() *
            resultAttempt.getMultiplication().getFactorB();
}
```

In the v3 code folder, you can also find the RandomGeneratorService interface and the corresponding implementation, as was covered in the previous chapter.

The Presentation Layer (REST API)

Now that we have our domain entities and our simple business logic in place, we'll expose the supported interactions through a REST API so a Web client or any other application can interact with our functionality. REST is a well-known standard for web services in the industry because of its simplicity: it's just basic interfaces on top of HTTP.

It's important to note here that we don't strictly need a REST layer for our application since we could use Spring MVC[2] and then return the view names and rendering our models directly in HTML or any other view layer implementation. But then we would need to design views in our codebase. That would make it harder to change the UI technology (for instance migrating to AngularJS or having a mobile app). Besides,

---

[2]https://docs.spring.io/spring/docs/current/spring-framework-reference/html/mvc.html

with REST, we're providing an interface that doesn't require an UI, just basic HTTP. Furthermore, this same API can be accessed from a different backend service in the future (e.g., if another application wants to get a random multiplication).

Spring has good support to build a REST API in a very fast manner, but keep in mind that you should follow some conventions for URLs and HTTP verbs that have become the de facto standard (see *http://tpd.io/ rest-methods*). In this book, we'll use these standard mappings of actions to URLs and HTTP verbs.

What are the interfaces that we want to expose for this application? We can get them from the requirements:

- We want users to solve a multiplication so we want to read a random, medium complexity multiplication as consumers of the REST API.

- In order to solve the multiplication, we want to send a result for a given multiplication, and because we want to know who is solving it, we want to send it together with the user's alias.

So far that's what we need: a read operation and a send action. After having clarified the interactions, we can design our REST API, keeping in mind the standards:

- `GET /multiplications/random` will return the random multiplication.

- `POST /results/` will be our endpoint to send results.

- `GET /results?user=[user_alias]` will be our way of retrieving results of a particular user.

As you can see, we design the API in two main contexts for the endpoints: `multiplications` and `results`. This is a good practice. Don't try to put everything into the same context and controller. It's better to separate interfaces based on the business entities they relate to. We'll create two different `Controller` classes.

The Multiplication Controller

Let's follow TDD again and write the unit test as usual. First, we need an empty implementation of the controller class to compile the code, as shown in Listing 3-15.

Listing 3-15. MultiplicationController.java Initial Version (social-multiplication v3)

```
package microservices.book.multiplication.controller;

import microservices.book.multiplication.service.
        MultiplicationService;
import org.springframework.beans.factory.annotation.Autowired;
import org.springframework.web.bind.annotation.RestController;

@RestController
public class MultiplicationController {

    private final MultiplicationService multiplicationService;

    @Autowired
    public MultiplicationController(final MultiplicationService
            multiplicationService) {
        this.multiplicationService = multiplicationService;
    }

}
```

Now we build the unit test to check that the `MultiplicationController` will return a random multiplication when performing a GET to the location `/multiplication/random`, as shown in Listing 3-16.

Listing 3-16. MultiplicationControllerTest.java (social-multiplication v3)

```java
// import statements...

@RunWith(SpringRunner.class)
@WebMvcTest(MultiplicationController.class)
public class MultiplicationControllerTest {

    @MockBean
    private MultiplicationService multiplicationService;

    @Autowired
    private MockMvc mvc;

    // This object will be magically initialized by the
    // initFields method below.
    private JacksonTester<Multiplication> json;

    @Before
    public void setup() {
        JacksonTester.initFields(this, new ObjectMapper());
    }

    @Test
    public void getRandomMultiplicationTest() throws Exception{
        // given
        given(multiplicationService.createRandomMultiplication())
                .willReturn(new Multiplication(70, 20));
```

```
// when
MockHttpServletResponse response = mvc.perform(
        get("/multiplications/random")
                .accept(MediaType.APPLICATION_JSON))
        .andReturn().getResponse();

// then
assertThat(response.getStatus()).isEqualTo(HttpStatus.
OK.value());
assertThat(response.getContentAsString())
        .isEqualTo(json.write(new Multiplication
        (70, 20)).getJson());
    }

}
```

Let's look at the main changes introduced in this test:

1. It's a @WebMvcTest, so it will initialize the Spring's web application context. However, it will only load the configuration related to the MVC layer (controllers), in contrast to @SpringBootTest, which loads the entire configuration. By using this annotation, we also get the MockMvc bean loaded.

2. Do you remember @MockBean from the previous chapter? We use it here again instead of @Mock since we need to tell Spring not to inject the real bean (MultiplicationServiceImpl) but a mock object, which we configure later with given() to return the expected Multiplication. What we're doing here is isolating layers: we only want to test the controller, not the service.

3. The JacksonTester object will provide useful
    methods to check JSON contents. It can be
    automatically configured and autowired when
    using @JsonTest annotation, but since we're writing
    a @WebMvcTest, we need to configure it manually
    (within the method annotated with Before).

GOOD PRACTICES: @WEBMVCTEST AND @SPRINGBOOTTEST

MVC tests are intended to cover just the controller piece of your application.
HTTP requests and responses are mocked so the real connections are not
created. On the other hand, when you use @SpringBootTest, all the
configuration for the web application context is loaded and the connections
are going through the real web server. In that case, you don't use the
MockMvc bean but a standard RestTemplate instead (or the new alternative
TestRestTemplate).

So, when should we choose one or the other? @WebMvcTest is intended to
test unitarily the controller from the server side. @SpringBootTest, on the
other hand, should be used for *integration tests*, when you want to interact
with the application from the client side.

That doesn't mean that you can't use mocks with @SpringBootTest; if
you're writing an integration test, that could still be necessary. In any case,
it's better not to use it just for a simple controller's unit test.

If you execute the test now, you will get a 404 status code. That's not
surprising, because the implementation of the logic is not there yet.
Listing 3-17 shows how to build the controller.

Listing 3-17. MultiplicationController.java Adding Logic (social-multiplication v3)

```
/**
 * This class implements a REST API for our Multiplication
application.
 */
@RestController
@RequestMapping("/multiplications")
final class MultiplicationController {

    private final MultiplicationService multiplicationService;

    @Autowired
    public MultiplicationController(final MultiplicationService
            multiplicationService) {
        this.multiplicationService = multiplicationService;
    }

    @GetMapping("/random")
    Multiplication getRandomMultiplication() {
        return multiplicationService.createRandomMultiplication();
    }

}
```

It's a very simple class (even shorter than the test!). That's because with some Spring annotations and a few lines of code, you can get all you need:

1. The @RestController annotation specifies that the class is a controller and all the @RequestMapping (or @GetMapping in our case) annotated methods will return the content in the response body. If we use a plain @Controller annotation instead, we need to

annotate our class (or every corresponding method) with @ResponseBody. Thus, @RestController is a *shortcut* annotation.

2. The @RequestMapping annotation at the class level is setting the root context for all the methods (in our case, *multiplications*).

3. Another shortcut annotation is @GetMapping, and it's equivalent to using @RequestMapping(method = RequestMethod.GET). So, the resulting endpoint will perform a GET operation to the URL composed by the class' specified context plus the method's request mapping, which results in /multiplications/random.

That's how easily we can build a REST API with Spring. If you run it now, the test will pass as expected.

Some of you might think that writing unit tests for the controller layer *is not really important*, because of the simplicity of these classes. That is a good point, actually. However, if you write unit tests for this layer you ensure a double check for changes in the API contract, which becomes really useful especially in a microservices environment where multiple teams can be managing different services. If you accidentally change /multiplications/random for /multiplication/random, your test will fail, same as if you change HTTP verbs or the data the endpoints handle. Your REST API consumers will appreciate that you need to think twice before changing the API contract.

The Results Controller

This controller will check the results being POSTed by our users and tell them if they are correct or not. We could choose from many different ways to return the response but a good approach is to create a basic class that will wrap the result, by now consisting only of a boolean field: correct. Bear in mind that if you return a boolean directly in the response instead of wrapping it into a class, the default JSON serializer will not work.[3]

The first, empty version of the controller is shown in Listing 3-18.

Listing 3-18. MultiplicationResultAttemptController.java Initial Version (social-multiplication v3)

```
@RestController
@RequestMapping("/results")
final class MultiplicationResultAttemptController {

    private final MultiplicationService multiplicationService;

    @Autowired
    MultiplicationResultAttemptController(final
    MultiplicationService multiplicationService) {
        this.multiplicationService = multiplicationService;
    }

    // Here we'll implement our POST later

    @RequiredArgsConstructor
    @NoArgsConstructor(force = true)
    @Getter
    private static final class ResultResponse {
        private final boolean correct;
    }
}
```

---

[3]https://stackoverflow.com/questions/33185217/is-it-possible-in-spring-mvc-4-return-boolean-as-json

Having modeled the ResultResponse, let's write our unit test for
MultiplicationResultAttemptController. We'll include the scenarios
of sending a correct attempt and a wrong attempt. Since there is no
mapping for the POST request we're performing, the tests will fail throwing
a predictable 404 (not found), as shown in Listing 3-19.

Listing 3-19. MultiplicationResultAttemptControllerTest.java
(social-multiplication v3)

```java
@RunWith(SpringRunner.class)
@WebMvcTest(MultiplicationResultAttemptController.class)
public class MultiplicationResultAttemptControllerTest {

    @MockBean
    private MultiplicationService multiplicationService;

    @Autowired
    private MockMvc mvc;

    // This object will be magically initialized by the
    // initFields method below.
    private JacksonTester<MultiplicationResultAttempt> jsonResult;
    private JacksonTester<ResultResponse> jsonResponse;

    @Before
    public void setup() {
        JacksonTester.initFields(this, new ObjectMapper());
    }

    @Test
    public void postResultReturnCorrect() throws Exception {
        genericParameterizedTest(true);
    }

    @Test
```

```java
public void postResultReturnNotCorrect() throws Exception {
    genericParameterizedTest(false);
}

void genericParameterizedTest(final boolean correct) throws
Exception {
    // given (remember we're not testing here the service
    itself)
    given(multiplicationService
            .checkAttempt(any(MultiplicationResultAttempt.
            class)))
            .willReturn(correct);
    User user = new User("john");
    Multiplication multiplication = new Multiplication(50, 70);
    MultiplicationResultAttempt attempt = new
    MultiplicationResultAttempt(
            user, multiplication, 3500);

    // when
    MockHttpServletResponse response = mvc.perform(
            post("/results").contentType(MediaType.
            APPLICATION_JSON)
                    .content(jsonResult.write(attempt).
                    getJson()))
            .andReturn().getResponse();

    // then
    assertThat(response.getStatus()).isEqualTo(HttpStatus.
    OK.value());
    assertThat(response.getContentAsString()).isEqualTo(
            jsonResponse.write(new
            ResultResponse(correct)).getJson());
}

}
```

We create a convenience method `genericParameterizedTest` just to extract the common behavior to test that, when the service considers the result correct, we'll receive `true` as a response and `false` otherwise. As mentioned, the main purpose of this test is to check the API.

Next, we can implement the `POST` mapping in the `MultiplicationResultAttemptController` class to receive new attempts from users, as shown in Listing 3-20.

Listing 3-20. MultiplicationResultAttemptController.java Adding the POST Method (social-multiplication v3)

```
@PostMapping
ResponseEntity<ResultResponse> postResult(@RequestBody
MultiplicationResultAttempt multiplicationResultAttempt) {
    return ResponseEntity.ok(
            new ResultResponse(multiplicationService
                    .checkAttempt(multiplicationResultAttempt)));
}
```

It's quite straightforward: `@PostMapping` annotation does a similar thing to `@GetMapping`, but in this case handling a `POST` request. And, because we want to receive the attempt data as part of the body of the request, we need to annotate the method argument with `@RequestBody`. In this case, the Spring developers decided not to infer this one even when using `@RestController`, since the requests might come with parameters as well and then that assumption would make things harder (magic has a limit).

Now we can safely run the test with a successful result.

Hey, we just finished with the backend part for our first business requirement! Now it's time to play with a basic user interface.

The Frontend (Web Client)

Since you have finished your first REST API, you're ready to build a basic UI on top of it. You'll provide a user-friendly interface for the application (humans don't like interacting with REST APIs in general). There are many options but taking into account the simplicity of the application we're building, we'll use just HTML and jQuery for communication with the REST web services.

We could separate this part into a new project since we don't have any dependency thanks to our REST API. However, to start with, we'll do that inside the same project since then we can use the same embedded Tomcat server used by Spring Boot to serve our static content. We'll cover this decision with more detail at the beginning of the next chapter, explaining why it's a good idea to follow this *mini-monolith-first approach*.

SPOILER ALERT: NOT A FRONTEND BOOK

You'll see in the JavaScript and HTML code that they are extremely basic. The reason is that this book is mainly focused on the backend services and how to connect everything together. On the other hand, we can't simply skip the user interface since this book wouldn't be so practical then, and we need to deliver our user story with a screen to interact with. The advantage of having our REST API in place is that we can change the frontend anytime without impacting any other functionality: it's good that we have loose coupling!

As you've no doubt learned in this book, it's a good idea to start simple and build from there. In this case, we'll start with a basic `index.html` file, a minimal amount of styles in `styles.css`, and some behavior for the web page implemented in JavaScript using jQuery: `multiplication-client.js`. We'll place all these files in the `static` folder inside `main/resources`, created the first time when we generated the project using Spring Initializr. Remember: The folder v3 of the code included with the book also contains the full contents of these files. Let's look at them one by one and add some comments. See Listing 3-21.

Listing 3-21. index.html (social-multiplication v3)

```html
<!DOCTYPE html>
<html>
<head>
    <title>Multiplication v1</title>
    <link rel="stylesheet" type="text/css" href="styles.css">
    <script src="https://ajax.googleapis.com/ajax/libs/
    jquery/3.1.1/jquery.min.js"></script>
    <script src="multiplication-client.js"></script>
</head>

<body>
<div>
    <h1>Welcome to Social Multiplication</h1>
    <h2>This is your challenge for today:</h2>
    <h1>
        <span class="multiplication-a"></span> x <span
        class="multiplication-b"></span> =
    </h1>
    <p>
        <form id="attempt-form">
            Result? <input type="text" name="result-
            attempt"><br>
            Your alias: <input type="text" name="user-alias"><br>
            <input type="submit" value="Check">
        </form>
    </p>
```

```
<h2><span class="result-message"></span></h2>
</div>
</body>
</html>
```

Listing 3-21 is a simple landing page. We import the JavaScript file and the styles (see Listing 3-22), and we include the reference to the jQuery library (see Listing 3-23). Then we have the text in which we show the challenge to the users, and next to it, the form from which the users can fill their alias and send their attempts to solve the multiplication. Remember that the user should do the operation mentally!

Listing 3-22. styles.css (social-multiplication v3)

```
html, body {
    height: 100%;
}

html {
    display: table;
    margin: auto;
}

body {
    display: table-cell;
    vertical-align: middle;
}
```

Surely it's not the fanciest CSS in the world: we are just making sure the contents are shown in the center of the page, to avoid the feeling of emptiness and to focus attention even on big screens. We'll improve it in coming chapters.

Listing 3-23. multiplication-client.js (social-multiplication v3)

```javascript
function updateMultiplication() {
    $.ajax({
        url: "http://localhost:8080/multiplications/random"
    }).then(function(data) {
        // Cleans the form
        $("#attempt-form").find( "input[name='result-attempt']" )
        .val("");
        $("#attempt-form").find( "input[name='user-alias']" )
        .val("");
        // Gets a random challenge from API and loads the data
        in the HTML
        $('.multiplication-a').empty().append(data.factorA);
        $('.multiplication-b').empty().append(data.factorB);
    });
}

$(document).ready(function() {

    updateMultiplication();

    $("#attempt-form").submit(function( event ) {

        // Don't submit the form normally
        event.preventDefault();

        // Get some values from elements on the page
        var a = $('.multiplication-a').text();
        var b = $('.multiplication-b').text();
        var $form = $( this ),
            attempt = $form.find( "input[name='result-
            attempt']" ).val(),
```

```
    userAlias = $form.find( "input[name='user-alias']" )
    .val();

// Compose the data in the format that the API is
expecting
var data = { user: { alias: userAlias}, multiplication:
{factorA: a, factorB: b}, resultAttempt: attempt};

// Send the data using post
$.ajax({
    url: '/results',
    type: 'POST',
    data: JSON.stringify(data),
    contentType: "application/json; charset=utf-8",
    dataType: "json",
    success: function(result){
        if(result.correct) {
            $('.result-message').empty().append("The
            result is correct! Congratulations!");
        } else {
            $('.result-message').empty().append("Oops
            that's not correct! But keep trying!");
        }
    }
});

updateMultiplication();
});
});
```

What we do here with jQuery is two main things:

- When the content is loaded, we perform a REST API call to get a random multiplication. Then we show the factors in the placeholders using the class to locate them.

- We register a listener for the submit event in our form to intercept it and prevent it from doing the default operation. We then get the data from the form, post the data to the API to check the resulting attempt, and then show a friendly message with the result to the users.

As mentioned, it's not the nicest web application ever, but it does the trick for the first deliverable we want to accomplish.

WE DID IT! USER STORY 1 IS FINISHED

We just finished our first user story! We implemented solutions for all the requirements. And we made it using TDD, a proper REST API, and with a three-tier design—this application follows good standards and is ready to be extended!

Playing with the Application (Part I)

You can now execute the application using mvnw `spring-boot:run`. You can also package and send it to your business people for them to play with (if they have a Java runtime environment installed). All you need is Maven and Java (make sure you change the JAR filename if you're using your own versioning). See Listing 3-24.

Listing 3-24. Console: Packaging and Executing the Application (social-multiplication v3)

```
$ mvnw package
...
$ cd ./target
$ java -jar social-multiplication-v3-0.3.0-SNAPSHOT.jar
...
INFO 12484 --- [              main] m.book.
SocialMultiplicationApplication   : Started
SocialMultiplicationApplication in 3.171 seconds (JVM running
for 3.77)
```

To play with it, you can navigate with a browser to localhost:8080/ index.html. Then you can play around with the operations and exercise your mind a little bit: you'll see different messages when you pass or fail the operation. Figure 3-2 shows how it looks right now.

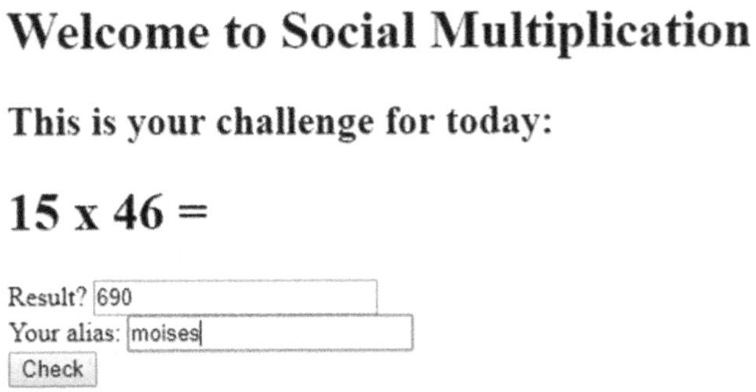

Welcome to Social Multiplication

This is your challenge for today:

15 x 46 =

Result? 690
Your alias: moises
Check

Figure 3-2. *The application's entry screen*

New Requirements for Data Persistence

So far we've designed and implemented a service that is not keeping any state at all: there is no database, file storage, etc. We are missing one of the layers commonly present in many software applications: *the data layer*.

Because we're lucky and have plenty of work to do, our business users come with this new requirement in the form of a user story.

USER STORY 2

As a user of the application, I want it to show me my last attempts, so I can see how good or bad I'm doing over time.

We need some data storage for this request, since we need to keep track of the user attempts. We'll take several steps to accomplish this requirement:

- Store all instances of the `MultiplicationResultAttempt` class. That way, we can extract them later.

- Expose a new REST endpoint to get the latest attempts for a given user.

- Create a new service (business logic) to retrieve those attempts.

- Show that attempts' history to the users on the web page after they send a new one.

Note that this user story impacts our code in a different way: we were checking the correctness of the attempt *on the fly*, so our `MultiplicationResultAttempt` class doesn't include a flag to indicate if it's correct or not. That was perfectly fine to cope with the requirements we had, but now, if we use the same approach, our application would be very inefficient and would have to calculate every time to extract the results. That's why we need a *refactoring* task, which must be included as part of this user story.

AGILE AND REFACTORING

When we work following the Agile methodology, we need to embrace refactoring as a normal part of our tasks. We want to deliver value as soon as possible, and then evolve the application in small increments. *That means that investing too much time at the beginning of the project to design the final status of our application would be wrong: the requirements might change.*

Finding a good balance is the key. Meet with your product owner or business users and ask them their vision: what they want to have at the end of the project. Then invest time in determining the minimum deliverable that gives them value, the first chunk of the entire project that they could use and still save time, make money, etc. This is the most difficult part when following Agile, because normally the business stakeholders don't want to sacrifice any functionality, and you might face an *I-want-all-or-nothing* problem. But this situation can be unlocked with effort and good communication between the business end and the project execution en (project manager, product owners, architects, and/or developers). After you define the vision and the MVP (Minimum Viable Product) the iterative work starts—meetings with the stakeholders to define the next portions of value to reach the target. The earlier you do this, the better.

It's critical to have a perfectly clear vision of what do you want to achieve from the business point of view at the end of the project and also a perfectly defined MVP with descriptive use cases. Then, since we'll work with Sprints, the work of the upcoming three-four Sprints should be more or less defined as well. *Total improvisation* and changing direction in every Sprint are very bad for a project unless it is based on experimenting.

Having said that, it's critical that your business stakeholders understand what refactoring is and embrace it as well. While working with Agile, there will be situations in which the increment of value might be very little, but the amount of effort to deliver it is big. You can't be too strict in following the Agile manifesto and argue that refactoring doesn't add value. When you see your plan for the next three-four Sprints and you can see clearly that a change in software design or architecture is needed, better plan it as early as you can. If you skip it, you will regret later when the *technical debt* consumes your project's resources.

We could challenge this book too: in our application we could argue that the persistence requirement should have been clear from the beginning and thus we should have designed the attempts in a different way. That's right, however, we're using it to conduct this explanation as an example of Agile refactoring.

Let's try to summarize what our refactoring task should include:

1. The attempt (`MultiplicationResultAttempt`) should include a `boolean` to indicate if it's correct or not. We'll store it and later we'll be able to query the database.

2. The service (`MultiplicationServiceImpl`) should not only return the result calculated "on the fly" but save it in the attempt too.

3. The client shouldn't be able to flag an attempt as correct, so this field should not be read from the REST API but instead calculated internally.

4. The tests need to be changed to reflect our new circumstances.

Let's divide the work between refactoring and changes to implement persistence.

SOURCE CODE AVAILABLE WITH THE BOOK

You can find all the code referenced from here in the v4 repository on GitHub: `https://github.com/microservices-practical`.

Refactoring the Code

As explained, we need to perform some changes to the code to avoid unnecessary calculations—we'll store a boolean value in the attempt, so we can query the database for the correct ones. See Listing 3-25.

Listing 3-25. MultiplicationResultAttempt.java (social-multiplication v4)

```java
// Imports, annotations...
public final class MultiplicationResultAttempt {

    private final User user;
    private final Multiplication multiplication;
    private final int resultAttempt;

    private final boolean correct;

    // Empty constructor for JSON (de)serialization
    MultiplicationResultAttempt() {
        user = null;
        multiplication = null;
        resultAttempt = -1;
        correct = false;
    }

}
```

Because we added this new field to our class, Lombok will now generate the new constructor and the getter. It will also take care of updating the equals(), hashCode(), and toString() methods, which is why Lombok is great for refactoring works. That also means that we need to change the MultiplicationServiceImplTest and MultiplicationResultAttemptControllerTest classes to adapt them to the new constructor. See Listing 3-26.

Listing 3-26. MultiplicationServiceImplTest.java (social-multiplication v4)

```
@Test
public void checkCorrectAttemptTest() {
    // given
    Multiplication multiplication = new Multiplication(50, 60);
    User user = new User("john_doe");
    MultiplicationResultAttempt attempt = new
    MultiplicationResultAttempt(
            user, multiplication, 3000, false);

    // when
    boolean attemptResult = multiplicationServiceImpl.check
    Attempt(attempt);

    // then
    assertThat(attemptResult).isTrue();
}

@Test
public void checkWrongAttemptTest() {
    // given
    Multiplication multiplication = new Multiplication(50, 60);
    User user = new User("john_doe");
    MultiplicationResultAttempt attempt = new
    MultiplicationResultAttempt(
            user, multiplication, 3010, false);
    given(userRepository.findByAlias("john_doe")).
    willReturn(Optional.empty());

    // when
    boolean attemptResult = multiplicationServiceImpl.
    checkAttempt(attempt);
```

```
    // then
    assertThat(attemptResult).isFalse();
}
```

How do we set the proper value for the new correct field? Let's add that to our business logic inside the service implementation. See Listing 3-27.

Listing 3-27. MultiplicationServiceImpl.java (social-multiplication v4)

```
@Override
public boolean checkAttempt(final MultiplicationResultAttempt
attempt) {
    // Checks if it's correct
    boolean correct = attempt.getResultAttempt() ==
                        attempt.getMultiplication().
                        getFactorA() *
                        attempt.getMultiplication().
                        getFactorB();

    // Avoids 'hack' attempts
    Assert.isTrue(!attempt.isCorrect(), "You can't send an
    attempt marked as correct!!");

    // Creates a copy, now setting the 'correct' field
    accordingly
    MultiplicationResultAttempt checkedAttempt =
            new MultiplicationResultAttempt(attempt.getUser(),
                attempt.getMultiplication(),
                attempt.getResultAttempt(),
                correct);

    // Returns the result
    return correct;
}
```

Note that the method argument, `attempt`, may contain a `true` value for the `correct` field (in case we're dealing with a smart user who wants to cheat the application). What we do in this case is calculate the right value for `correct` and set it in a new instance, `checkedAttempt`. We need to create a copy since we want to keep our class immutable. As you can see in our logic, we also throw an error to a potential cheater thanks to the convenient `Assert` class included in Spring;[4] the assertion will trigger an `IllegalArgumentException`.

We also have the opportunity to get rid of the inner class `ResultResponse` we used in our controller. With our previous change to include `correct`, it makes much more sense to return the same `MultiplicationResultAttempt` type in our REST call, with the boolean value indicating if the attempt was correct or not. See Listing 3-28.

Listing 3-28. MultiplicationResultAttemptController.java (social-multiplication v4)

```
@PostMapping
ResponseEntity<MultiplicationResultAttempt>
postResult(@RequestBody MultiplicationResultAttempt
multiplicationResultAttempt) {
    boolean isCorrect = multiplicationService.checkAttempt
    (multiplicationResultAttempt);
    MultiplicationResultAttempt attemptCopy = new
    MultiplicationResultAttempt(
            multiplicationResultAttempt.getUser(),
            multiplicationResultAttempt.getMultiplication(),
            multiplicationResultAttempt.getResultAttempt(),
            isCorrect
    );
    return ResponseEntity.ok(attemptCopy);
}
```

---

[4]https://docs.spring.io/spring/docs/current/javadoc-api/org/springframework/util/Assert.html

To complete the refactoring, we apply the corresponding changes to our `MultiplicationResultAttemptControllerTest` to use the new constructor and to verify the returned `MultiplicationResultAttempt` object, instead of the former boolean. See Listing 6-29.

Listing 3-29. MultiplicationResultAttemptControllerTest.java (social-multiplication v4)

```
void genericParameterizedTest(final boolean correct) throws
Exception {
    // given (remember we're not testing here the service
    itself)
    // ...
    MultiplicationResultAttempt attempt = new
    MultiplicationResultAttempt(
            user, multiplication, 3500, correct);

    // when
    // ...

    // then
    assertThat(response.getStatus()).isEqualTo(HttpStatus.
    OK.value());
    assertThat(response.getContentAsString()).isEqualTo(
            jsonResult.write(
                    new MultiplicationResultAttempt(attempt.
                    getUser(),
                            attempt.getMultiplication(),
                            attempt.getResultAttempt(),
                            correct)
            ).getJson());
}
```

Normally, if you change a return type for a response in your REST API, you would need to change your frontend as well. However, in our case we don't need to change anything by now. We used to return a simple JSON object with a correct boolean inside; now we return a bigger JSON (from MultiplicationResultAttempt) that also has a correct boolean. Luckily for us, our multiplication-client.js will keep working. See Listing 3-30.

Listing 3-30. multiplication-client.js (social-multiplication v4)

```
// Send the data using post
$.ajax({
    url: '/results',
    type: 'POST',
    data: JSON.stringify(data),
    contentType: "application/json; charset=utf-8",
    dataType: "json",
    async: false,
    success: function(result){
        if(result.correct) {
            $('.result-message').empty().append("The result is
            correct! Congratulations!");
        } else {
            $('.result-message').empty().append("Oops that's
            not correct! But keep trying!");
        }
    }
});
```

The Data Layer

The refactoring task is finished, so now let's continue layering our Spring Boot application introducing our data layer. For this use case, we'll benefit from an ORM framework like Hibernate: we'll persist data in our database following a model that can be mapped to the Java objects. If you keep the model not too complex, it's a solution that makes the work with the persistence layer very straightforward. To achieve this, we'll make use of the starter package of Spring Boot for the Java Persistence API (JPA), which includes Hibernate. JPA is just the standard specification for persistence that is implemented by many different providers (Hibernate is one of them), and it's always a good idea to use standards instead of binding ourselves to a specific implementation. If you want to know more about JPA you can read the official documentation or visit the ObjectDB site at `http://www.objectdb.com/api/java/jpa/annotations`.

The first step we need to take is to include two new dependencies in our `pom.xml` file:

- The `spring-boot-starter-data-jpa` dependency will give us access to the Spring Data JPA[5] tooling, like creating repositories in an easy and fast manner. This starter provides support for JPA using Hibernate.

- The h2 artifact includes a lightweight, embedded database engine called H2. We could have used MySQL, PostgreSQL, or any other database engine, but this one fits our requirements and makes our service easier to explain for the book. See Listing 3-31.

Listing 3-31. pom.xml Adding Data-Related Dependencies (social-multiplication v4)

```
<dependency>
  <groupId>org.springframework.boot</groupId>
  <artifactId>spring-boot-starter-data-jpa</artifactId>
</dependency>

<dependency>
```

---

[5]`http://projects.spring.io/spring-data-jpa/`

```
<groupId>com.h2database</groupId>
<artifactId>h2</artifactId>
<scope>runtime</scope>
</dependency>
```

Then we fill the configuration in the `application.properties` file. Since we used Spring Initializr to generate our project, this file should be located in `src/main/resources`. If you prefer, you can also use YAML format, but then rename the file to `application.yml`. See Listing 3-32.

Listing 3-32. application.properties (social-multiplication v4)

```
# Gives us access to the H2 database web console
spring.h2.console.enabled=true
# Generates the database *only* if it's not there yet
spring.jpa.hibernate.ddl-auto=update
# Creates the database in a file
spring.datasource.url=jdbc:h2:file:~/social-multiplication;
DB_CLOSE_ON_EXIT=FALSE;
# For educational purposes we will show the SQL in console
spring.jpa.properties.hibernate.show_sql=true
```

The H2 console is a lightweight web UI for us to manage and query the H2 database. The instructions about how to configure it with Spring Boot can be found at *https://tpd.io/h2-spring*. As you can see, we only needed to specify some basic properties; everything else is being auto-configured by Spring Boot. An important part of the configuration is the URL. We specify there that we want the database to be stored in a file and the name of the database. If we don't set it to `file`, we'd have an in-memory database, and we'd lose our data every time we shut down the service. Note that we're using ~/, so the file will be located in your operating system's user home folder.

PRODUCTION READINESS: USING A DIFFERENT DB ENGINE

H2 is a valid engine for the goals of our application, also because the intention of this book is to not go into database details. You might want to explore some better alternatives for a production database, and then you can configure it following the instructions from the official Spring Boot documentation page for that (see https://tpd.io/boot-prod-db). The good news is that they're configured in a very similar way to H2.

The Data Model

This is the most important task we accomplish to model our persistence layer: designing the data model. We defined previously how our business entities look; now we need to define how we want them to relate from the data's point of view.

Sometimes data models don't match the domain models: for example, you may have in your domain CustomerWithPersonalDetails and EmployeeWithPersonalDetails because you want to keep them simple, but you may want to keep the customer, employee, and personal_details tables separate to avoid data replication and save some space in the future. In this case, we'll do a direct mapping: domain entities match with data entities. Figure 3-3 shows the data model.

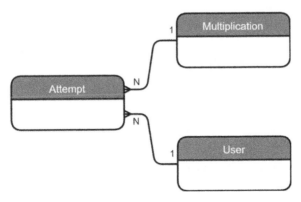

Figure 3-3. *The current data model*

Not really complex, but it is a good example. We can explain it from the User entity: they can have many attempts. At the same time, attempts coming from different users may have a relation with the same multiplication (if they have equal factors).

How can we model this with JPA? The easiest way is to use the provided annotations. We won't go into details about JPA because that could cover an entire book, but we'll cover the basics by looking at the changes to our entities and explaining them. Let's start with the Multiplication class, as shown in Listing 3-33.

Listing 3-33. Multiplication.java (social-multiplication v4)

```java
package microservices.book.multiplication.domain;

import lombok.EqualsAndHashCode;
import lombok.Getter;
import lombok.RequiredArgsConstructor;
import lombok.ToString;

import javax.persistence.Column;
import javax.persistence.Entity;
import javax.persistence.GeneratedValue;
import javax.persistence.Id;

/**
 * This class represents a Multiplication (a * b).
 */
@RequiredArgsConstructor
@Getter
@ToString
@EqualsAndHashCode
@Entity
public final class Multiplication {
```

```
@Id
@GeneratedValue
@Column(name = "MULTIPLICATION_ID")
private Long id;

// Both factors
private final int factorA;
private final int factorB;

// Empty constructor for JSON/JPA
Multiplication() {
    this(0, 0);
}
}
```

- The @Entity annotation is used to specify that the class should be considered a JPA entity, so it can be stored in a JPA repository. Note that we also have an empty constructor, which is required by JPA to be able to instantiate objects via reflection.

- We'll use unique identifiers as primary keys, and for that we'll use the Java Long class. The annotation @Id tells JPA that it's going to be the primary key identifier, and the @GeneratedValue indicates that it should be autogenerated (we're not setting it).

- In some cases we may want to explicitly set the column name instead of letting JPA do it. To do so, we can use the @Column annotation. Sometimes it's useful because we want to give a fixed name to a column and then use it from a different entity to join two tables (which will be the case here). We could also omit this annotation and reference to this id field later using the field and table names from MultiplicationResultAttempt.

We need to make very similar changes to the User class, as shown in Listing 3-34.

Listing 3-34. User.java (social-multiplication v4)

```java
@RequiredArgsConstructor
@Getter
@ToString
@EqualsAndHashCode
@Entity
public final class User {

    @Id
    @GeneratedValue
    @Column(name = "USER_ID")
    private Long id;

    private final String alias;

    // Empty constructor for JSON/JPA
    protected User() {
        alias = null;
    }
}
```

The most interesting changes are in MultiplicationResultAttempt, since it's the part in the model that links the other entities. See Listing 3-35.

Listing 3-35. MultiplicationResultAttempt.java (social-multiplication v4)

```java
package microservices.book.multiplication.domain;

import lombok.EqualsAndHashCode;
import lombok.Getter;
```

```java
import lombok.RequiredArgsConstructor;
import lombok.ToString;

import javax.persistence.*;

/**
 * Identifies the attempt from a {@link User} to solve a
 * {@link Multiplication}.
 */
@RequiredArgsConstructor
@Getter
@ToString
@EqualsAndHashCode
@Entity
public final class MultiplicationResultAttempt {

    @Id
    @GeneratedValue
    private Long id;

    @ManyToOne(cascade = CascadeType.PERSIST)
    @JoinColumn(name = "USER_ID")
    private final User user;

    @ManyToOne(cascade = CascadeType.PERSIST)
    @JoinColumn(name = "MULTIPLICATION_ID")
    private final Multiplication multiplication;
    private final int resultAttempt;

    private final boolean correct;

    // Empty constructor for JSON/JPA
    MultiplicationResultAttempt() {
        user = null;
```

```
        multiplication = null;
        resultAttempt = -1;
        correct = false;
    }

}
```

- In order to specify the relation between entities, JPA
  provides several annotations: @OneToOne, @OneToMany,
  @ManyToOne, and @ManyToMany. With some of these
  annotations you can define also the details for how
  you want to link them. Check the documentation if you
  want to know more about this. With the configuration
  above, our attempts table will have two foreign keys to
  the respective identifiers of User and Multiplication
  (if you need more knowledge about the *primary key*
  and *foreign key* concepts, read the article at *https://
  tpd.io/ms-pk-fk*).

- For our MultiplicationResultAttempt we choose a
  cascade type PERSIST. What we want to achieve with
  this is that we can store from our Java code directly the
  attempts, and any other linked entity will be persisted
  (if it's not already there) in their corresponding tables
  as well.

- As shown, we use @JoinColumn to reference other
  entities using their identifiers (using the name provided
  there via @Column).

Tables 3-1 through 3-3 show an example of how these entities look in
the different tables for a given iteration of the game (an attempt to solve a
multiplication sent by a given user).

Table 3-1. *USER Table (social-multiplication v4)*

USER_ID	ALIAS
3	john

Table 3-2. *MULTIPLICATION Table (social-multiplication v4)*

MULTIPLICATION_ID	FACTORA	FACTORB
8	41	54

Table 3-3. *MULTIPLICATION_RESULT_ATTEMPT Table (social-multiplication v4)*

ID	CORRECT	RESULT_ATTEMPT	MULTIPLICATION_ID	USER_ID
11	true	2214	8	3

The Repositories

Now that we have the needed tools in our project to implement persistence and have our model designed, we can create our JPA repositories so we can store and read our Java objects. Following our packaging structure and the layered application pattern, we'll create repositories in a new repository package.

Let's start with the repository to store MultiplicationResultAttempt objects, as shown in Listing 3-36.

Listing 3-36. MultiplicationResultAttemptRepository (social-multiplication v4)

```
package microservices.book.multiplication.repository;

import microservices.book.multiplication.domain.
MultiplicationResultAttempt;
```

```java
import org.springframework.data.repository.CrudRepository;

import java.util.List;

/**
 * This interface allow us to store and retrieve attempts
 */
public interface MultiplicationResultAttemptRepository
        extends CrudRepository<MultiplicationResultAttempt,
Long> {

    /**
     * @return the latest 5 attempts for a given user,
     * identified by their alias.
     */
    List<MultiplicationResultAttempt> findTop5ByUserAliasOrder
    ByIdDesc(String userAlias);
}
```

Once again, a simple solution: just by creating an interface that extends one of the provided interfaces in Spring Data JPA, we'll have all the functionality that we need in our application. In this case, CrudRepository is a convenient solution (kind of magic interface) provided by Spring to implement the operations to create, read, update, and delete entities (CRUD). It uses Java generics so we just need to pass as parameters the class annotated with @Entity for which we want a repository (the first one), and the identifier type (in our case, we declared them as Long). PagingAndSortingRepository is also an useful one which, besides CRUD operations, provides pagination and sorting capabilities.

Have you noticed the findTop5ByUserAliasOrderByIdDesc method? It's using another cool feature from Spring Data JPA: query methods. Just by following some given naming patterns, you can easily create custom queries by defining the method in the interface. You can get more information about this on the official documentation page.[6] If you don't like such magic, you can also create your method (name it whatever you like) and use the @Query annotation with your custom JPQL (we'll cover some cases in the next chapter). You can find more information about this alternative on the same page.

We can apply what we know now to create our UserRepository and MultiplicationRepository classes. The latter one does not need any custom query method, so it's just the interface declaration (and yet we have the power of all the predefined methods in CrudRepository). See Listings 3-37 and 3-38.

Listing 3-37. UserRepository (social-multiplication v4)

```
package microservices.book.multiplication.repository;

import microservices.book.multiplication.domain.User;
import org.springframework.data.repository.CrudRepository;

import java.util.Optional;

/**
 * This interface allows us to save and retrieve Users
 */
public interface UserRepository extends CrudRepository<User,
Long> {

    Optional<User> findByAlias(final String alias);

}
```

[6]https://docs.spring.io/spring-data/jpa/docs/current/reference/
html/#repositories.query-methods

Listing 3-38. MultiplicationRepository (social-multiplication v4)

```
package microservices.book.multiplication.repository;

import microservices.book.multiplication.domain.Multiplication;
import org.springframework.data.repository.CrudRepository;

/**
 * This interface allows us to save and retrieve
Multiplications
 */
public interface MultiplicationRepository extends
CrudRepository<Multiplication, Long> {
}
```

You might be wondering at this point why we're not following TDD for the repositories. The answer is simple: there is no new code, and we trust the implementation provided by Spring, so we don't need to include unit tests for these *skinny* repositories.

CHOOSING WHICH METHODS TO EXPOSE

The Repository interface has a hidden trick: if you create interface methods matching the signature of CrudRepository, the result is a partial CrudRepository solution with only the methods you want to expose. You can find this trick documented on the Javadoc.

Once we have our repositories, we want to use them. Our business logic should take care of calling them to persist our entities. Back to TDD: let's include that in our unit test by verifying the attempt logic (MultiplicationServiceImplTest), both for a correct and a wrong one. See Listing 3-39.

Listing 3-39. MultiplicationServiceImplTest (social-multiplication v4)

```java
// package, imports...
public class MultiplicationServiceImplTest {

    private MultiplicationServiceImpl
multiplicationServiceImpl;

    @Mock
    private RandomGeneratorService randomGeneratorService;

    @Mock
    private MultiplicationResultAttemptRepository
    attemptRepository;

    @Mock
    private UserRepository userRepository;

    @Before
    public void setUp() {
        // With this call to initMocks we tell Mockito to
        process the annotations
        MockitoAnnotations.initMocks(this);
        multiplicationServiceImpl = new MultiplicationService
        Impl(randomGeneratorService, attemptRepository,
        userRepository);
    }

    @Test
    public void createRandomMultiplicationTest() {
        // [...] no changes here, keep it as it was before
    }
```

```java
@Test
public void checkCorrectAttemptTest() {
    // given
    Multiplication multiplication = new Multiplication
    (50, 60);
    User user = new User("john_doe");
    MultiplicationResultAttempt attempt = new
    MultiplicationResultAttempt(
            user, multiplication, 3000, false);
    MultiplicationResultAttempt verifiedAttempt = new
    MultiplicationResultAttempt(
            user, multiplication, 3000, true);
    given(userRepository.findByAlias("john_doe")).
    willReturn(Optional.empty());

    // when
    boolean attemptResult = multiplicationServiceImpl.
    checkAttempt(attempt);

    // then
    assertThat(attemptResult).isTrue();
    verify(attemptRepository).save(verifiedAttempt);
}

@Test
public void checkWrongAttemptTest() {
    // given
    Multiplication multiplication = new Multiplication
    (50, 60);
    User user = new User("john_doe");
    MultiplicationResultAttempt attempt = new
    MultiplicationResultAttempt(
            user, multiplication, 3010, false);
    given(userRepository.findByAlias("john_doe")).
    willReturn(Optional.empty());
```

```
// when
boolean attemptResult = multiplicationServiceImpl.
checkAttempt(attempt);

// then
assertThat(attemptResult).isFalse();
verify(attemptRepository).save(attempt);
    }
}
```

- We need to mock MultiplicationResultAttempt Repository and UserRepository to keep the unit test focused on the service layer. Note in the code that they are also passed in the MultiplicationServiceImpl constructor. You may want to update that line later, when you modify that class, or you can also create the new constructor at this point.

- In our checkCorrectAttemptTest() we're including a copy of the attempt (verifiedAttempt) to make it closer to reality: the one sent by the user should have a false value for the correct field. Then, in the last line, we verify (using Mockito) that we call the repository to store the one with correct set to true.

- The checkWrongAttemptTest() needs an update to check that the repository is also called for wrong attempts. Remember that the real call is not executed: we're just verifying that the mock objects are called with those arguments.

So now we have a failing test again (the repositories are never called). We need to add the repositories to our MultiplicationServiceImpl and save the attempts in both cases. Listing 3-40 shows the changes.

Listing 3-40. MultiplicationServiceImpl (social-multiplication v4)

```
// [...]
@Service
class MultiplicationServiceImpl implements
    MultiplicationService {

    private RandomGeneratorService randomGeneratorService;
    private MultiplicationResultAttemptRepository
            attemptRepository;
    private UserRepository userRepository;

    @Autowired
    public MultiplicationServiceImpl(final
            RandomGeneratorService randomGeneratorService,
                                    final Multiplication
                                    ResultAttemptRepository
                                    attemptRepository,
                                    final UserRepository
                                    userRepository) {
        this.randomGeneratorService = randomGeneratorService;
        this.attemptRepository = attemptRepository;
        this.userRepository = userRepository;
    }

    // [...]

    @Transactional
    @Override
    public boolean checkAttempt(final Multiplication
    ResultAttempt attempt) {
        // Check if the user already exists for that alias
        Optional<User> user = userRepository.findBy
        Alias(attempt.getUser().getAlias());
```

```
// Avoids 'hack' attempts
Assert.isTrue(!attempt.isCorrect(), "You can't send an
attempt marked as correct!!");

// Check if the attempt is correct
boolean isCorrect = attempt.getResultAttempt() ==
                attempt.getMultiplication().
                getFactorA() *
                attempt.getMultiplication().
                getFactorB();

MultiplicationResultAttempt checkedAttempt = new
MultiplicationResultAttempt(
        user.orElse(attempt.getUser()),
        attempt.getMultiplication(),
        attempt.getResultAttempt(),
        isCorrect
);

// Stores the attempt
attemptRepository.save(checkedAttempt);

return isCorrect;
    }
}
```

- An important concept to understand here is that we don't really need to use all the new repositories. Since we introduced before our CascadeType.PERSIST in the MultiplicationResultAttempt entity, whenever we save an attempt, the linked Multiplication and User objects will be persisted too.

- However, we still need the `UserRepository` to get the user identifier given the alias. Every time we receive an attempt it's a new one from the REST API's point of view, so it's linked to a `Multiplication` and `User` with null IDs. If the user is an existing one, they will be already in our database. We want to link this attempt to the user so we need to retrieve the existing identifier from database given the user's alias. Using Java's `Optional`, we can later resolve nicely if it's a new (null ID) or an existing user with `user.orElse(attempt. getUser())`.

- We changed the constructor so now the repository implementations are also injected by Spring (we don't develop them; they are *automagically* generated).

- We store the attempt using the attempt's repository. As mentioned before, JPA will also store the linked entities.

EXERCISE (OPTIONAL)

Time for you to accept a challenge! With the current implementation, we have a small issue with multiplications. We will persist every one of them as if they were new, even if there are existing ones with the same combination of factorA and factorB. Are you ready to solve it? We just covered the main idea so… go for it!

Completing User Story 2: Going Through the Layers

We have almost completed user story 2. Remember: we wanted to show the users their last attempts. We're now saving them, so we can create a REST API endpoint to retrieve the latest ones for a given user. We partially covered this when we introduced the query method `findTop5ByUserAliasOrderByIdDesc()` in `MultiplicationResultAttemptRepository`. Let's link it back through all layers to the UI.

The next layer is the service. Since this one does not contain much business logic, let's write our implementation first and then add our new test case. See Listing 3-41.

Listing 3-41. MultiplicationServiceImpl Adding a New Method (social-multiplication v4)

```
@Service
class MultiplicationServiceImpl implements
MultiplicationService {

    // [...]

    @Override
    public List<MultiplicationResultAttempt>
getStatsForUser(String userAlias) {
        return attemptRepository.findTop5ByUserAliasOrderBy
IdDesc(userAlias);
    }
}
```

Listing 3-42. MultiplicationServiceImplTest Adding a Test (social-multiplication v4)

```java
public class MultiplicationServiceImplTest {

    // [...]

    @Test
    public void retrieveStatsTest() {
        // given
        Multiplication multiplication = new Multiplication
        (50, 60);
        User user = new User("john_doe");
        MultiplicationResultAttempt attempt1 = new
        MultiplicationResultAttempt(
                user, multiplication, 3010, false);
        MultiplicationResultAttempt attempt2 = new
        MultiplicationResultAttempt(
                user, multiplication, 3051, false);
        List<MultiplicationResultAttempt> latestAttempts =
        Lists.newArrayList(attempt1, attempt2);
        given(userRepository.findByAlias("john_doe")).
        willReturn(Optional.empty());
        given(attemptRepository.findTop5ByUserAliasOrderById
        Desc("john_doe"))
                .willReturn(latestAttempts);

        // when
        List<MultiplicationResultAttempt> latestAttemptsResult =
                multiplicationServiceImpl.
                getStatsForUser("john_doe");
```

```
    // then
    assertThat(latestAttemptsResult).isEqualTo
    (latestAttempts);
  }
}
```

It's the same for the Controller layer: all the logic is coming from the query so we just need to pass the result. In this case, we need to make a slight modification to the test class to include a new JacksonTester to assert results using a list of attempts. See Listings 3-43 and 3-44.

Listing 3-43. MultiplicationResultAttemptController Adding a New Method (social-multiplication v4)

```
@RestController
@RequestMapping("/results")
final class MultiplicationResultAttemptController {

    // [...]

    @GetMapping
    ResponseEntity<List<MultiplicationResultAttempt>>
    getStatistics(@RequestParam("alias") String alias) {
        return ResponseEntity.ok(
                multiplicationService.getStatsForUser(alias)
        );
    }
}
```

Listing 3-44. MultiplicationResultAttemptControllerTest - adding a test (social-multiplication v4)

```
@RunWith(SpringRunner.class)
@WebMvcTest(MultiplicationResultAttemptController.class)
```

```java
public class MultiplicationResultAttemptControllerTest {

    // [...]

    // These objects will be magically initialized by the
    // initFields method below.
    private JacksonTester<MultiplicationResultAttempt>
    jsonResultAttempt;
    private JacksonTester<List<MultiplicationResultAttempt>>
    jsonResultAttemptList;

    @Before
    public void setup() {
        JacksonTester.initFields(this, new ObjectMapper());
    }

    // [...]

    @Test
    public void getUserStats() throws Exception {
        // given
        User user = new User("john_doe");
        Multiplication multiplication = new Multiplication
        (50, 70);
        MultiplicationResultAttempt attempt = new
        MultiplicationResultAttempt(
                user, multiplication, 3500, true);
        List<MultiplicationResultAttempt> recentAttempts =
        Lists.newArrayList(attempt, attempt);
        given(multiplicationService
                .getStatsForUser("john_doe"))
                .willReturn(recentAttempts);
```

```
        // when
        MockHttpServletResponse response = mvc.perform(
                get("/results").param("alias", "john_doe"))
                .andReturn().getResponse();

        // then
        assertThat(response.getStatus()).isEqualTo(Http
        Status.OK.value());
        assertThat(response.getContentAsString()).isEqualTo(
                jsonResultAttemptList.write(
                        recentAttempts
                ).getJson());
    }

}
```

On the UI side, we need to call this new REST API and present the results on the screen. First, we add the logic to `multiplication-client.js` to call the backend service for every attempt sent, as shown in Listing 3-45.

Listing 3-45. multiplication-client.js Adding Attempts (social-multiplication v4)

```
// [...]
function updateStats(alias) {
    $.ajax({
        url: "http://localhost:8080/results?alias=" + alias,
    }).then(function(data) {
        $('#stats-body').empty();
        data.forEach(function(row) {
            $('#stats-body').append('<tr><td>' + row.id +
            '</td>' +
                '<td>' + row.multiplication.factorA + ' x ' +
                row.multiplication.factorB + '</td>' +
```

```
                    '<td>' + row.resultAttempt + '</td>' +
                    '<td>' + (row.correct === true ? 'YES' : 'NO')
                    + '</td></tr>');
        });
    });
}

$(document).ready(function() {

    updateMultiplication();

    $("#attempt-form").submit(function( event ) {

        // [...]

        updateStats(userAlias);
    });
});
```

Then we add a pretty basic table to the HTML code to render the results, as shown in Listing 3-46.

Listing 3-46. index.html Adding Attempts Table (social-multiplication v4)

```
<!DOCTYPE html>
<html>
<head>
    <title>Multiplication v1</title>
    <link rel="stylesheet" type="text/css" href="styles.css">
    <script src="https://ajax.googleapis.com/ajax/libs/
            jquery/3.1.1/jquery.min.js"></script>
    <script src="multiplication-client.js"></script>
</head>
```

```html
<body>
<div>
    <h1>Welcome to Social Multiplication</h1>
    <h2>This is your challenge for today:</h2>
    <h1>
        <span class="multiplication-a"></span> x <span
class="multiplication-b"></span> =
    </h1>
    <p>
        <form id="attempt-form">
            Result? <input type="text" name="result-
            attempt"><br>
            Your alias: <input type="text" name="user-
            alias"><br>
            <input type="submit" value="Check">
        </form>
    </p>
    <h2><span class="result-message"></span></h2>
    <h2>Stats</h2>
    <table id="stats" style="width:100%">
        <tr>
            <th>Attempt ID</th>
            <th>Multiplication</th>
            <th>You entered</th>
            <th>Correct?</th>
        </tr>
        <tbody id="stats-body"></tbody>
    </table>
</div>
</body>
</html>
```

```
WE DID IT AGAIN! USER STORY 2 IS FINISHED
```

We completed our new requirements! We created our data model,
implemented it on our entities, and created the repositories to persist and
collect our data. We also exposed a new endpoint to retrieve these latest
attempts and included a new component in the UI. Time to play with our new
functionality!

Playing with the Application (Part II)

Finally! We have a second version of the application, now with persistence
included. You already looked at the multiplication logic before, so now you
can focus on the new feature—persistence and displaying attempts.

Run the application either using the code or packaging it, as you saw
earlier. Then navigate to `http://localhost:8080/index.html` with your
browser. Try to solve some multiplications, making sure you try at least five
times. You'll get something like Figure 3-4.

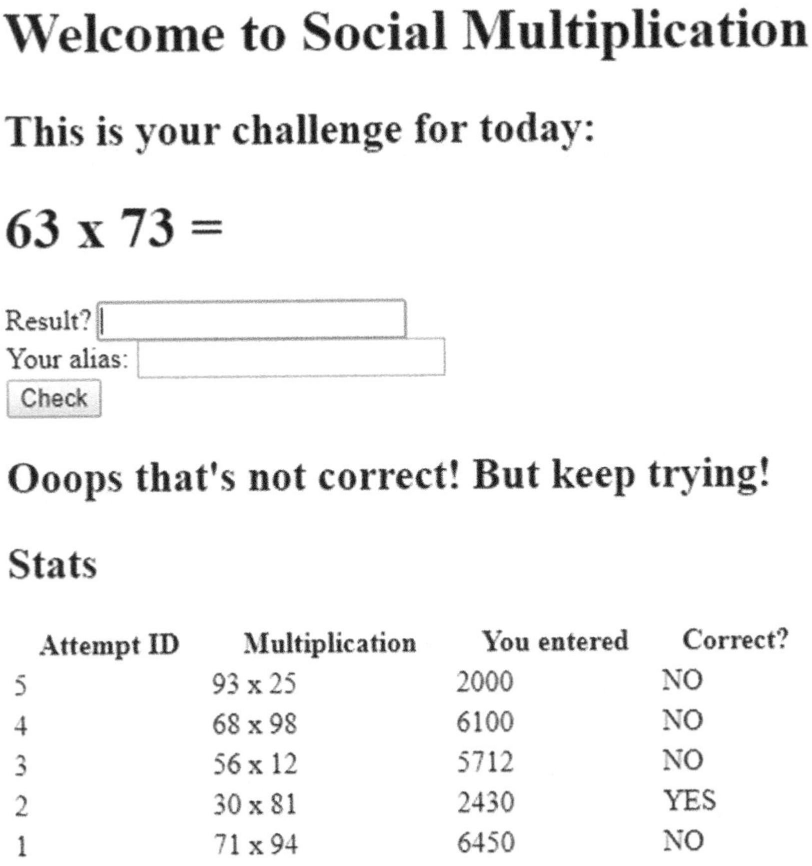

Welcome to Social Multiplication

This is your challenge for today:

63 x 73 =

Result? |
Your alias: |
[Check]

Ooops that's not correct! But keep trying!

Stats

Attempt ID	Multiplication	You entered	Correct?
5	93 x 25	2000	NO
4	68 x 98	6100	NO
3	56 x 12	5712	NO
2	30 x 81	2430	YES
1	71 x 94	6450	NO

Figure 3-4. Improved application that lists previous tries

Looking better! The interface is simple, but it's good enough. Anyway, we'll improve it in a later chapter. If you want to look at the data, you can navigate to http://localhost:8080/h2-console/. You'll see the H2 Console login screen, where you can enter the JDBC URL (in case it's not already there): jdbc:h2:file:~/social-multiplication. Leave the other fields as they are. See Figure 3-5.

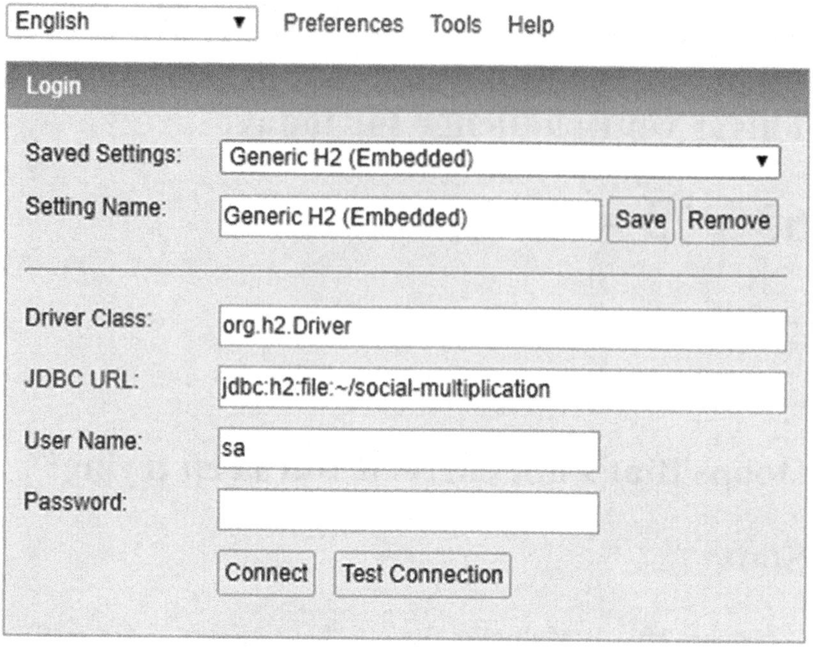

Figure 3-5. *Enter the JDBC URL here*

When you click Connect, you are presented with a rudimentary interface from which you can execute all kind of commands to the database (see Figure 3-6). If you click on a table name, the console will generate a standard `select-all` query for you that you can then execute by clicking the Run button.

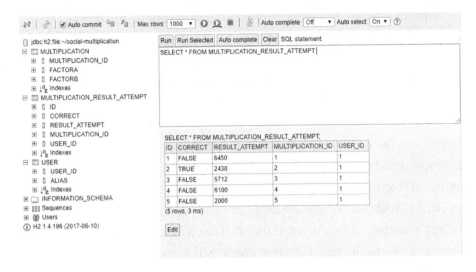

Figure 3-6. *You can execute commands to the database from this screen*

Summary

In this chapter, you learned how to build your first real-life application using Spring Boot. You'll use it as one of your microservices in a later chapter, when you'll learn about functionality spread across multiple applications.

We used a simulated Agile approach to deliver value as early as possible and built a complete web application in just two iterations (represented as two user stories). This chapter tried to show you how it's preferable to start simple and then apply modifications when they're needed: we started without a database, and later we evolved our code to include it.

Another important concept in this chapter was test-driven development: we took the use case and implemented the unit test, before coding the implementation. If you get used to this approach, you'll see how many advantages it brings you—one of the the most important is the improvement of your functional requirements' definition.

Without a doubt, the most important topic has been the proper software design of the application: you used a three-tier approach, layering it in domain, application, presentation, and data. This is a well-known pattern for its benefits related to loose coupling and clear separation of responsibilities. The first part of the chapter focused on the business logic and the presentation layers, including a simple frontend to allow user interaction. Then, we got new requirements that drove us to design and develop a data layer. But, before that, we needed to stop for a while to prepare our application for that—we needed a refactoring task, as usually happens in real life. Finally, we designed and implemented our data model and repositories, and connected them all the way up the layers to the user interface to show the latest attempts sent by the users.

You can apply now the knowledge from this book to write well-designed, layered Spring Boot applications. But there is still much more to learn: once you get several of these applications, how are they going to connect to each other? How do they see each other's instances if they start to scale up? These are the questions we'll cover in coming chapters. It's time to move to *microservices*.

CHAPTER 4

Starting with Microservices

The Small Monolith Approach

Chapter 3 ended with a single deployable application that contained not only the different backend functionalities but also the frontend side. Our application is a *small monolith*. As an alternative, we could have started designing a complete system, identifying the different contexts (or bounded contexts)[1] in it, mapping them to microservices, and then developing all of them from the beginning, at the same time.

You might be tempted to follow that strategy. One good reason to do it is that you could have multiple teams working in parallel in different microservices, so you could take advantage of mapping microservices to teams from the beginning—happy days, you could finish earlier. My experience says don't do that, and I'm not the only one advocating for a monolith-first approach (see https://tpd.io/monofirst).

When you develop software the Agile way, you can't wait a long time to deliver your software. Neither can you spend weeks designing your complete system in advance, with details. Within the product or project execution time, you better deliver full-working slices of your software. If you start splitting your project into microservices from the beginning

---

[1]https://tpd.io/bounded-ctx

© Moises Macero 2017
M. Macero, *Learn Microservices with Spring Boot*,
https://doi.org/10.1007/978-1-4842-3165-4_4

using a sheet of paper (or a nice digital drawing), that won't be the case: it will take much longer than building a monolith. Why? Because it's technically more difficult to deploy, orchestrate, and test a system based on microservices.

There is another good reason for you not to start from scratch with microservices: your system will likely have poor software design, worse than when building a monolith. This prediction has more to do with the way people work: when you divide the work into different pieces and assign them to different teams, the teams often start caring about their pieces of work and not about the entire system. Design, as it was done at the beginning, can be corrupted easily. Teams can start ignoring the company's common guidelines and principles unless you keep all microservices in control (and that is a very hard work for architects). End-to-end testing is much more difficult to set up with all those pieces evolving on their own. In this scenario, I'm assuming you already had a clear picture of the APIs and ways of communication between your different microservices. If you don't even have that, I'd stick to the monolith to start with, no doubt.

That's not to say that you can't be successful in predicting your microservice boundaries in advance and developing them in parallel but, in that case, you should pay much more attention to deployment, integration testing, common standards compliance, clear APIs, logging and monitoring, error handling, communication channels between teams, etc. Failing only in one of these topics can jeopardize your project if you start directly with microservices.

Consider a better approach: plan a monolithic application first. Plan it in a way that it can be split later with little effort:

- *Compartmentalize your code in root packages defining your domain contexts.* For instance, your application may have functionalities related to customers (person, company, address, etc.) and others related to orders (order generation, dispatch, handling, etc.). Instead of packaging your root structure directly by layers, you can create top levels where you first split customers and orders. Then, replicate the layering for each of them (e.g., controller, repository, domain, and service) and make sure you follow good practices for class visibility (implementations are package-private). The main advantages you get with this structure are that you keep business logic inaccessible across domain contexts, and that later you should be able to extract one complete root package as a microservice if you need it, with less refactoring.

- *Take advantage of dependency injection: base your code on interfaces, and let Spring do its job injecting the implementations.* Refactoring using this pattern is much easier. For example, you may change an implementation to call to a different microservice instead of keeping all the business logic in one place (if that makes sense for you when you design your boundaries).

- *Once you have identified the contexts (e.g., customers and orders) give them a consistent name across your application.* Move your domain logic here and there (easier with a small monolith) during the design phase until boundaries are clear, and then respect the boundaries. Never take shortcuts tangling business logic across contexts just because you can. Always keep in mind that the monolith should be prepared to evolve.

- *Find common patterns and identify what can be later extracted as common libraries, for example.*

- *Use peer reviews[2] to make sure the architecture designs are understood and followed.*

- *Clearly communicate to the project manager to plan time in later releases to split the monolith.* Explain the strategy and create the culture: refactoring is going to be necessary and there is nothing wrong with it.

Try to keep a small monolith at least until your first release. Don't be afraid of it—a small monolith will bring you lots of advantages:

- You make progress and have something to play with: business users can start checking if that's what they wanted and make adjustments.

- You can easily change the Domain Model you made: check if it's good enough or not, and adapt it.

- Your team(s) will get used to the common technical and functional company guidelines for the project.

- Common cross-domain functionality can be identified and extracted as libraries.

- Everybody works with the first version of the complete system, so it's easier that they get to understand the complete view and not just parts.

On the other hand, there are some disadvantages that you can try to palliate:

- You know you're building a monolith, and that does not feel good. However, this shouldn't bother you too much if you're following good design patterns to help you to split it later (compartmentalize, use interfaces, etc.).

---

[2]If you are not familiar with peer reviews, see https://www.atlassian.com/agile/code-reviews.

- Your first deployment strategy will be partly obsolete.
  But you can reuse your existing tools the same way, just
  adapting them to multiple services.

- Too many people working at the same time in the
  same codebase can be noisy and inefficient. My
  recommendation here is to start small with the team
  as well. Work with project managers: if the scope is
  planned to deliver a good, small monolith, the team
  doesn't need to be big for the first release. Resources can
  be employed in a different way: it would be even a better
  idea to start in parallel two different alternatives for the
  small monolith, with the same functionality, and then
  discard one of them when you reach the first release.

Analyzing the Monolith

Figure 4-1 depicts how the application looks like up to now.

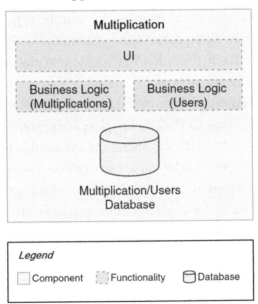

Figure 4-1. *The application thus far*

103

So far we have been building a small monolith. After extracting the requirements for the first user story, we can identify at least three parts:

- The *multiplication domain*, which handles generation and verification of operations.

- The *user domain*, which handles information related to users.

- The *UI component*, which communicates with the REST API and holds the web page.

These are the parts that could have been started independently, and deployed as such, with some redesign of the references between the multiplication's domain objects and the user's. Note that we're not considering UI a domain; it's just a technical component of our application that can be extracted separately. We're exposing our application behavior through a REST API so it makes more sense to have the Web UI in a different, independently-deployable component. One of the reasons is that we could have a mobile app consuming the same API, which doesn't need the Web interfaces. Also, the UI could evolve to a single page application consuming APIs from different services (e.g., multiplication and user). For all these reasons, you'll see that UI code is often placed into a different service in many software projects.

In any case, we didn't split anything from scratch when creating our application. The reasons, as you can imagine, are the ones covered in the previous subsection about the advantages of a monolith-first approach. Note that book examples can be traps: you can't live the complete process of design and development, so it's more difficult to sell you the idea of a better match between the small monolith and fast experimenting. You could still be wondering why this book didn't start directly with a predefined set of services that work perfectly all together. I could have skipped the monolith to make the code nicer, but that would go against the basic idea of this book: being a practical, evolving a software project as you would do in reality. But not only that, if we would have started with the complete ecosystem of services and the needed tools to support them, the entire business goal of our example application would have been *diluted by technical details*. To explain it better in practice, if we would have taken the decision of starting directly with microservices for our first requirements (user story 1), we would have needed to go through almost the entire book before delivering our first working application.

Moving Forward

What are the next steps to evolve our application? We're keeping the multiplication application as it is for a little bit longer, since before doing the complete refactor, we'll introduce a second Spring Boot application in our system. And that, as always, is driven by a new functionality.

USER STORY 3

As a user of the application, I want to be more motivated to participate every day, so I don't give up easily.

Note that this one can be also written from another perspective: "As the administrator of the application, I want users to come back every day so I can later monetize the recurrent visits."

In this fictional scenario, there could be some people on the team who know about *gamification techniques* and want to apply them here to encourage users to come back every day to the page. Let's say that the idea sinks in, so now the architecture team decides how to solve it: that's us.

Gamification seems a completely different world, nothing to do with solving multiplications. It's our perfect opportunity to design our model and then make it a reality as a separate Spring Boot application, now that we have the first version of the current application already up and running.

105

We're moving to a microservices architecture now, in which our existing Spring Boot application will become the *multiplication microservice*, and the new application would become the *gamification microservice*.

But before going into more detail, let me introduce some basic concepts about gamification techniques and discuss how we're going to apply them to our system.

Gamification Basics

Gamification is the design process in which you apply techniques used commonly in games to some other field, which was not initially a game. Normally you do that because you want to get some well-known benefits from games, among others getting players motivated and interacting with your process, application, or whatever you're *gamifying*.

It's also important to clarify what is **not** gamification: it's not about trying to manipulate people. It's not magic you can apply everywhere to make people like something.

Applying game techniques can be rather complex, and goes easily into big knowledge areas like motivation, personal interests, and psychology, in general. We'll cover a simplification of it based on some basic tools available for the game designer—points, badges, and leaderboards.

Points, Badges, and Leaderboards

One basic idea about making things a game is introducing *points*: every time you perform an action, and you do well, you get some points. You can even get points if you didn't perform so well, but it should be a fair mechanism: you get more if you do better. Winning points make the player feel as if they're progressing, which gives them *feedback*.

Leaderboards make the points visible to everybody, so they motivate players by activating feelings of competition. We want to get more points than the person above us and rank higher. This is even more fun if you play with friends.

Last but not least, *badges* are virtual symbols of achieving a *status*. We like badges; they say more than points. Also, they can represent different things: you can have same points as another player (e.g., five correct answers), but you could have won them in a different way (e.g., *five in a minute!*).

There are different software applications that are not games but that use these elements very well, StackOverflow being my favorite. You can look at the stackoverflow.com web page if you don't know it yet: everything is designed with game elements to encourage people to keep participating.

It's important to note that using these tools won't make your application a nicely designed game since there are many other aspects that should be taken into account as well if we want to achieve a better result. However, for the sake of the main goal of this book, this is more than enough.

Applying It to the Example

What we'll do is assign points to every correct answer that users submit. To keep it simple, we'll only give points if they send a correct answer. Instead of giving one point, which doesn't feel as good, we'll make it 10 points per correct answer.

A *leaderboard* with the top scores will be shown on the page, so players can find themselves in the ranking and compete with others.

We'll create also some basic badges: *Bronze* (10 correct attempts), *Silver* (25 correct attempts), and *Gold* (50 correct attempts). The badges should not be extraordinarily difficult to obtain, because that wouldn't motivate our users. Because the first correct attempt can be hard to achieve, we'll also introduce the badge called *First Correct!*, to give quick positive feedback.

We could introduce more badges in the future, some other game mechanics, etc. But with these basics, we already have something that may motivate our users to come back and keep playing, competing with their peers.

Moving to a Microservices Architecture

So we decided to move to a microservices architecture: we'll create a different part of our system that's independently deployable and decoupled from the previous business logic (the *gamification microservice*). We'll need to connect the existing Spring Boot application (that now we can call the *multiplication microservice*) with the new one and make sure that they can scale up independently. And the big question is: why should we do that? Why not continue just with the one-project (monolithic) approach? As usual, we'll answer that question from a practical point of view, based on some strong reasons.

Separation of Concerns and Loose Coupling

If we put together the gamification logic with the existing logic, within the same codebase and the same deployable artifact, we run the risk of mixing them up in the future, throwing away all the advantages of the separation of concerns. You may think that this won't happen, but in reality the longer you have these domains together, the higher the risk somebody will take shortcuts. Especially if you also store your data in the same database.

As we saw when we were describing the advantages of a monolith-first approach, keeping everything together eases the design and development during the first phase of the project. However, if you want to migrate to microservices for its advantages, it's critical to find the proper timing along the project's lifecycle to stop growing your monolith. Otherwise, you'll find yourself traveling from a small-monolith to a medium-size-monolith, and from there to a "certified monolith". Of course, the risk is tenfold if the software project is being managed under high pressure and tight guidelines. This is a perfect environment for shortcuts and for the monolith to grow without control.

Achieving loose coupling is hard. Let's use the example in which new requirements say that you want to show in a table every multiplication with the number of points won: it's so easy to write a *join query* that many developers will use it. Even if you have different data stores, somebody could write a class using the different domains together and add some extra business logic on top of that. The problem is much more visible if you think of a system with multiple domain contexts: soon you would have *spaghetti services* mixing domain objects and business logic here and there. The jungle. And then you'd need your machete and a lot of patience to untangle everything. Having multiplication and gamification separated in different microservices will force you to think of a loosely-coupled solution: you can replicate part of the data, or have one service calling the other one whenever it's needed. We'll see an example of this in our system.

Independent Changes

Having independently deployable services for the multiplication and gamification domains will allow us to test them separately, using their APIs. In the future, we could have the gamification team evolving their services without interfering in the development cycle of the multiplication team. If they need new interfaces for communication, they can just create fake calls or messages—therefore defining their API changes—and move forward. Note again the main advantage here: they know for sure that they won't break anything in the multiplication service, and they are not blocking each other. This peace of mind makes project managers sleep at night.

Scalability

Imagine that we make a great success with the multiplication game. Users start using it from thousands to millions, and soon enough the cloud server we chose starts running low on resources and not responding on time to the multiplication checks. So we want to scale our system up and apply some load balancing techniques.

If we would have one single deployable artifact (the entire system) the only thing we can do is create several instances of that one. But that could imply wasting resources, or at least not being as flexible as we could. If we have multiple services, we can choose how to scale up, and a valid strategy for this case could be scaling the multiplication service up to cope with our new needs, but not the gamification one since it's not so important if points and leaderboards are calculated with a delay. Of course, that strategy is more complex to achieve than the previous one, but let's not forget that servers and cloud computing cost money, and saving money is good for every software project.

Connecting Microservices

We will create gamification logic in a separate microservice. It should *somehow* connect with our existing business process of *solving an attempt and getting feedback*, extending it to be *solving an attempt, getting feedback, and winning points*.

How do we span our process across those two microservices? If you ask this question to people who never worked with an event-driven approach, you'll get usually some of these answers:

1. They could share the database so the gamification service can use the data there directly.

2. The gamification service could poll data periodically from the multiplication service and process it as needed to assign points, badges, etc. That could be done by exposing some extra REST APIs in our existing service.

3. When something happens in the multiplication service (i.e., an attempt is sent), this one will call gamification service and pass the data, so this one can update the game stats. This is a kind of Remote Procedure Call (RPC) approach.

Let's analyze these alternatives. Option 1 is not a good approach since many of the advantages of decoupling contexts would be lost the very moment that services can access and mix up each other's data.

Option 2 sounds better, but requires constant polling for new data and keeping track of which attempts have been already processed (for instance, by asking for attempts sent since the last time gamification processed them).

Option 3 could be preferred over Option 2 since, in this case, we don't need the polling mechanism. But there is still one thing that can be improved: multiplication service does not need to know about gamification service. We should be able to design a system in which our multiplication service can live without gamification and still behave as it is now in the current status of the application.

So we can go for an improved variation of the third option, designing a way of communication in which services are as decoupled as possible. Multiplication will notify—to whoever is interested—that a new multiplication attempt has been entered in the system, by sending an event to a message bus. In the future, other pieces of logic could connect their business processes in a transparent way to the existing one without an impact on the others:

- Do we want to send an e-mail to the administrator whenever a user exhibits a suspicious behavior, meaning too many consecutive correct attempts? We subscribe to the same `MultiplicationSolvedEvent` and perform our business logic in a different microservice.

- Do we want to gather analytics and build statistics like correct attempts per user, per time of the day, etc.? It's also possible with a new microservice, without impacting the others.

111

- Do we want to add a social network plugin to post new correctly-solved attempts? Great, that's another microservice consuming the same event and doing its part independently.

As you can see, designing our functionality following these reactive patterns give us a lot of flexibility. This way of modeling our architecture is known as *event-driven architecture* or *reactive systems*.

However, the event-driven strategy doesn't fit in all the interactions required between microservices. Within our business processes we may have scenarios in which services need data from each other, not necessarily related to an event. In those cases, we can't use an event-driven approach since they're matching a request-response pattern. An example of that, based on our previous examples, would be the social network service. That one would need to access the user alias (and probably some other to-be-implemented details). To illustrate how this way of communication combines with an event-driven approach, we cover a practical case using our application.

Event-Driven Architecture

In this type of architecture, the different microservices send *events* whenever an important action happens. Those events are exchanged between microservices through a message broker (also called sometimes *event bus*). Others can subscribe to events for which they are interested and *react* to them.

Note an important concept: an action that already happened. Others can't change it and can't prevent it from happening. That's why event names are commonly given as past actions: `MultiplicationSolvedEvent`. What other microservices will do (if they are *subscribed* to this event) is process it according to their own business logic, which could lead to other events being published (e.g., `ScoreUpdatedEvent`). Systems based on this action-reaction pattern are also known as *reactive systems*, a concept that should not be confused with *reactive programming* (*see* `https://tpd.io/ rprogsys`), which is a programming style applied at a different level.

Related Techniques

Event-driven architecture has an affinity for some other techniques: event sourcing, domain-driven design, and CQRS. You can apply them independently and you should always use them reasonably. When designing your system, try not to be seduced by technology hypes, but use them as tools to solve your problems.

Event sourcing is an approach to persist business entities. Instead of modeling them with a static state that you can change over time, you model them as sequences of immutable events. If we use a common example such as `Customer`, there wouldn't be a `Customer` table in your data but a sequence of `CustomerChanged` events. Let's imagine the case in which we create a customer with given value `name: John`. We change it to `name: Jhonas` and we notice we made a mistake and change it back to `name: John`. In a traditional persistence method, if you check the data after applying these changes, you will only see the `name: John` state. Using event sourcing, your entity is the final status of reproducing the sequence of events `CustomerChanged -> name: John` (created), `CustomerChanged -> name: Jhonas` (mistake), `CustomerChanged -> name: John` (correction). The common examples normally used for event sourcing are based on banking applications, for which this pattern makes a lot of sense. Your account is a compilation of transactions over time.

As you can imagine, event sourcing can be implemented easier in a system that is based on events. However, it does not come for free: you can design your event-driven architecture with a few events, but going full event sourcing can increment significantly the number of events that you need to model. The system will use event-driven architecture, but our persistence is not based on event sourcing.

If you want to learn more about event sourcing, the article at `https://tpd.io/evsrc` is a good starting point.

Domain-driven design (sometimes abbreviated as DDD) is a pattern applied to software, first described by Eric Evans in his book *Domain-Driven Design: Tackling Complexity in the Heart of Software*. More than a pattern could be even defined as a philosophy for designing software, in which your business domain is the core of your system.

When you follow DDD patterns, you can identify *bounded contexts*, which are like subdomains that can be treated separately in your system. This is very useful when designing microservices, since they can easily be mapped to bounded contexts and benefit from the DDD approach. In this book, we're following some of these principles.

For extra reading about DDD, you can buy Eric Evans' book or download for free the InfoQ minibook at `https://www.infoq.com/minibooks/domain-driven-design-quickly`.

CQRS (Command-Query Responsibility Segregation) is a pattern in which the *query model* (for reading) and the *command model* (for writing) are separated, thus enabling a very fast reading approach at the expense of having a much more complex system. It can be used together with event sourcing, being the event store the write model.

This article from Martin Fowler is a good starting point if you want to read more about CQRS: `https://martinfowler.com/bliki/CQRS.html`.

Pros and Cons of Event-Driven Architecture

Let's use our application to explain the advantages and disadvantages of an event-driven architecture in a practical way. Our scenario is the following: if we send an attempt to solve a multiplication problem, we'll process it in the multiplication microservice and then send a `MultiplicationSolvedEvent`. The new gamification microservice will consume these types of events and assign a new score to the proper user. They keep their data and their functionality separate.

As you'll see, some of the following topics can't be immediately mapped to *advantage* or *disadvantage*. Those are characteristics of your system that, on the one hand, may give you more work to do, but on the other hand, you can benefit from.

Loose Coupling

With event-driven architecture, we can achieve loose coupling between our services, as described in the previous section when analyzing the options to connect them. You can also split big processes into smaller pieces, having them completed by multiple services in an independent manner. In our system, the *attempt-to-points* process is divided into two microservices.

This is a great advantage: we have our processes there, but they are *distributed*. There is no place in the system that controls—and potentially tangles—everything else.

Transactions

On the other hand, in an architecture based on events you need to assume that you don't have ACID[3] transactions across services anymore (or understand that, if you want to support them, you need to introduce complexity). Instead, you have eventual consistency, if you stop all interactions with the system and let all the events propagate and be consumed, you'll get to a consistent state.

In our scenario, if the gamification service is down and we don't implement any mechanism to prevent it, the score will not be updated. This means that there is no atomicity in the transaction Solve Multiplication - Get Points. A solution for this is using a message broker implementation that guarantees delivery of the events at least once.

---

[3]https://en.wikipedia.org/wiki/ACID

Not having transactions across services is not bad per se. The big risk here is that it requires a change in the way you design and translate your functional requirements (e.g., what happens if the process is interrupted at step N?).

Fault Tolerance

As a consequence of not having (or minimizing) transactions, fault tolerance becomes more important in these systems. One of the services might not be able to complete its part of the process, but that shouldn't make the whole system fail. You need to prevent that from happening (e.g., by aiming for high availability with microservice redundancy and load-balancing) and also think of a way to recover from possible errors (e.g., by having a maintenance console from which you can recreate events).

In any case, including fault tolerance is good in any kind of system, not only those using an event-driven approach. If you implement it properly, your distributed system can reach higher availability than a monolith. Big transaction scopes failing in a monolith will be rolled-back and users can't do anything. Events are queued for later processing so small parts of the system can die independently and restart automatically. That's much more powerful.

Orchestration and Monitoring

Not having a *centralized orchestration layer* might be problematic in systems where it's critical to have process monitoring. In an event-driven architecture, you span processes across services that are triggering and reacting to events. You can't follow them in a centralized way: they're distributed across your microservices. To monitor such processes, you need to implement mechanisms to trace the flow of events and you need a common logging system where you can keep track of what's going on between services.

Let's imagine that the system evolves and there are four different services reacting to the first event (`MultiplicationSolvedEvent`), with some other subsequent events happening after that (`ScoreUpdatedEvent ->`

`LeaderboardPositionChangedEvent -> CongratulationsEmailSent`).
It would be difficult to keep track of what's happening as an end-to-end
business process, unless we manually maintain good documentation or
introduce something else that does automatic tracing in our code. How
do we know, by just looking at the system from a high perspective, that an
e-mail might be sent when a multiplication is solved? We can implement
our own integrated mechanism to correlate events (by tagging them as
they cross the services), or we can use an existing tool like Zipkin.[4]

Evaluate Before Making a Decision

To sum up, it's important for you to weigh these factors (and their
advantages and disadvantages) when you consider implementing a system
using an event-driven approach. If you go for it because of the advantages,
keep the drawbacks in mind and prepare the solutions.

Further Reading

To avoid breaking the practical approach of this book, you won't find here
an extensive description of event-driven architecture concepts, but I provide
you with some good articles in case you're eager to dive into the topics:

- This article from nginx describes the basics
  about event-driven architecture in the context of
  microservices. The full series is great for grasping the
  important concepts. *https://tpd.io/edd-mgm*

- This article from Microsoft is a little bit more technical,
  but it provides extra insight into the communication.
  Some parts are not easy to read though. *https://tpd.
  io/ms-ev-arc*

---

[4]`https://github.com/openzipkin/zipkin`

- This article from O'Reilly is also interesting since it shows two different variations you can implement depending on your orchestration needs. *https://tpd. io/edvars*

Applying Event-Driven Architecture to the Application

At this point of the chapter, it's clear that we'll use a new Spring Boot application to implement the gamification logic. We decided to move to microservices: our functionality is split into the multiplication application (now the *multiplication microservice*) and the gamification application (*gamification microservice*).

Besides, we'll use an event-driven architecture applied to our microservices, so we need now to model the interactions between these two different contexts (multiplication and gamification) as events.

Figure 4-2 shows the logical view that illustrates what we want to achieve in the chapter.

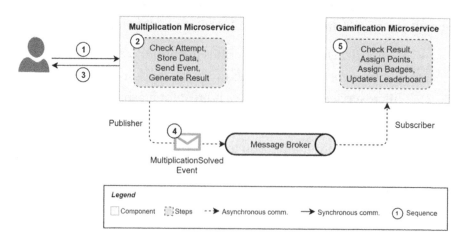

Figure 4-2. *Logical view of the interactions between the two contexts*

We want the multiplication service to behave as it is now, with the only difference that we need to communicate to interested parties that a multiplication has been solved correctly. In order to do that, we model the MultiplicationSolvedEvent, which represents that business action in the system.

Then, we'll model the new business logic for gamification in a new service, which will consume events of our new type from the event bus. When a new event is received, it processes the data contained in it and assigns points and badges to the user.

INCREMENTAL CHANGE

Note that we don't expose the gamification functionality to the user interface in this chapter since that would mean lots of refactoring. We want to keep the focus on the event-driven architecture patterns and respect the incremental/Agile mindset of this book, so the needed changes to expose that functionality will be covered in the next chapter. Spoiler: we won't finish our new user story by the end of this chapter. But no worries, you'll get there soon.

Going Event-Driven with RabbitMQ and Spring AMQP

RabbitMQ is an open source message broker that is nicely integrated with Spring Boot. It is the perfect tool to send and receive messages in this application. Besides, it implements AMQP (*Advanced Message Queuing Protocol*) so we can write our code in a generic way, avoiding coupling with the tool itself.

If you want to get full details about the AMQP Model in RabbitMQ, the official tutorial is a good starting point, where you can learn more about the concepts of queue, exchange, and route, and also learn about the different types of exchanges: *Direct, Fanout, Topic, and Headers*. See https://www.rabbitmq.com/tutorials/amqp-concepts.html.

Using RabbitMQ in Your System

Let's start with defining what we need from RabbitMQ to achieve what we defined in our logical view. Don't worry about the concepts now; we'll extend them through this chapter.

- We'll create an *exchange*, which is a channel to which multiplication will send basic MultiplicationSolvedEvent messages. We choose JSON to serialize them, since it's a widely-extended format and also human-readable.

- Our exchange will be of type *topic*. This is to illustrate the most flexible way of sending messages.

- We'll send our event message with a routing key called multiplication.solved.

- On the subscriber side (the gamification microservice), we'll create a queue and bind it to our topic exchange to receive the messages we're interested in.

- We'll make our queues durable. By doing this, we make sure that even if the broker (RabbitMQ) goes down, we'll be able to process the events whenever they are back (because the messages are persisted).

The flexibility of *topic exchanges* and *routing keys* comes from the fact that multiple subscribers can bind queues to the same exchange with different routing keys, thus potentially receiving a different subset of messages. Think of the example of an online store: a microservice in charge of canceling orders would subscribe to order.cancelled, while the one responsible for sending e-mails would subscribe to order.* (which means whatever happens to orders: cancel, delayed, etc.). As you may guess, designing exchanges, queues, and routing keys is not easy, especially if you want to achieve optimal performance. I recommend that you go through the Spring AMQP tutorial[5] on the RabbitMQ web site to get familiar with all these concepts. Anyway, we cover this practical example while implementing the subscriber's side within the gamification microservice.

Spring AMQP

We'll interact with our RabbitMQ broker using Spring AMQP. All we need to do from our Spring Boot applications to start using it is to include the `spring-boot-starter-amqp` dependency.

We could configure our exchange and queue directly through RabbitMQ (using the command line or the UI), but instead we'll do that from the Java code using Spring AMQP. The main advantage is that every service keeps its AMQP configuration in control, not needing to depend on a central place to maintain it.

However, the main drawback of not starting RabbitMQ *fully-configured* is that services can't assume, for instance, that the exchange is there before they start. Our gamification microservice should contain configuration to create the topic exchange, just in case it starts before the multiplication microservice. However, that's not a big issue since Spring AMQP will not create duplicated exchanges or queues but take the existing ones if they are already there.

Sending Events from Multiplication

Let's get practical! We want to make our existing multiplication microservice work in an event-driven ecosystem. We made our technical choices: RabbitMQ as a broker and Spring AMQP to interact with it from the Java code.

---

[5]https://www.rabbitmq.com/tutorials/tutorial-three-spring-amqp.html

Remember: we're aiming to have multiplication sending a MultiplicationSolvedEvent every time a new attempt is sent by a user. Later we'll implement our new gamification microservice, which will subscribe to that event and react upon it.

RabbitMQ Configuration

As mentioned, we need to edit the pom.xml file to include the new dependency spring-boot-starter-amqp. This starter contains the dependencies to use Spring AQMP (spring-messaging) and RabbitMQ (spring-rabbit). See Listing 4-1.

Listing 4-1. pom.xml (social-multiplication v5)

```
<dependency>
        <groupId>org.springframework.boot</groupId>
        <artifactId>spring-boot-starter-amqp</artifactId>
</dependency>
```

Now we can start modifying our code. We create a new class called RabbitMQConfiguration under a new package called configuration. We add the @Configuration annotation so Spring will use it when setting up the application context to generate the beans that we'll define. This class will be automatically processed since it's located in a child package with respect to our main Application class, and our @SpringBootApplication annotation includes @ComponentScan.

From our publisher's side (multiplication), the minimum configuration we need is a TopicExchange to send our event. But we'll also add configuration to change the default message format to JSON; later we'll see why. See Listing 4-2.

122

Listing 4-2. RabbitMQConfiguration.java (social-multiplication v5)

```java
/**
 * Configures RabbitMQ to use events in our application.
 */
@Configuration
public class RabbitMQConfiguration {

    @Bean
    public TopicExchange multiplicationExchange(@
    Value("${multiplication.exchange}") final String
    exchangeName) {
        return new TopicExchange(exchangeName);
    }

    @Bean
    public RabbitTemplate rabbitTemplate(final
    ConnectionFactory connectionFactory) {
        final RabbitTemplate rabbitTemplate = new Rabbit
        Template(connectionFactory);
        rabbitTemplate.setMessageConverter(producerJackson2
        MessageConverter());
        return rabbitTemplate;
    }

    @Bean
    public Jackson2JsonMessageConverter producer
    Jackson2MessageConverter() {
        return new Jackson2JsonMessageConverter();
    }

}
```

- We create the `TopicExchange` bean using a name
  defined by us in a property that we need to add
  to our `application.properties` file (a new line
  `multiplication.exchange=multiplication_`
  `exchange`). The name itself is not important but take
  into account that we'll need to use the same one when
  we configure our new gamification microservice. The
  `@Value` annotation and the syntax inside are the way to
  inject a property value in Spring Boot.

- With the second and third methods, we change the
  default serialization mechanism. The last one injects
  a `Jackson2JsonMessageConverter`, which takes
  Java objects and serializes them to JSON. With the
  `rabbitTemplate()` bean declaration, we override the
  default `RabbitTemplate` injected by Spring. We take
  as an argument the `ConnectionFactory` (injected
  by Spring in the application context) and create a
  `RabbitTemplate` bean that uses our JSON message
  converter. Later we'll inject that `RabbitTemplate` and
  use it to publish our event message.

Changing the serialization method to JSON instead of using the
default Java serialization mechanism is good practice in general for several
reasons:

- Java serialization of messages uses a header
  (`__TypeId__`) to tag the full name of the class. That
  means we need all subscribers that are going to
  deserialize the message to use the same class name,
  in the same package. This introduces tight coupling
  between services.

- If we want to connect in the future with other polyglot services, we can't rely on a Java serialization.

- Trying to analyze possible errors in the channel (queues and exchanges) is a nightmare if you don't use a human-readable format (at least in early stages of development).

If you want to check in detail the technical differences between these two serialization mechanisms (JSON and Java Serialized Object), you can read the article at *https://tpd.io/rmqjson*.

Modeling the Event

Let's create the piece of information that will be exchanged by these two microservices: the event. Keep in mind the principles of the event-driven architecture: an event happens in the past and should be generic (unaware of the subscribers). We'll indicate that a multiplication attempt has been solved and whoever is subscribed to that is irrelevant for our multiplication microservice.

We create this new class under a new package called event and make it implement Serializable since that's a requirement of the JSON message converter. See Listing 4-3.

Listing 4-3. MultiplicationSolvedEvent.java (social-multiplication v5)

```
package microservices.book.multiplication.event;

import lombok.EqualsAndHashCode;
import lombok.Getter;
import lombok.RequiredArgsConstructor;
import lombok.ToString;

import java.io.Serializable;
```

```
/**
 * Event that models the fact that a {@link microservices.book.
multiplication.domain.Multiplication}
 * has been solved in the system. Provides some context
information about the multiplication.
 */
@RequiredArgsConstructor
@Getter
@ToString
@EqualsAndHashCode
public class MultiplicationSolvedEvent implements Serializable
{

    private final Long multiplicationResultAttemptId;
    private final Long userId;
    private final boolean correct;

}
```

Let's focus now on the contents. When modeling events, you have a wide spectrum of options regarding the information you put there. In this case, we could have included the whole `MultiplicationResultAttempt` object. That would travel in the message together with the contents of the referenced `User` and `Multiplication` objects. But why would you that? People who follow that approach are normally based on the "just in case we need it" idea.

To illustrate the risks of *fat events,* I'll use another example. Imagine that we are receiving events when user details are updated, and we decided to model the event including the changes made to the user. Think of the case in which there are multiple subscribers, one of them is failing and the broker is dispatching those rejected messages back again. Now the order of events is not the real sequence of the changes. We can't be sure on the consumer's side if that change reflects the latest status. As a possible solution, we could use a timestamp on events, but then extra logic is needed on the consumer's end to handle time: discarding older changes, etc.

Including data in events modeling changes in a mutable object is risky. In this case, it might be better to notify that the user with the given identifier has been updated, and leave the consumers to ask for the latest state whenever they decide to process their logic.

Another potential drawback of including too much data in events can be shown in the following example: if in future we include an extra microservice (e.g., a *stats analyzer*) and it needs to use the timestamp of attempts, we could just add the timestamp to MultiplicationSolvedEvent. But, in that case, we would be tailoring the events from the publisher's side to the needs of all our consumers. We would have not only a fat event but also a smart publisher who knows too much about the business logic of their consumers: an anti-pattern of event-driven architecture. In general, it's more advisable to let the consumers ask for the data they need and avoid including it as part of the event's content.

Going back to our case, we have the advantage that our *attempt* represents a reality that's immutable: we don't expect to modify attempts once they're processed by multiplication service. Using that in our benefit, we can include a reference to the user (userId) and also pass a boolean value indicating if the attempt was correct or not. This chunk of information is generic and immutable, and can save some extra REST requests from potential consumers (which is the side effect of having *too skinny* events).

As you can see, there is no black and white approach, but it should be clear at this point that modeling events is as important as modeling your domain. Think carefully about which ones you need to start with (don't include too many of them at once) and try to keep them as simple as possible, creating small, generic contents that are good enough for the subscribers and consistent if they are received in an unexpected order.

Sending the Event: Dispatcher Pattern

The event dispatcher (or event publisher) and event handler (or event subscriber) are two common patterns for asynchronous communication. Instead of having events being published or consumed across all your classes, these centralized points for event input/output make your service interactions easier to find and understand.

On the other hand, having all the event dispatchers or listeners in a single class may end up with a huge class and a lot of redirection logic. However, this can be seen as an advantage in a microservices architecture: if the EventDispatcher or the EventHandler classes become too big, it's probably because your microservice is not so *micro* anymore. Why would you deal with so many events within a single microservice? You should reflect on that and try to identify if it is the case that your microservice has too many responsibilities. It could also be that the microservice really needs to handle many events; then a good solution is just split event dispatchers/handlers into multiple classes, based on the business logic.

Let's focus first on the multiplication microservice and see how to implement the Dispatcher pattern there. Later in this chapter, we'll cover the subscriber's logic when we navigate through the gamification microservice's codebase. See Listing 4-4.

Listing 4-4. EventDispatcher.java (social-multiplication v5)

```
package microservices.book.multiplication.event;

import org.springframework.amqp.rabbit.core.RabbitTemplate;
import org.springframework.beans.factory.annotation.Autowired;
import org.springframework.beans.factory.annotation.Value;
import org.springframework.stereotype.Component;
/**
 * Handles the communication with the Event Bus.
 */
```

```java
@Component
public class EventDispatcher {

    private RabbitTemplate rabbitTemplate;

    // The exchange to use to send anything related to
    Multiplication
    private String multiplicationExchange;

    // The routing key to use to send this particular event
    private String multiplicationSolvedRoutingKey;

    @Autowired
    EventDispatcher(final RabbitTemplate rabbitTemplate,
                   @Value("${multiplication.exchange}") final
                   String multiplicationExchange,
                   @Value("${multiplication.solved.key}")
                   final String multiplicationSolved
                   RoutingKey) {
        this.rabbitTemplate = rabbitTemplate;
        this.multiplicationExchange = multiplicationExchange;
        this.multiplicationSolvedRoutingKey = multiplication
        SolvedRoutingKey;
    }

    public void send(final MultiplicationSolvedEvent
    multiplicationSolvedEvent) {
        rabbitTemplate.convertAndSend(
                multiplicationExchange,
                multiplicationSolvedRoutingKey,
                multiplicationSolvedEvent);
    }
}
```

The class gets the RabbitTemplate from the Spring's application context, together with the name of the exchange, and the routing key from the application properties. Then we use the template to convertAndSend our object (in this case, converted to JSON based on the provided configuration). Besides, our MultiplicationSolvedEvent will use the routing key multiplication.solved. Remember that this event will be captured by the consumer's queue using the routing pattern multiplication.*. We'll cover that later in the chapter. See Listing 4-5.

Listing 4-5. Application.Properties: Adding RabbitMQ Values (social-multiplication v5)

```
# ... (other properties)
## RabbitMQ configuration
multiplication.exchange=multiplication_exchange
multiplication.solved.key=multiplication.solved
```

The only part we're missing in our code is sending the event from our business logic. As introduced in previous subsections, we'll do that for every attempt received from users. The change is very straightforward: we just inject the EventDispatcher and use it to send a new MultiplicationSolvedEvent.

It's important to point out that Spring AMQP supports transactions. Since we have our method annotated with @Transactional, the event will not be sent in case of an exception even if we placed our eventDispatcher.send() at the beginning of the method and the exception happened afterward. For better readability, place the event senders at the end of the logic, or at least after the action happens. See Listing 4-6.

Listing 4-6. MultiplicationServiceImpl.java: Adding Event Logic (social-multiplication v5)

```
@Service
class MultiplicationServiceImpl implements
MultiplicationService {

    private RandomGeneratorService randomGeneratorService;
    private MultiplicationResultAttemptRepository
    attemptRepository;
    private UserRepository userRepository;
    private EventDispatcher eventDispatcher;

    @Autowired
    public MultiplicationServiceImpl(final RandomGenerator
    Service randomGeneratorService,
                                    final MultiplicationResult
                                    AttemptRepository attempt
                                    Repository,
                                    final UserRepository
                                    userRepository,
                                    final EventDispatcher
                                    eventDispatcher) {
        this.randomGeneratorService = randomGeneratorService;
        this.attemptRepository = attemptRepository;
        this.userRepository = userRepository;
        this.eventDispatcher = eventDispatcher;
    }

    @Override
    public Multiplication createRandomMultiplication() {
        int factorA = randomGeneratorService.generateRandom
        Factor();
```

```java
    int factorB = randomGeneratorService.
    generateRandomFactor();
    return new Multiplication(factorA, factorB);
}

@Transactional
@Override
public boolean checkAttempt(final
MultiplicationResultAttempt attempt) {
    // Check if the user already exists for that alias
    Optional<User> user = userRepository.
    findByAlias(attempt.getUser().getAlias());
    // Avoids 'hack' attempts
    Assert.isTrue(!attempt.isCorrect(), "You can't send an
    attempt marked as correct!!");

    // Check if the attempt is correct
    boolean isCorrect = attempt.getResultAttempt() ==
                    attempt.getMultiplication().
                    getFactorA() *
                    attempt.getMultiplication().
                    getFactorB();

    MultiplicationResultAttempt checkedAttempt = new
    MultiplicationResultAttempt(
            user.orElse(attempt.getUser()),
            attempt.getMultiplication(),
            attempt.getResultAttempt(),
            isCorrect
    );
```

```java
        // Stores the attempt
        attemptRepository.save(checkedAttempt);

        // Communicates the result via Event
        eventDispatcher.send(
                new MultiplicationSolvedEvent(checkedAttempt.
                getId(),
                        checkedAttempt.getUser().getId(),
                        checkedAttempt.isCorrect())
        );

        return isCorrect;
    }

    @Override
    public List<MultiplicationResultAttempt> getStatsForUser
    (String userAlias) {
        return attemptRepository.findTop5ByUserAliasOrderBy
        IdDesc(userAlias);
    }
}
```

EXERCISE

We updated the logic to include the EventDispatcher and our tests
will still pass, but it's not complete anymore. We want to use Mockito
to verify that, within our logic, a correct event is sent. Update the test to
include that assertion. If you need help, you can check the solution in the
MultiplicationServiceImplTest class (social-multiplication v5).

Deeper Look at the New Gamification Microservice

Code Overview

Within this section, we'll cover the implementation of our new Gamification microservice and we will see how to receive events from the existing multiplication microservice, which we just modified.

Given that this is the second Spring Boot application we build, we won't review all the details. Instead, we'll focus on the most interesting parts. In any case, the Exercise blocks will guide you through the rest of the changes needed.

SOURCE CODE AVAILABLE WITH THE BOOK: V5

You can find all the code related to this chapter (both multiplication and gamification microservices) inside the v5 repository on GitHub (the `social-multiplication` and `gamification` projects) at: `https://github.com/microservices-practical`.

Exercise

Prior to starting coding the new microservice, you need to create a project for it. As you did before, you can use Spring Initializr (http://start.spring.io). Call the new application `gamification` and use the `microservices.book.gamification` package. Besides the Web dependency, you should also include Lombok, H2, and AMQP.

After extracting the project, open the `pom.xml` and align the dependency versions to the ones in the multiplication application. This way, you avoid a potentially different behavior from the one described in this book.

The Domain

First, let's take some time to understand the gamification domain model. It consists of the following:

- ScoreCard: Models one incremental set of points that a given user gets at a given time.

- Badge: An enumeration of all possible badges in the game.

- BadgeCard: Represents a badge linked to a certain user, won at a certain time.

- LeaderBoardRow: A position in the leaderboard that is the total score together with the user.

- GameStats: Score and badges for a given user. It can be used for a given game iteration (one attempt's result) or for a collection of attempts (aggregating score and badges).

Cards (score and badge) contain the moment in time they were obtained. The result of a game iteration may contain one or more ScoreCards and one or more BadgeCards. See Figure 4-3.

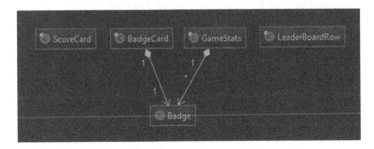

Figure 4-3. *The gamification domain model*

Let's take a quick look at the codebase for these domain classes. See Listings 4-7 through 4-11.

Listing 4-7. Badge.java (gamification v5)

```java
package microservices.book.gamification.domain;

/**
 * Enumeration with the different types of Badges that a user
   can win.
 */
public enum Badge {

    // Badges depending on score
    BRONZE_MULTIPLICATOR,
    SILVER_MULTIPLICATOR,
    GOLD_MULTIPLICATOR,

    // Other badges won for different conditions
    FIRST_ATTEMPT,
    FIRST_WON

}
```

Listing 4-8. BadgeCard.java (gamification v5)

```java
/**
 * This class links a Badge to a User. Contains also a
   timestamp with the moment in which the user got it.
 */
@RequiredArgsConstructor
@Getter
@ToString
@EqualsAndHashCode
@Entity
```

```java
public final class BadgeCard {

    @Id
    @GeneratedValue
    @Column(name = "BADGE_ID")
    private final Long badgeId;

    private final Long userId;
    private final long badgeTimestamp;
    private final Badge badge;

    // Empty constructor for JSON / JPA
    public BadgeCard() {
        this(null, null, 0, null);
    }

    public BadgeCard(final Long userId, final Badge badge) {
        this(null, userId, System.currentTimeMillis(), badge);
    }

}
```

Listing 4-9. ScoreCard.java (gamification v5)

```java
/**
 * This class represents the Score linked to an attempt in the game,
 * with an associated user and the timestamp in which the score
 * is registered.
 */
@RequiredArgsConstructor
@Getter
@ToString
@EqualsAndHashCode
@Entity
```

```java
public final class ScoreCard {

    // The default score assigned to this card, if not
    specified.
    public static final int DEFAULT_SCORE = 10;

    @Id
    @GeneratedValue
    @Column(name = "CARD_ID")
    private final Long cardId;

    @Column(name = "USER_ID")
    private final Long userId;

    @Column(name = "ATTEMPT_ID")
    private final Long attemptId;

    @Column(name = "SCORE_TS")
    private final long scoreTimestamp;

    @Column(name = "SCORE")
    private final int score;

    // Empty constructor for JSON / JPA
    public ScoreCard() {
        this(null, null, null, 0, 0);
    }

    public ScoreCard(final Long userId, final Long attemptId) {
        this(null, userId, attemptId, System.current
        TimeMillis(), DEFAULT_SCORE);
    }

}
```

Listing 4-10. GameStats.java (gamification v5)

```
/**
 * This object contains the result of one or many iterations of
   the game.
 * It may contain any combination of {@link ScoreCard} objects
   and {@link BadgeCard} objects.
 *
 * It can be used as a delta (as a single game iteration) or to
   represent the total amount of score / badges.
 */
@RequiredArgsConstructor
@Getter
@ToString
@EqualsAndHashCode
public final class GameStats {

    private final Long userId;
    private final int score;
    private final List<Badge> badges;

    // Empty constructor for JSON / JPA
    public GameStats() {
        this.userId = 0L;
        this.score = 0;
        this.badges = new ArrayList<>();
    }

    /**
     * Factory method to build an empty instance (zero points
       and no badges)
     * @param userId the user's id
     * @return a {@link GameStats} object with zero score and
       no badges
```

```
    */
  public static GameStats emptyStats(final Long userId) {
      return new GameStats(userId, 0, Collections.
      emptyList());
  }

  /**
    * @return an unmodifiable view of the badge cards list
    */
  public List<Badge> getBadges() {
      return Collections.unmodifiableList(badges);
  }
}
```

Listing 4-11. LeaderBoardRow.java (gamification v5)

```
/**
  * Represents a line in our Leaderboard: it links a user to a
total score.
  */
@RequiredArgsConstructor
@Getter
@ToString
@EqualsAndHashCode
public final class LeaderBoardRow {

    private final Long userId;
    private final Long totalScore;

    // Empty constructor for JSON / JPA
    public LeaderBoardRow() {
        this(0L, 0L);
    }
}
```

The Data

Strictly speaking, what we need to persist from our model is the total score of a user and the linked badges. Instead of accumulating the score in a single object/row, we will store the cards and aggregate them when querying the total score of a user. This way, we keep the traceability of user's score over time.

Therefore, our persisted data will be composed of two tables, which are direct representations of ScoreCard and BadgeCard classes.

First, let's look at our repository for BadgeCard objects. Nothing new there, using the CrudRepository from Spring Data and a query method which, by naming conventions, will be processed as a query to get badges for a given user, most recent first. See Listing 4-12.

Listing 4-12. BadgeCardRepository.java (gamification v5)

```
package microservices.book.gamification.repository;

import microservices.book.gamification.domain.BadgeCard;
import org.springframework.data.repository.CrudRepository;

import java.util.List;
/**
 * Handles data operations with BadgeCards
 */
public interface BadgeCardRepository extends
CrudRepository<BadgeCard, Long> {

    /**
     * Retrieves all BadgeCards for a given user.
     * @param userId the id of the user to look for BadgeCards
     * @return the list of BadgeCards, sorted by most recent.
     */
```

```
List<BadgeCard> findByUserIdOrderByBadgeTimestampDesc
(final Long userId);
```

}

ScoreCardRepository is a little bit more interesting since in this case we need an aggregation for the total score. For the sake of learning, the result of the query will be mapped to a new object: a LeaderBoardRow. This is an example of how *the business model (the leaderboard) doesn't need to map one to one to the data model (an aggregation of scores)*. See Listing 4-13.

Listing 4-13. ScoreCardRepository.java (gamification v5)

```
package microservices.book.gamification.repository;

import microservices.book.gamification.domain.LeaderBoardRow;
import microservices.book.gamification.domain.ScoreCard;
import org.springframework.data.jpa.repository.Query;
import org.springframework.data.repository.CrudRepository;
import org.springframework.data.repository.query.Param;

import java.util.List;

/**
 * Handles CRUD operations with ScoreCards
 */
public interface ScoreCardRepository extends
CrudRepository<ScoreCard, Long> {

    /**
     * Gets the total score for a given user, being the sum of
     * the scores of all his ScoreCards.
     * @param userId the id of the user for which the total
     * score should be retrieved
     * @return the total score for the given user
     */
```

```
@Query("SELECT SUM(s.score) FROM microservices.book.
gamification.domain.ScoreCard s WHERE s.userId = :userId
GROUP BY s.userId")
int getTotalScoreForUser(@Param("userId") final Long
userId);

/**
 * Retrieves a list of {@link LeaderBoardRow}s representing
   the Leader Board of users and their total score.
 * @return the leader board, sorted by highest score first.
 */
@Query("SELECT NEW microservices.book.gamification.domain.
LeaderBoardRow(s.userId, SUM(s.score)) " +
        "FROM microservices.book.gamification.domain.
        ScoreCard s " +
        "GROUP BY s.userId ORDER BY SUM(s.score) DESC")
List<LeaderBoardRow> findFirst10();

/**
 * Retrieves all the ScoreCards for a given user,
   identified by his user id.
 * @param userId the id of the user
 * @return a list containing all the ScoreCards for the
   given user, sorted by most recent.
 */
List<ScoreCard> findByUserIdOrderByScoreTimestampDesc(final
Long userId);
}
```

This class gets closer to a real-life example, in which the *magical* query methods based on naming patterns are not enough to accomplish our goal. We need to use queries written in the Java Persistence Query Language (JPQL). They are not native queries (specific of the underlying database engine) but generic ones, based on the code. That's a big power of JPQL: we can use queries and still keep the database implementation abstraction. JPQL provides a set of functions, operators, expressions, etc., that should suffice to perform most queries. However, take into account that this language is a specification and there are some database implementations that may not support it completely.

Our query will create new LeaderBoardRow objects for the query results, using the userId and the aggregation of the score for a given user. It also covers the sorting of results with the highest score first.

The Business Logic

There will be two main parts of the code in charge of the business logic of the gamification microservice:

- The GameService interface and its implementation GameServiceImpl: Used to calculate score and badges, based on the received attempts.

- LeaderBoardService and LeaderBoardServiceImpl: Used to retrieve the top 10 users with the highest score.

Let's define the interfaces first. See Listings 4-14 and 4-15.

Listing 4-14. GameService.java (gamification v5)

```java
package microservices.book.gamification.service;

import microservices.book.gamification.domain.GameStats;

/**
 * This service includes the main logic for gamifying the
system.
 */
public interface GameService {
```

144

```
/**
 * Process a new attempt from a given user.
 *
 * @param userId    the user's unique id
 * @param attemptId the attempt id, can be used to retrieve
 * extra data if needed
 * @param correct   indicates if the attempt was correct
 *
 * @return a {@link GameStats} object containing the new
 * score and badge cards obtained
 */
GameStats newAttemptForUser(Long userId, Long attemptId,
boolean correct);

/**
 * Gets the game statistics for a given user
 * @param userId the user
 * @return the total statistics for that user
 */
GameStats retrieveStatsForUser(Long userId);

}
```

Listing 4-15. LeaderBoardService.java (gamification v5)

```
package microservices.book.gamification.service;

import microservices.book.gamification.domain.LeaderBoardRow;

import java.util.List;

/**
 * Provides methods to access the LeaderBoard with users and scores.
 */
public interface LeaderBoardService {
```

```
/**
  * Retrieves the current leader board with the top score
    users
  * @return the users with the highest score
  */
  List<LeaderBoardRow> getCurrentLeaderBoard();
}
```

EXERCISE

It's TDD time! Now that you know how the interfaces look, write the unit tests to verify their functionality before writing the real implementation. Remember these tips:

- First, write empty implementation classes of the interfaces.

- Use when/given/then structure for better readability.

- Cover all the use cases, including the badge scenarios: First Won, Bronze (100 points or more), Silver (500 points or more), and Gold (999 points or more).

You can find the completed tests in the v5 code repository, within the gamification project.

The main game logic is inside the GameServiceImpl class. More specifically, it's inside the newAttemptForUser() method. Let's go through the implementation, shown in Listing 4-16.

Listing 4-16. GameServiceImpl.java newAttemptForUser() (gamification v5)

```
@Service
@Slf4j
class GameServiceImpl implements GameService {
```

146

```java
private ScoreCardRepository scoreCardRepository;
private BadgeCardRepository badgeCardRepository;

GameServiceImpl(ScoreCardRepository scoreCardRepository,
            BadgeCardRepository badgeCardRepository,
    this.scoreCardRepository = scoreCardRepository;
    this.badgeCardRepository = badgeCardRepository;
}

@Override
public GameStats newAttemptForUser(final Long userId,
                                    final Long attemptId,
                                    final boolean correct) {
    // For the first version we'll give points only if it's
    correct
    if(correct) {
        ScoreCard scoreCard = new ScoreCard(userId,
        attemptId);
        scoreCardRepository.save(scoreCard);
        log.info("User with id {} scored {} points for
        attempt id {}",
                userId, scoreCard.getScore(), attemptId);
        List<BadgeCard> badgeCards =
        processForBadges(userId, attemptId);
        return new GameStats(userId, scoreCard.getScore(),
                badgeCards.stream().
                map(BadgeCard::getBadge)
                    .collect(Collectors.toList()));
    }
    return GameStats.emptyStats(userId);
}
```

```
/**
 * Checks the total score and the different score cards
   obtained
 * to give new badges in case their conditions are met.
 */
private List<BadgeCard> processForBadges(final Long userId,
                                         final Long
                                         attemptId) {
    List<BadgeCard> badgeCards = new ArrayList<>();

    int totalScore = scoreCardRepository.
    getTotalScoreForUser(userId);
    log.info("New score for user {} is {}", userId,
    totalScore);

    List<ScoreCard> scoreCardList = scoreCardRepository
            .findByUserIdOrderByScoreTimestampDesc(userId);
    List<BadgeCard> badgeCardList = badgeCardRepository
            .findByUserIdOrderByBadgeTimestampDesc(userId);

    // Badges depending on score
    checkAndGiveBadgeBasedOnScore(badgeCardList,
            Badge.BRONZE_MULTIPLICATOR, totalScore, 100,
            userId)
            .ifPresent(badgeCards::add);
    checkAndGiveBadgeBasedOnScore(badgeCardList,
            Badge.SILVER_MULTIPLICATOR, totalScore, 500,
            userId)
            .ifPresent(badgeCards::add);
    checkAndGiveBadgeBasedOnScore(badgeCardList,
            Badge.GOLD_MULTIPLICATOR, totalScore, 999,
            userId)
            .ifPresent(badgeCards::add);
```

```
    // First won badge
    if(scoreCardList.size() == 1 &&
            !containsBadge(badgeCardList, Badge.
            FIRST_WON)) {
        BadgeCard firstWonBadge = giveBadgeToUser(Badge.
        FIRST_WON, userId);
        badgeCards.add(firstWonBadge);
    }

    return badgeCards;
}

@Override
public GameStats retrieveStatsForUser(final Long userId) {
    int score = scoreCardRepository.
    getTotalScoreForUser(userId);
    List<BadgeCard> badgeCards = badgeCardRepository
            .findByUserIdOrderByBadgeTimestampDesc(userId);
    return new GameStats(userId, score, badgeCards.stream()
            .map(BadgeCard::getBadge).collect
            (Collectors.toList()));
}

/**
 * Convenience method to check the current score against
 * the different thresholds to gain badges.
 * It also assigns badge to user if the conditions are met.
 */
private Optional<BadgeCard> checkAndGiveBadgeBasedOnScore(
        final List<BadgeCard> badgeCards, final Badge
        badge,
        final int score, final int scoreThreshold, final
        Long userId) {
```

```java
    if(score >= scoreThreshold &&
    !containsBadge(badgeCards, badge)) {
        return Optional.of(giveBadgeToUser(badge, userId));
    }
    return Optional.empty();
}

/**
 * Checks if the passed list of badges includes the one
 being checked
 */
private boolean containsBadge(final List<BadgeCard>
badgeCards,
                                   final Badge badge) {
    return badgeCards.stream().anyMatch(b -> b.getBadge().
    equals(badge));
}

/**
 * Assigns a new badge to the given user
 */
private BadgeCard giveBadgeToUser(final Badge badge, final
Long userId) {
    BadgeCard badgeCard = new BadgeCard(userId, badge);
    badgeCardRepository.save(badgeCard);
    log.info("User with id {} won a new badge: {}", userId,
    badge);
    return badgeCard;
}
}
```

If we focus on the newAttemptForUser, we'll understand the game logic: when we receive a correct attempt, we create a ScoreCard object (with a default score of 10) and persist it in the database. Then, we invoke the method processForBadges(), which will query the database for a given user ID and assign new badges when necessary. Finally, we combine the scores with badges in a GameStats object and return this result. The rest of the class is intended to help that method and a simple retrieveStatsForUser() implementation.

Note that we haven't covered yet the interaction of this microservice with the multiplication microservice: there is no event logic. This is a good practice to keep layers isolated: we don't make our service layer dependent on the interface, so we don't pass the event as an argument. The link between the event bus and the business logic is the EventHandler. This way, we can replace the interface of our microservice without needing changes in other layers (e.g., if we decide to remove the events and put something else there).

EXERCISE

The service implementation LeaderBoardServiceImpl is pretty straightforward: it will use its existing repository method to return the 10 users with the highest score. Try to build it. If you need help, you can find the solution in the v5 code repository, within the gamification project.

The REST API (Controllers)

An incoming event will trigger the main business logic in the gamification service but still, we need to expose the results of the game. How many points does a user have? What is the current leaderboard? These requests will come from a user interface or client service accessing our system, so we'll create a REST API for them.

The LeaderBoardController exposes an endpoint called /leaders, which will retrieve the current leaderboard. See Listing 4-17.

Listing 4-17. LeaderBoardController.java (gamification v5)

```java
/**
 * This class implements a REST API for the Gamification
   LeaderBoard service.
 */
@RestController
@RequestMapping("/leaders")
class LeaderBoardController {

    private final LeaderBoardService leaderBoardService;

    public LeaderBoardController(final LeaderBoardService
    leaderBoardService) {
        this.leaderBoardService = leaderBoardService;
    }

    @GetMapping
    public List<LeaderBoardRow> getLeaderBoard() {
        return leaderBoardService.getCurrentLeaderBoard();
    }
}
```

On the other hand, UserStatsController is taking care of the endpoint /stats, and it returns a JSON representation of the GameStats object: score and badges. Here we use a parameter userId to query for the statistics of a given user. In this case, if we want statistics for a user with ID 9, we need to request GET /stats?userId=9. See Listing 4-18.

Listing 4-18. UserStatsController.java (gamification v5))

```java
/**
 * This class implements a REST API for the Gamification User
   Statistics service.
 */
@RestController
@RequestMapping("/stats")
class UserStatsController {

    private final GameService gameService;

    public UserStatsController(final GameService gameService) {
        this.gameService = gameService;
    }

    @GetMapping
    public GameStats getStatsForUser(@RequestParam("userId")
    final Long userId) {
        return gameService.retrieveStatsForUser(userId);
    }
}
```

Besides the code, we're going to change the default HTTP application) port to 8081, to avoid a collision when we start them together on the local machine. To get this working, you need to set the Spring Boot's property server.port in gamification's application.properties:

```
server.port=8081
```

Receiving Events with RabbitMQ
The Subscriber's Side

Early in this chapter, we saw how to connect the multiplication microservice with RabbitMQ and publish an event when a user sends an attempt. Now let's see how the subscriber looks (our gamification service).

RabbitMQ Configuration

We'll need to place a new class `RabbitMQConfiguration` as we did for multiplication. But in this case, it's going to be a little bit more complicated. We have six methods: five declare beans and the last one implements the interface `RabbitListenerConfigurer`.

To understand this configuration, the concept of *binding a queue to an exchange* is an important one here. Our subscriber creates a queue from which it's going to consume messages. Those messages are published to an exchange with a *routing key* (in our case `multiplication.solved`). This is where the flexibility of a *topic exchange* resides: all the messages sent through the exchange are "tagged" with a routing key, and the consumers can select the messages that go to their queues by specifying either an explicit routing key or a pattern (like in our case, `multiplication.*`) when they bind their queues to the exchange. You can look at the official RabbitMQ tutorial page[6] to learn more about topics and to see various examples of routing. See Listing 4-19.

Listing 4-19. RabbitMQConfiguration.java (gamification v5)

```
/**
 * Configures RabbitMQ to use events in our application.
 */
```

---

[6]https://www.rabbitmq.com/tutorials/tutorial-five-spring-amqp.html

```java
@Configuration
public class RabbitMQConfiguration implements
RabbitListenerConfigurer {

    @Bean
    public TopicExchange multiplicationExchange
    (@Value("${multiplication.exchange}") final String
    exchangeName) {
        return new TopicExchange(exchangeName);
    }

    @Bean
    public Queue gamificationMultiplicationQueue
    (@Value("${multiplication.queue}") final String
    queueName) {
        return new Queue(queueName, true);
    }

    @Bean
    Binding binding(final Queue queue, final TopicExchange
    exchange,
                    @Value("${multiplication.anything.routing-
                    key}") final String routingKey) {
        return BindingBuilder.bind(queue).to(exchange).
        with(routingKey);
    }

    @Bean
    public MappingJackson2MessageConverter consumer
    Jackson2MessageConverter() {
        return new MappingJackson2MessageConverter();
    }
```

```java
@Bean
public DefaultMessageHandlerMethodFactory message
HandlerMethodFactory() {
    DefaultMessageHandlerMethodFactory factory = new
    DefaultMessageHandlerMethodFactory();
    factory.setMessageConverter(consumerJackson2MessageConv
    erter());
    return factory;
}

@Override
public void configureRabbitListeners(final Rabbit
ListenerEndpointRegistrar registrar) {
    registrar.setMessageHandlerMethodFactory(messageHandler
    MethodFactory());
}
}
```

Let's review some important parts within this class:

- The first three methods are to connect a new queue
  (declared by gamificationMultiplicationQueue())
  and a TopicExchange (declared by
  multiplicationExchange()) by binding them together
  (binding(), which takes the exchange and the queue
  as arguments).

- We make the Queue durable (the second true argument
  when creating it). We introduced this idea before: by
  doing this we can process pending events even after the
  broker goes down, given that they are persisted.

- Note that the value of the property multiplication.
  exchange must be the same as defined in multiplication:
  multiplication_exchange). We use the pattern

multiplication.* for the value of the routing key
property (multiplication.anything.routing-key).
For the queue name (multiplication.queue property),
we can use any convention we prefer. All these values
should be defined in the application.properties file.

- The last three methods configure JSON deserialization
in the subscriber. In this case, it's done differently
if you compare it with our multiplication's
RabbitMQConfiguration. Now we don't use a
RabbitTemplate (since we're not sending messages
from this microservice) but methods annotated with
@RabbitListener. Therefore we need to configure the
RabbitListenerEndpointRegistrar in a way that uses
a MappingJackson2MessageConverter.

Listing 4-20. application.properties changes (gamification v5)

```
## Other properties ...
## RabbitMQ configuration
multiplication.exchange=multiplication_exchange
multiplication.solved.key=multiplication.solved
multiplication.queue=gamification_multiplication_queue
multiplication.anything.routing-key=multiplication.*
```

The Event Handler

Remember that, when we introduced the event handler pattern, we did it
together with the event dispatcher. The goal is similar: having a centralized
place from where we can process the received events and trigger the
corresponding business logic.

We create as many methods annotated with @RabbitListener as events to be consumed. This annotation handles all the complexity of receiving a message from the broker through the queue that we defined (we need to pass the queue name as a parameter to the annotation).

Since we're passing the argument type MultiplicationSolvedEvent, the message converter (set up in RabbitMQConfiguration) will deserialize the received JSON to an object of this class. To avoid inter-dependencies between our microservices, we copy our MultiplicationSolvedEvent class to the gamification project. We'll cover this idea more in detail at the end of this chapter when we talk about *domain isolation*. See Listing 4-21.

Listing 4-21. EventHandler.java (gamification v5)

```java
package microservices.book.gamification.event;

import lombok.extern.slf4j.Slf4j;
import microservices.book.gamification.service.GameService;
import org.springframework.amqp.
AmqpRejectAndDontRequeueException;
import org.springframework.amqp.rabbit.annotation.RabbitListener;
import org.springframework.stereotype.Component;

/**
 * This class receives the events and triggers the associated
 * business logic.
 */
@Slf4j
@Component
class EventHandler {

    private GameService gameService;

    EventHandler(final GameService gameService) {
        this.gameService = gameService;
    }
```

```
@RabbitListener(queues = "${multiplication.queue}")
void handleMultiplicationSolved(final Multiplication
SolvedEvent event) {
    log.info("Multiplication Solved Event received: {}",
    event.getMultiplicationResultAttemptId());
    try {
        gameService.newAttemptForUser(event.getUserId(),
                event.getMultiplicationResultAttemptId(),
                event.isCorrect());
    } catch (final Exception e) {
        log.error("Error when trying to process
        MultiplicationSolvedEvent", e);
        // Avoids the event to be re-queued and
        reprocessed.
        throw new AmqpRejectAndDontRequeueException(e);
    }
  }
}
```

Note that we're also wrapping the logic inside a try-catch block and throwing an AmqpRejectAndDontRequeueException in case an exception is thrown. By doing that, we make sure the event is not repeatedly requeued whenever something is wrong (which is the default behavior), but directly rejected. Since we don't have anything in place to handle rejected events, they will be simply discarded. If you want to get deeper into good practices with RabbitMQ, you can look at how to configure a dead letter exchange and put our failing messages there for further processing (like retrying, logging, or raising alerts).[7]

---

[7]https://www.rabbitmq.com/dlx.html

Requesting Data Between Microservices

Combining Reactive Patterns and REST

In the section "Connecting Microservices", we briefly introduced the concept of microservices calling each other to gather data. In this section, we expand on the idea by using our architecture as a reference.

Imagine that we get a change to our gamification design. Our game designers come up with a new badge called *Lucky Number*. They tell us that the users can only get this badge if they solve a multiplication attempt involving the number 42 (which seems to be a lucky number—at least for them).

Let's apply what we know so far to fit the new requirement into our design. First, we can conclude that the context of that new business logic is our gamification microservice: it's the one that assigns badges and this is a badge's logic. However, we have a small issue: gamification doesn't know anything about the factors. They are not coming inside the MultiplicationSolvedEvent.

Also, we know that doesn't sound good to include the factors in our event just because now it's required in our consumer. In this case, it might be simple and yet look like a generic event, but if you follow the approach of tailoring publishers to consumers, you may end up with *fat, too smart events.*

When you want to share data across microservices, you don't do that using your reactive patterns (*event-has-happened*) but use a request/response pattern instead. You could also do that using the same underlying technologies (AMQP/RabbitMQ), but it's much easier to use one of the most common implementations of the request/response pattern to transfer objects: REST APIs.

To solve this new challenge, the gamification microservice can contact the multiplication microservice and ask for the factors of the multiplication given the identifier of the attempt (contained in the event). Then, if it finds the lucky number, it will assign the badge. Don't get nervous if you're already visualizing this architecture and thinking that we're going to couple our microservices; in the next chapter, you'll see how this approach doesn't prevent you from having a loosely coupled system. See Figure 4-4.

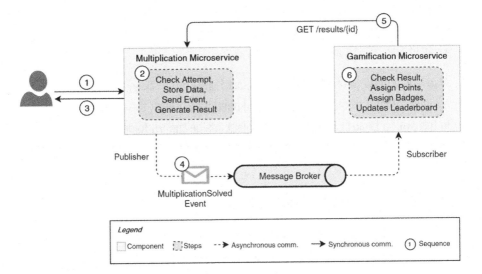

Figure 4-4. *Updated logical view*

As you can see in the updated logical view, we need to expose a new endpoint in the multiplication microservice to give access to multiplication attempts (which include the multiplication factors) by their attempt's identifier. Then, we need to create a REST client in gamification to retrieve the factors. Finally, we use them in our logic to assign the badge if one of them is the lucky number.

EXERCISE

At this point in the book, creating an endpoint in the multiplication service to retrieve a `MultiplicationResultAttempt` by ID should be very easy. Make sure that it responds to `GET /results/{id}` and don't forget to include the tests. Hint: This time you should use a

@PathVariable annotation in the controller since the ID is embedded in the URI and is not a parameter. Your new method's declaration in MultiplicationResultAttemptController should be:

```
@GetMapping("/{resultId}")
ResponseEntity getResultById(@PathVariable("resultId") Long
resultId)
```

Also, you'll need to use the MultiplicationRepository, which will cause a minor refactor of other classes. If you need help, check the solution located in the social-multiplication project, inside the v5 folder.

Keeping Domains Isolated

There is a major effect of including this new functionality in our system that deserves some lines in the book: the gamification microservice will need to handle attempts, so the attempt's business concept needs to be understood by both microservices. That means that we need to model a MultiplicationResultAttempt inside gamification *somehow*.

Even though this might not seem a complex issue, it's one of the key factors of success or failure when you design a microservices architecture.

A common pitfall is thinking of extracting the domain package from the multiplication microservice as a separate library that can be shared with gamification, thus having access to MultiplicationResultAttempt. It's a very bad idea though—your domain would be out of control and other microservices could potentially start relying on it for their logic, thus introducing multiple inter-dependencies if you (or others) need updates in the model. You should always keep ownership of the domain entities in one microservice, so there is only one source of truth.

162

A better alternative is to generate *simple copies* of your model and share them with others. This is actually an approach based on Data Transfer Objects (DTOs). If you go this way, bear in mind that maintaining those DTOs takes time and might also introduce dependencies if you don't follow some other good practices. For example, if those DTOs are Java representations of JSON objects that you're transferring through a REST API, you should maintain different DTO packages per API version or you'll create a lot of headaches for your consumers (they won't be able to deserialize the JSON if you introduce changes in the structure). On the other hand, having these DTO packages can save a lot of development time if you have many API consumers, because they won't need to replicate data structures.

If you don't mind dealing with bare responses (let's say JSON) in your consumers, the ideal approach is to keep the microservices as isolated as possible: *don't share anything*. This has the advantage of minimizing dependencies: if you need only a couple of fields, you deserialize those and ignore everything else. That way, your microservice will be impacted only if those specific fields change.

An extra advantage of not sharing is that you can adapt the foreign model entities as you wish: in this case, we'll flatten the *Attempt-Multiplication-User* structure to a single class, given that multiplication doesn't need such a structure.

Let's get practical. On the gamification side, we're going to create this `MultiplicationResultAttempt` version in a new `client.dto` package. This class contains `factorA` and `factorB` as fields. See Listing 4-22.

Listing 4-22. MultiplicationResultAttempt.java (gamification v5)

```java
package microservices.book.gamification.client.dto;

import com.fasterxml.jackson.databind.annotation.JsonDeserialize;
import lombok.EqualsAndHashCode;
import lombok.Getter;
```

```java
import lombok.RequiredArgsConstructor;
import lombok.ToString;
import microservices.book.gamification.client.
        MultiplicationResultAttemptDeserializer;

/**
 * Identifies the attempt from a user to solve a multiplication.
 */
@RequiredArgsConstructor
@Getter
@ToString
@EqualsAndHashCode
@JsonDeserialize(using =
MultiplicationResultAttemptDeserializer.class)
public final class MultiplicationResultAttempt {

    private final String userAlias;

    private final int multiplicationFactorA;
    private final int multiplicationFactorB;
    private final int resultAttempt;

    private final boolean correct;

    // Empty constructor for JSON/JPA
    MultiplicationResultAttempt() {
        userAlias = null;
        multiplicationFactorA = -1;
        multiplicationFactorB = -1;
        resultAttempt = -1;
        correct = false;
    }

}
```

A simplified version of the original: flattened and without identifiers. Note the @JsonDeserialize annotation pointing to a class that we don't have yet: it's to instruct our @RestTemplate's message converter to use a special deserializer to read the JSON data. We need this since the JSON structure we'll receive doesn't match with our Java class (since it's matching *the original* MultiplicationResultAttempt in the multiplication microservice), so the default deserializer won't work. We'll cover that implementation in the following subsection.

Implementing the REST Client

To start with, we need to tell gamification how to find multiplication: we'll use a new line in our application.properties and reference it from the code. For now, we will point it directly to the host and port in which we know that the microservice is deployed. We'll learn how to do this properly in the next chapter when we go through service discovery and routing. See Listing 4-23.

Listing 4-23. application.properties (gamification v5)

```
# REST client settings
multiplicationHost=http://localhost:8080
```

Let's now implement the custom JSON deserializer for the MultiplicationResultAttempt. We use some classes from the *Jackson library*, which is included inside Spring Boot. See Listing 4-24.

Listing 4-24. MultiplicationResultAttemptClient.java (gamification v5)

```
package microservices.book.gamification.client;

import com.fasterxml.jackson.core.JsonParser;
import com.fasterxml.jackson.core.JsonProcessingException;
import com.fasterxml.jackson.core.ObjectCodec;
```

165

```java
import com.fasterxml.jackson.databind.DeserializationContext;
import com.fasterxml.jackson.databind.JsonDeserializer;
import com.fasterxml.jackson.databind.JsonNode;
import microservices.book.gamification.client.dto.
     MultiplicationResultAttempt;

import java.io.IOException;

/**
 * Deserializes an attempt coming from the Multiplication
   microservice
 * into the Gamification's representation of an attempt.
 */
public class MultiplicationResultAttemptDeserializer
       extends JsonDeserializer<MultiplicationResultAttempt> {
   @Override
   public MultiplicationResultAttempt deserialize(JsonParser
          jsonParser,
                              DeserializationContext
                              deserializationContext)
          throws IOException, JsonProcessingException {
      ObjectCodec oc = jsonParser.getCodec();
      JsonNode node = oc.readTree(jsonParser);
      return new MultiplicationResultAttempt(node.
             get("user").get("alias").asText(),
          node.get("multiplication").get("factorA").asInt(),
          node.get("multiplication").get("factorB").asInt(),
          node.get("resultAttempt").asInt(),
          node.get("correct").asBoolean());
   }
}
```

As you can see, it's pretty readable. We need to create a subclass of JsonDeserializer, passing the type we want to use as a result. Then, we implement the deserialize() method, from which we get a JsonParser that we can use to traverse the JSON node tree and get the values we're looking for.

The next step is to write an interface to abstract the communication logic. From the business logic point of view, we just want to retrieve the attempt, no matter which kind of technical interface we're using. See Listing 4-25.

Listing 4-25. MultiplicationResultAttemptClient.java (gamification v5)

```
package microservices.book.gamification.client;

import microservices.book.gamification.client.dto.
MultiplicationResultAttempt;

/**
 * This interface allows us to connect to the Multiplication
   microservice.
 * Note that it's agnostic to the way of communication.
 */
public interface MultiplicationResultAttemptClient {

    MultiplicationResultAttempt retrieveMultiplicationResultAtt
    emptbyId(final Long multiplicationId);

}
```

For the implementation, we use RestTemplate, a class provided by Spring that makes it very easy to communicate with REST APIs. To have it available in our Spring's application context, we need to configure it as a bean. We'll create a new configuration class to keep our code organized (in the configuration package). See Listing 4-26.

167

Listing 4-26. RestClientConfiguration.java (gamification v5)

```java
package microservices.book.gamification.configuration;

import org.springframework.boot.web.client.RestTemplateBuilder;
import org.springframework.context.annotation.Bean;
import org.springframework.context.annotation.Configuration;
import org.springframework.web.client.RestTemplate;

/**
 * Configures the REST client in our application
 */
@Configuration
public class RestClientConfiguration {

    @Bean
    public RestTemplate restTemplate(RestTemplateBuilder builder) {
        return builder.build();
    }

}
```

Then, we can inject the RestTemplate in MultiplicationResult AttemptClientImpl, together with the multiplicationHost property, and perform a GET request with the passed identifier. See Listing 4-27.

Listing 4-27. MultiplicationResultAttemptClientImpl.java (gamification v5)

```java
package microservices.book.gamification.client;

import microservices.book.gamification.client.dto.
       MultiplicationResultAttempt;
import org.springframework.beans.factory.annotation.Autowired;
import org.springframework.beans.factory.annotation.Value;
import org.springframework.stereotype.Component;
```

```java
import org.springframework.web.client.RestTemplate;

/**
 * This implementation of MultiplicationResultAttemptClient
   interface connects to
 * the Multiplication microservice via REST.
 */
@Component
class MultiplicationResultAttemptClientImpl implements
     MultiplicationResultAttemptClient {

   private final RestTemplate restTemplate;
   private final String multiplicationHost;

   @Autowired
   public MultiplicationResultAttemptClientImpl
          (final RestTemplate restTemplate,
           @Value("${multiplicationHost}") final String
           multiplicationHost) {
      this.restTemplate = restTemplate;
      this.multiplicationHost = multiplicationHost;
   }

   @Override
   public MultiplicationResultAttempt retrieveMultiplication
   ResultAttemptbyId(final Long multiplicationResultAttemptId) {
      return restTemplate.getForObject(
             multiplicationHost + "/results/" +
             multiplicationResultAttemptId,
             MultiplicationResultAttempt.class);
   }
}
```

We don't need to link the deserializer here, since we set the annotation inside `MultiplicationResultAttempt`. The `getForObject()` method takes the class as an argument, then infers that it should use the custom deserializer.

EXERCISE

You can try to finish this task by yourself! You can follow TDD again, updating `GameServiceImplTest` to verify that the new badge is assigned to the users whenever they're sending an attempt with the number 42 as one of the factors. You'll need to create the new badge and adapt the `GameServiceImpl` class.

We will cover the business logic implementation but will leave the tests out of the book (since they are easy and don't add new concepts). If you want to look at them, they are located in the v5 repository, under the `gamification` project.

Updating Gamification's Business Logic

Now that we have all the pieces we need to connect both services, we can update our business logic in gamification to check if conditions are set to assign the new badge called *Lucky Number* to the user.

First, we need to create the new badge by adding a value to our enumeration, as shown in Listing 4-28.

Listing 4-28. MultiplicationResultAttemptClientImpl.java (gamification v5)

```java
public enum Badge {
    // ...
    FIRST_WON,
    LUCKY_NUMBER
}
```

Now we can inject the client in the game logic and process the returned attempt to assign the badge if the lucky number is present. See Listing 4-29.

Listing 4-29. MultiplicationResultAttemptClientImpl.java (gamification v5)

```
@Service
@Slf4j
class GameServiceImpl implements GameService {

    public static final int LUCKY_NUMBER = 42;

    private ScoreCardRepository scoreCardRepository;
    private BadgeCardRepository badgeCardRepository;
    private MultiplicationResultAttemptClient attemptClient;

    GameServiceImpl(ScoreCardRepository scoreCardRepository,
                    BadgeCardRepository badgeCardRepository,
                    MultiplicationResultAttemptClient
                     attemptClient) {
        this.scoreCardRepository = scoreCardRepository;
        this.badgeCardRepository = badgeCardRepository;
        this.attemptClient = attemptClient;
    }

    // ...

    /**
     * Checks the total score and the different score cards obtained
     * to give new badges in case their conditions are met.
     */
    private List<BadgeCard> processForBadges(final Long userId,
                                             final Long
                                              attemptId) {
```

```java
        List<BadgeCard> badgeCards = new ArrayList<>();

        int totalScore = scoreCardRepository.getTotal
        ScoreForUser(userId);
        log.info("New score for user {} is {}", userId, totalScore);

        List<ScoreCard> scoreCardList = scoreCardRepository
                .findByUserIdOrderByScoreTimestampDesc(userId);
        List<BadgeCard> badgeCardList = badgeCardRepository
                .findByUserIdOrderByBadgeTimestampDesc(userId);

        // Badges depending on score ...

        // First won badge ...

        // Lucky number badge
        MultiplicationResultAttempt attempt = attemptClient
                .retrieveMultiplicationResultAttemptbyId(attemp
                tId);
        if(!containsBadge(badgeCardList, Badge.LUCKY_NUMBER) &&
                (LUCKY_NUMBER == attempt.getMultiplication
                FactorA() ||
                LUCKY_NUMBER == attempt.getMultiplication
                FactorB())) {
            BadgeCard luckyNumberBadge = giveBadgeToUser(
                    Badge.LUCKY_NUMBER, userId);
            badgeCards.add(luckyNumberBadge);
        }

        return badgeCards;
    }
    // ...
}
```

Playing with the Microservices

In spite of not having finished user story 3, we can already test if our microservices are working fine together.

If you didn't do it yet, you need to download and install RabbitMQ. Just follow the web site's instructions for your operating system. Once you install it, start the broker (the installation guides include instructions for that as well). Make sure you also enable the `rabbitmq_management` plugin with the command `rabbitmq-plugins enable rabbitmq_management` (see `https://www.rabbitmq.com/management.html` if you need more details). That will give you access to a Web UI to manage RabbitMQ (on `http://localhost:15672/` if you installed it on your local machine). Keep the configuration as it is by default.

Once the RabbitMQ server is up, you can start both Spring Boot applications. Remember that you can do that from your IDE by running the class annotated with `@SpringBootApplication` or by packaging the applications with `mvn package` and then running the resulting JAR files with `java -jar your_jar_file`. If everything goes well, multiplication should start on port 8080 and gamification on port 8081.

You can navigate to `http://localhost:8080/index.html` and start trying to solve some multiplications, as you did in the previous chapter. The difference now is that every time you send an attempt, a new event is published. You can notice that by looking at the Gamification log, as shown in Listing 4-30.

Listing 4-30. Gamification Logging After Received Attempt (gamification v5)

```
2017-09-15 18:43:25.050  INFO 16276 --- [          main]
m.book.GamificationApplication          : Started
GamificationApplication in 8.225 seconds (JVM running for 8.938)
2017-09-15 18:43:34.351  INFO 16276 --- [cTaskExecutor-1]
m.book.gamification.event.EventHandler   : Multiplication
Solved Event received: 65
```

173

```
2017-09-15 18:43:58.194  INFO 16276 --- [cTaskExecutor-1]
m.book.gamification.event.EventHandler    : Multiplication
Solved Event received: 66
Hibernate: insert into score_card (card_id, attempt_id, score,
score_ts, user_id) values (null, ?, ?, ?, ?)
2017-09-15 18:43:58.253  INFO 16276 --- [cTaskExecutor-1]
m.b.g.service.GameServiceImpl            : User with id 1
scored 10 points for attempt id 66
Hibernate: select sum(scorecard0_.score) as col_0_0_ from
score_card scorecard0_ where scorecard0_.user_id=? group by
scorecard0_.user_id
2017-09-15 18:43:58.274  INFO 16276 --- [cTaskExecutor-1]
m.b.g.service.GameServiceImpl            : New score for user 1
is 50
Hibernate: select scorecard0_.card_id as card_id1_1_,
scorecard0_.attempt_id as attempt_2_1_, scorecard0_.score as
score3_1_, scorecard0_.score_ts as score_ts4_1_, scorecard0_.
user_id as user_id5_1_ from score_card scorecard0_ where
scorecard0_.user_id=? order by scorecard0_.score_ts desc
Hibernate: select badgecard0_.badge_id as badge_id1_0_,
badgecard0_.badge as badge2_0_, badgecard0_.badge_timestamp
as badge_ti3_0_, badgecard0_.user_id as user_id4_0_ from
badge_card badgecard0_ where badgecard0_.user_id=? order by
badgecard0_.badge_timestamp desc
```

If you send successful attempts, you can also see how the data is persisted in the gamification database. Do you remember that you had access to the multiplication database through the H2 console? You do the same for gamification, but this time you'll find it on http://localhost:8081/h2-console/. Similarly, you need to make sure that you use the proper URL to access it: jdbc:h2:file:~/gamification. If you query the tables after sending correct attempts, you should see the different badges and scores linked to users. See Figure 4-5.

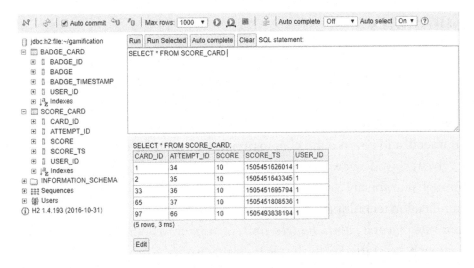

Figure 4-5. *You can query the gamification database using H2*

To try the lucky number, we need to cheat the system a bit. It's not so easy to get a multiplication with a 42 factor by accident (although you can try if you are a very patient person). If you prefer not to wait, you can use curl to post your own multiplication to the system, as shown in Listing 4-31.

Listing 4-31. Gamification: Posting a Multiplication with a Lucky Number (gamification v5)

```
$ curl -X POST -H "Content-Type: application/json" -d '{"user":
{"alias":"moises"},"multiplication":{"factorA":"42","factorB":"
10"},"resultAttempt":"420"}' http://localhost:8080/results
```

If you're running the application on a Windows machine, you can use a terminal emulator to run curl (like *Git Bash*, included if you install the Git package from https://git-scm.com). You can also use Postman,[8] which gives you a full UI from which you can send all types of requests. It's quite intuitive, but you can check the documentation if you need help.

---

[8]https://www.getpostman.com/

Summary

In this chapter, we introduced the concept of microservices. Before we delved into the microservices idea, we analyzed our plan to approach it: starting with a monolith. We used our application to compare how expensive it would have been to begin directly with a microservices approach, and covered the plan to prepare the monolith to be split later.

We received a new requirement in the form of a user story and went through it to specify a second service to design and implement, based on gamification techniques. We learned the basics of these techniques to motivate players: *points, badges, and leaderboards.* Following a pragmatic approach, we started with simple logic that works.

About microservice interactions, we saw that there are different ways of connecting microservices together to fulfill business processes, and we chose to go for an event-driven architecture. We reviewed its benefits and applied it directly to our application to see it in practice. We compared it to some other related techniques (event sourcing, CQRS, etc.) and saw how they can work together, very nicely in some cases, taking in consideration that a good evaluation of the technology versus the requirements is critical to avoid being misled by technology hypes.

The second part of the chapter explained how to implement the asynchronous communication that supports our event-driven architecture, using Spring AMQP with RabbitMQ as implementations. We did the first the change on the publisher's side, the multiplication microservice. Then, we went through the implementation of the new microservice, the gamification Spring Boot application. On our way, we not only saw how to implement the *subscriber's side*, but we also looked at new ways to send more advanced queries to the database and the gamification model and logic in code.

We ended this chapter with a system based on microservices, but we didn't finish our user story 3: we need to provide UI access to the leaderboard and, on the technical side, we need to fix some hard links we made between our applications (by pointing to specific host and port).

The next chapter covers a refactoring of the code to create a properly split system and, while we're doing that, we'll need to understand and apply two important concepts behind microservices: *routing and service discovery.*

CHAPTER 5

The Microservices Journey Through Tools

Introduction

We completed the previous chapter with a pending task: finishing user story 3 and letting our users see their progress in the game. The reason is that, in order to build a good microservices architecture, we need the UI part of the system extracted in a new service so it can interact as an independent party with our multiplication and gamification services. We'll cover the reasoning with more detail in the next section.

As soon as we put the UI aside and communicate it to the microservices, we'll find out that our environment is getting even more complicated. That shouldn't be a surprise though, since we know that's the case of any microservices architecture. Many advantages, at the expense of a more complex system.

If we do a rapid analysis of what's going to happen in this chapter, it will start with the UI calling two services by their specific hostname and ports, spreading the infrastructure of our services with tightly-coupled links between them, and creating a system that is not scalable and is very hard to maintain. Since that's a wrong approach, we'll introduce the

© Moises Macero 2017
M. Macero, *Learn Microservices with Spring Boot*,
https://doi.org/10.1007/978-1-4842-3165-4_5

concept of *service discovery* and how that can help us locate services by keeping them loosely coupled. Then we'll analyze how that scenario would perform if we aim for high availability by scaling up our services. Finally, after some evaluation of our architecture, we'll get to the conclusion that it's actually a good idea to include a routing service (gateway) that can handle the load balancing on the server side.

Most of the tools we'll cover to accomplish our mission are part of the Spring Cloud family: Eureka, Ribbon, Zuul, Hystrix, etc. We'll also explain how Sidecar and Feign work, which are part of Spring Cloud too. Don't you worry by the overwhelming amount of *tools with fancy names*, as we'll go through them one by one and explain why they're useful and under which circumstances you should rely on them. And, as usual, we'll analyze the problem we want to solve first and only after that we'll implement the solution.

Then we'll reach the end of the chapter knowing all these fantastic tools and where to find them and we'll ask ourselves a question: could we make it easier? Couldn't we just focus on microservices' business code and forget about all the tooling around? The answers to these questions are at the end of the chapter, when we'll explain how the fully integrated solutions for microservices work.

Extracting the UI and Connecting It to Gamification

First things first: I promised you good reasons for all the decisions we take along the book. It's time to explain why we want to extract our static content out of the multiplication microservice. An image can illustrate this very clearly, so look at Figure 5-1.

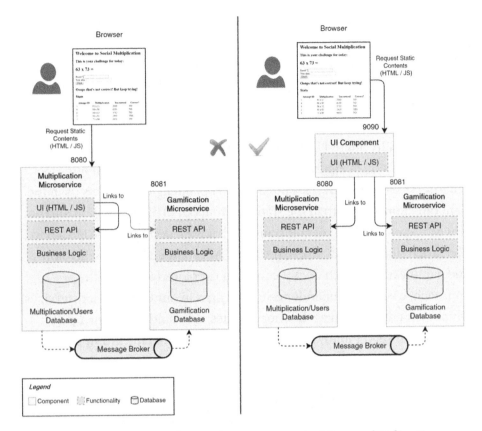

Figure 5-1. *Extracting the static content out of the multiplication microservice*

On the left side of Figure 5-1, we can see how our system would look if we move forward without the UI extraction. The static content will be served by the multiplication microservice, as before. If we include the new leaderboard table HTML/JavaScript, that code should have references to the gamification's REST API. That's not a good design pattern though: the UI would be no longer limited to multiplication functionalities since it would include functionality that spans both microservices.

The first disadvantage of that approach is inter-dependency: if we change the gamification API, we would also need to change the multiplication microservice and redeploy it afterward. The second disadvantage is that we would lose flexibility to scale: the availability of the UI server is linked to the availability of the multiplication microservice. Maybe we need more resources in the future to serve UI pages, but we may not want to scale all the functionality offered by the microservice.

The right side of Figure 5-1 shows the way to continue with our microservices adventure. (It's not a final step, but at least it takes us in the right direction.) We extract the static content out of multiplication and put it in a different web server component (that we'll deploy on the 9090 port). The JavaScript code will link to the REST APIs offered by multiplication and gamification, which do not contain a user interface. With this approach, we gain independence for changes in our UI and microservices, which don't depend on each other. Besides, we could now scale up or down our UI server following a different strategy than the multiplication microservice.

Now that we know our plan and the reasons behind it, let's execute it.

Moving the Static Content

The goal is to move all the static content (HTML, CSS, and JavaScript) to a separate service. We don't need Spring Boot for it: we just need a good, reliable and—if possible—lightweight web server. There are many good ones: Tomcat, Nginx, Jetty, etc. We'll use Jetty since it's built on top of Java, making it very easy to install and execute on both Linux and Windows platforms.[1]

---

[1]You could also choose Tomcat for consistency with the Spring Boot microservices but, in this case, I picked Jetty since it's really easy to explain how to download and configure it in the book.

SOURCE CODE AVAILABLE WITH THE BOOK: V6

You can find the first source code's upgrade of this chapter inside the v6 repository on GitHub: `https://github.com/microservices-practical`. It includes the UI extraction, so you'll find three folders with the different services: `Multiplication`, `Gamification`, and `UI`.

First, we need to download and install Jetty in our system. We'll use a helpful Jetty feature that allows us to create a new *Jetty Base* in a different folder, keeping separate the web server and the web app (and its configuration). This is a nice approach because we normally would like to keep our custom server configuration layer under version control and separated from the server binary files, making much easier a future solution for automated deployment.

We create a new jetty base (an `ui` folder) to place our static content following the instructions on the section, "Creating a New Jetty Base" (see *https://tpd.io/runjetty*). We'll get two folders as a result: `start.d` and `webapps`. This last one represents the root context of our server, so we'll create a new folder `ui` inside `webapps` and place there our static context. Listing 5-1 shows the resulting file structure.

Listing 5-1. UI File Structure (UI v6)

```
ui
├── start.d
|       deploy.ini
|       http.ini
|
└── webapps
    └── ui
```

```
index.html
multiplication-client.js
styles.css
```

The last step is to open the `http.ini` file in our favorite text editor and comment and change the value of the `jetty.http.port` to 9090 property, so we run the UI on a different port number, thus avoiding a clash with our Spring Boot applications.

Now we can run our Jetty server from the UI folder (the top-level one) and navigate to `http://localhost:9090/ui/index.html` to see our web page served from our new web server. See Listing 5-2.

Listing 5-2. Running Jetty (UI v6)

```
[/code/v6/ui]$ java -jar [YOUR_JETTY_HOME_FOLDER]/start.jar
```

Connecting UI with Gamification

Now it's time to create a new JavaScript file `gamification-client.js` in which will model our interactions with the gamification service. See Listing 5-3.

Listing 5-3. gamification-client.js (UI v6)

```javascript
function updateLeaderBoard() {
    $.ajax({
        url: "http://localhost:8081/leaders"
    }).then(function(data) {
        $('#leaderboard-body').empty();
        data.forEach(function(row) {
            $('#leaderboard-body').append('<tr><td>' + row.
            userId + '</td>' +
```

```
                    '<td>' + row.totalScore + '</td>');
        });
    });
}

function updateStats(userId) {
    $.ajax({
        url: "http://localhost:8081/stats?userId=" + userId,
        success: function(data) {
            $('#stats-div').show();
            $('#stats-user-id').empty().append(userId);
            $('#stats-score').empty().append(data.score);
            $('#stats-badges').empty().append(data.badges.
            join());
        },
        error: function(data) {
            $('#stats-div').show();
            $('#stats-user-id').empty().append(userId);
            $('#stats-score').empty().append(0);
            $('#stats-badges').empty();
        }
    });
}

$(document).ready(function() {

    updateLeaderBoard();

    $("#refresh-leaderboard").click(function( event ) {
        updateLeaderBoard();
    });

});
```

It consists of a couple of functions that will perform GET requests to the Gamification microservice (in this case running on port 8081) to retrieve the data and populate the tables. Also, we'll provide a button to refresh the leaderboard (not surprisingly named `refresh-leaderboard`), so we attach a `click` listener to it.

Note that we're using the URLs `http://localhost:8081/...` inside `gamification-client`, and `http://localhost:8080/...` in `multiplication-client.js`. We're not only hard-coding the URLs but also pointing to specific services by their host addresses and ports, which may be changing along with time. We should never use this approach, because if we move our microservices around, we'll need to change the host, port, URI context (e.g., `/results`), etc. Another problem we have when pointing at specific ports is that our system does not scale transparently. If we want to include an extra instance of the multiplication service, we should implement the logic to detect it and to do load balancing from our web client.

Luckily, there are solutions to solve this dangerous approach we just took. We'll cover a better alternative in a next section within this chapter, using service discovery and a gateway service. But before that, let's adapt our microservices to this new architecture and give a new look to our web client.

Changes to Existing Services

Even though splitting the UI service into a new project could seem harmless for multiplication and gamification, that's not the case. We'll serve now the static content from an *origin* (`localhost:9090`) which is different from where the backend services reside. In this case, port numbers are not the same (8080 and 8081). We'll have some issues with this if we don't apply changes in the backend, because Spring Security is using the Same-Origin Policy by default. Note that, in our case, it's about different ports but this issue would happen as well if you work with different hostnames.

You could see the issue by yourself if you skip this part, continue with the UI changes, and execute all the services as explained by the end of this section. Then, you should open the Development Tools within your browser (e.g., by pressing Ctrl+Shift+I in Chrome) and make sure that the console is visible (in Chrome it's one of the default tabs at the bottom). Now if you navigate to `http://localhost:9090/ui/index.html`, you'll see some red messages, as depicted in Figure 5-2.

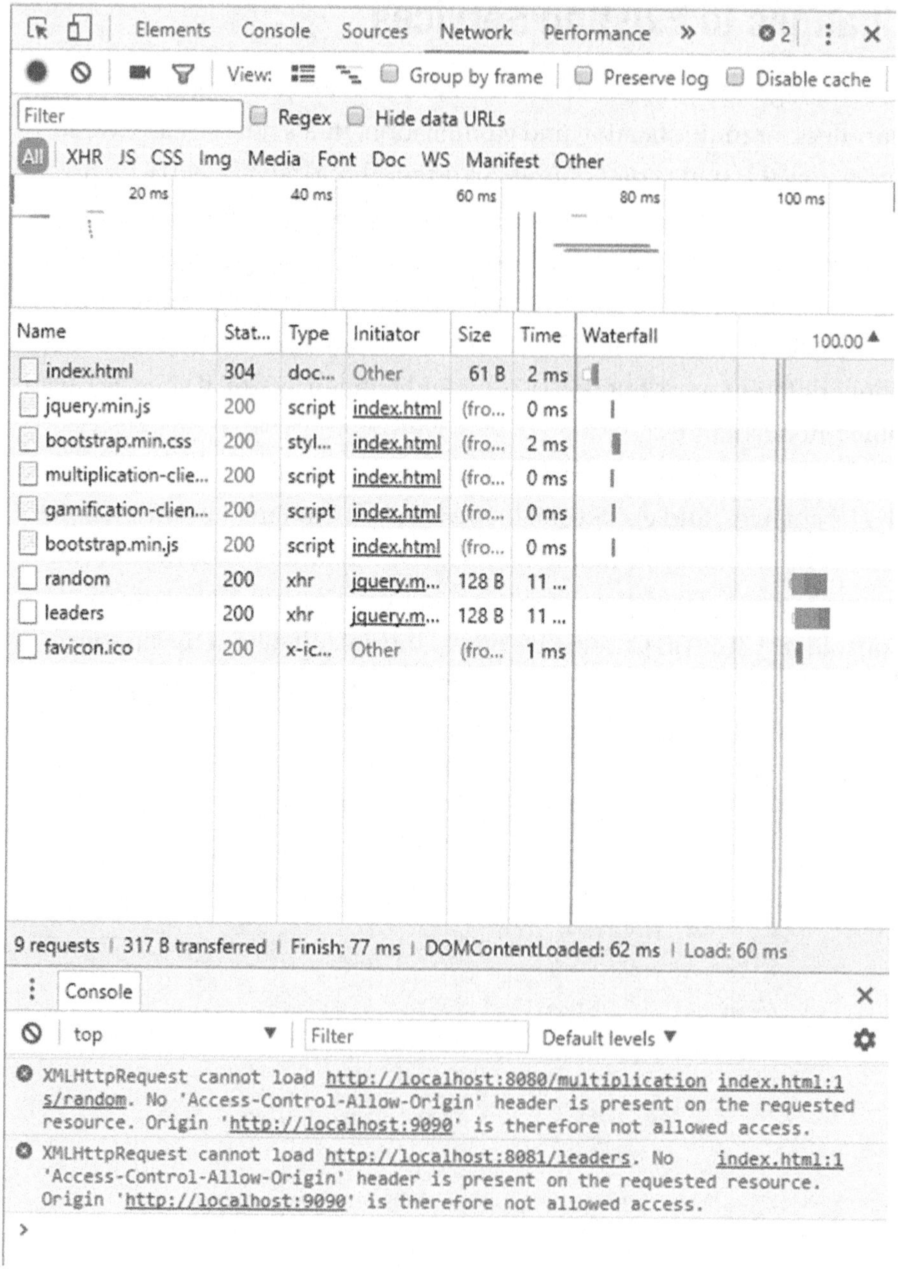

***Figure 5-2.** CORS error messages*

To fix this problem, we need to enable CORS (Cross-Origin Resource Sharing) for our backend services to allow requests coming from a different origin. To accomplish that, we need to add some Spring configuration to both of our services. Listing 5-4 shows the class added to gamification; we also need to create an identical class inside multiplication to enable CORS there as well.

Listing 5-4. WebConfiguration.java (gamification v6)

```java
package microservices.book.gamification.configuration;

import org.springframework.context.annotation.Configuration;
import org.springframework.web.servlet.config.annotation.
CorsRegistry;
import org.springframework.web.servlet.config.annotation.
EnableWebMvc;
import org.springframework.web.servlet.config.annotation.
WebMvcConfigurerAdapter;

/**
 * @author moises.macero
 */
@Configuration
@EnableWebMvc
public class WebConfiguration extends WebMvcConfigurerAdapter {

    /**
     * Enables Cross-Origin Resource Sharing (CORS)
     * More info: http://docs.spring.io/
     spring/docs/current/spring-framework-reference/html
     /cors.html
     * @param registry
     */
```

```
@Override
public void addCorsMappings(final CorsRegistry registry) {
    registry.addMapping("/**");
}
```
}

Note that, for simplicity, we're enabling CORS for every origin (we didn't specify any restriction) and for every mapping (with the pattern /**). When your system is mature and your infrastructure is set up, you may want to be stricter here by passing some property values to your applications to allow only some specific domains as origins. For extended details on how to fine-tune your configuration, read the official Spring documentation at *https://tpd.io/spr-cors*.

A New, Better UI with (Almost) No Effort

We have delivered so far a very minimalistic UI design to keep it simple and to release our first version of the application as soon as possible so our users can start playing. Now, taking advantage from the extraction and given that we need some room for our leaderboard, we'll update the design of our page using Bootstrap.

Regarding page layout, we'll split it into two different areas:

- On the left side, we'll place the multiplication attempt form, and we'll show the statistics to the user: total score and badges (coming from gamification).

- On the right side, we'll display the leaderboard with the top users (coming from Gamification) and, below that, the existing table with the latest attempts sent by the user who just played (provided by the Multiplication microservice).

We won't go into deep details about Bootstrap since they have a pretty good documentation that's very easy to follow (even for Java developers, see http://getbootstrap.com/css/). The *Grid system, Forms,* and *Buttons* will be the main features used in this application. See Listing 5-5.

Listing 5-5. index.html Adding Bootstrap (gamification v6)

```html
<!DOCTYPE html>
<html>
<head>
    <title>Multiplication v1</title>
    <link href="css/bootstrap.min.css" rel="stylesheet">
    <script src="https://ajax.googleapis.com/ajax/libs/
    jquery/3.1.1/jquery.min.js"></script>
    <script src="multiplication-client.js"></script>
    <script src="gamification-client.js"></script>
    <meta name="viewport" content="width=device-width,
    initial-scale=1">
</head>

<body>
<div class="container">
    <div class="row">
        <div class="col-md-12">
            <h1 class="text-center">Welcome to Social
            Multiplication</h1>
        </div>
    </div>
    <div class="row">
        <div class="col-md-6">
            <h3 class="text-center">Your new challenge is</h3>
            <h1 class="text-center">
```

```html
        <span class="multiplication-a"></span> x <span
        class="multiplication-b"></span>
    </h1>
    <p>
    <form id="attempt-form">
        <div class="form-group">
            <label for="result-attempt">Result?</label>
            <input type="text" name="result-attempt"
            id="result-attempt" class="form-control">
        </div>
        <div class="form-group">
            <label for="user-alias">Your alias:</label>
            <input type="text" name="user-alias"
            id="user-alias" class="form-control">
        </div>
        <input type="submit" value="Check" class="btn
        btn-default">
    </form>
    </p>
    <div class="result-message"></div>

    <div id="stats-div" style="display: none;">
        <h2>Your statistics</h2>
        <table id="stats" class="table">
            <tbody>
            <tr>
                <td class="info">User ID:</td>
                <td id="stats-user-id"></td>
            </tr>
            <tr>
                <td class="info">Score:</td>
                <td id="stats-score"></td>
```

```html
        </tr>
        <tr>
            <td class="info">Badges:</td>
            <td id="stats-badges"></td>
        </tr>
        </tbody>
    </table>
    </div>

</div>
<div class="col-md-6">
    <h3>Leaderboard</h3>
    <table id="leaderboard" class="table">
        <tr>
            <th>User ID</th>
            <th>Score</th>
        </tr>
        <tbody id="leaderboard-body"></tbody>
    </table>
    <div class="text-right">
        <button id="refresh-leaderboard" class="btn
        btn-default" type="submit">Refresh</button>
    </div>

    <div id="results-div" style="display: none;">
        <h2>Your latest attempts</h2>
        <table id="results" class="table">
            <tr>
                <th>Attempt ID</th>
                <th>Multiplication</th>
                <th>You entered</th>
                <th>Correct?</th>
```

```
                    </tr>
                    <tbody id="results-body"></tbody>
                </table>
            </div>
        </div>
    </div>
</div>
<script src="js/bootstrap.min.js"></script>
</body>
</html>
```

As promised, no significant effort: the HTML is still compact and readable. We removed the styles.css and now rely on the one provided by Bootstrap (which we need to download from their page and place inside our css folder). The main introduced changes are:

- There are new head and body inner tags to include Bootstrap and our new gamification-client.js.

- Grid system tags have been added to distribute the page in two areas, each of them taking half of the screen (6/12): it's just a set of divs and rows.

- The form has some style changes to make it look better than before.

- The leaderboard section is now a table similar to the latest attempts table, with a button to refresh it.

- The new stats table is now on the left side, and it uses the info class in Bootstrap to give some color to the first column.

- Both tables with statistics and latest attempts remain hidden until a first attempt is sent.

Besides that, we'll change our existing `multiplication-client.js` to support the new functionality. The main changes are:

- When the page loads, we retrieve the data not only for the latest results (now renamed to `updateResults`) but also for the information coming from Gamification—Score and Badges (the new Stats table) and the Leaderboard.

- Note that we introduced a delay (300 milliseconds) to retrieve information from the server. This is to make sure we give some time to the event to propagate and we get the updated information. We just want to keep the UI simple so this is a basic solution, but if you want to explore better options, you can read about how the server can notify the client when the data is ready using technologies like WebSockets.

- The `updateStats` function has been renamed to `updateResults` to avoid confusion. Also, this function now returns the user identifier since it's needed later by the new `updateStats` to retrieve the information from the server.

Listing 5-6. multiplication-client.js (gamification v6)

```
function updateMultiplication() {
    $.ajax({
        url: "http://localhost:8080/multiplications/random"
    }).then(function(data) {
        // Cleans the form
        $("#attempt-form").find( "input[name='result-attempt']" )
        .val("");
```

```
        $("#attempt-form").find( "input[name='user-alias']"
        ).val("");
        // Gets a random challenge from API and loads the data
        in the HTML
        $('.multiplication-a').empty().append(data.factorA);
        $('.multiplication-b').empty().append(data.factorB);
    });
}

function updateResults(alias) {
    var userId = -1;
    $.ajax({
        async: false,
        url: "http://localhost:8080/results?alias=" + alias,
        success: function(data) {
            $('#results-div').show();
            $('#results-body').empty();
            data.forEach(function(row) {
                $('#results-body').append('<tr><td>' + row.id +
                '</td>' +
                    '<td>' + row.multiplication.factorA + ' x '
                    + row.multiplication.factorB + '</td>' +
                    '<td>' + row.resultAttempt + '</td>' +
                    '<td>' + (row.correct === true ? 'YES' :
                    'NO') + '</td></tr>');
            });
            userId = data[0].user.id;
        }
    });
    return userId;
}
```

```javascript
$(document).ready(function() {

    updateMultiplication();

    $("#attempt-form").submit(function( event ) {
        // Don't submit the form normally
        event.preventDefault();

        // Get some values from elements on the page
        var a = $('.multiplication-a').text();
        var b = $('.multiplication-b').text();
        var $form = $( this ),
            attempt = $form.find( "input[name='result-
            attempt']" ).val(),
            userAlias = $form.find( "input[name='user-alias']" )
            .val();

        // Compose the data in the format that the API is expecting
        var data = { user: { alias: userAlias}, multiplication:
        {factorA: a, factorB: b}, resultAttempt: attempt};

        // Send the data using post
        $.ajax({
            url: 'http://localhost:8080/results',
            type: 'POST',
            data: JSON.stringify(data),
            contentType: "application/json; charset=utf-8",
            dataType: "json",
            async: false,
            success: function(result){
                if(result.correct) {
                    $('.result-message').empty()
```

```
                      .append("<p class='bg-success
                      text-center'>The result is correct!
                      Congratulations!</p>");
            } else {
                $('.result-message').empty()
                      .append("<p class='bg-danger
                      text-center'>Oops that's not correct!
                      But keep trying!</p>");
            }
        }
    });

    updateMultiplication();

    setTimeout(function(){
        var userId = updateResults(userAlias);
        updateStats(userId);
        updateLeaderBoard();
    }, 300);
  });
});
```

PRODUCTION READINESS: RESPONSIVE WEB DESIGN

Thanks to Bootstrap we added one key feature to our web application: now it's responsive. That means it will look good on smaller screens like smartphones, adapting the content to the screen size. You can test it by resizing the browser or using the web developer tools to simulate different devices.

After the changes, we can go to our page and see the renovated web client; it's looking much nicer thanks to Bootstrap (see Figure 5-3). Remember that now we have to include an extra stepto see our system running:

1. Start the RabbitMQ broker.

2. Run the Multiplication microservice (now without UI) from the IDE, or package it and run it from the command line.

3. Do the same for gamification microservice.

4. Execute the Jetty server from the root UI folder (running `java -jar [YOUR_JETTY_HOME_FOLDER]/start.jar`). Then you can navigate to `http://localhost:9090/ui/index.html`.

Welcome to Social Multiplication

Your new challenge is

88 x 34

Result?

Your alias:

| |

Check

The result is correct! Congratulations!

Leaderboard

User ID	Score
1	100
4	30
2	20
34	10
33	10

Refresh

Your statistics

User ID:	1
Score:	100
Badges:	BRONZE_MULTIPLICATOR,LUCKY_NUMBER,FIRST_WON

Your latest attempts

Attempt ID	Multiplication	You entered	Correct?
40	55 x 27	1485	YES
39	28 x 46	1287	NO
19	33 x 56	897654	NO
17	42 x 17	714	YES
16	89 x 93	8277	YES

Figure 5-3. *The renovated web client*

The Current Architecture

Let's revisit the logical view of our system, which now includes the UI server as a separate service and the browser, representing the real client making requests to the backend services.

Our architecture is growing toward a real microservice architecture, step by step. That's great, because we want to benefit from advantages like having more independent changes and a more flexible scalability. *But we're not there yet.*

As introduced when we connected the gamification's UI leaderboard to our backend services, we can still see two major issues with our current design:

- *Our UI page still knows the structure of the backend:* It needs to know that there is a gamification microservice and a multiplication microservice. The problem here is that, if we split or combine some of our microservices in the future, we will impact the UI, requiring modifications to align with the new backend structure.

- *The UI has hardcoded URLs to locate multiplication and gamification microservices.* The same happens with gamification and its link to multiplication. We should change those direct links, otherwise, our system won't scale.

This is when a major transition in our architecture occurs. To solve these problems, we need to introduce some patterns such as service discovery, load balancing, the API gateway (or routing), etc. In the world of microservices, they usually come together with the names of the tools or frameworks that implement those patterns: *Eureka, Consul, Ribbon, Zuul, etc.*

As mentioned earlier, it's difficult to find our way across these tools: when do we need them? Should we implement all of them to have a proper microservices architecture? Those are the questions that we'll answer in the coming sections. First, we'll introduce service discovery and load balancing. Once you understand how it works, we'll cover the API gateway pattern and see how all the pieces work together. Then, as usual, we'll apply these patterns to our code and see the benefits for our system.

PRODUCTION READINESS: DEPLOYMENT AND TESTING

You might have noticed that the system is getting more complex to manage. Our current architecture status is already showing how important automated deployment and testing become if we want to achieve success when implementing a microservices architecture:

- To start the full application, we need to start manually the many parts of it (as in the previous section). This is annoying. We could think of creating a script file to start up these different parts, and that would be really good since we would create our first automated deployment strategy. We won't cover that part within the book but, as you can imagine, deploying your microservices is not as easy as deploying a single monolith.

- To feed the system with data and start testing it, we need to go to our page and solve some attempts for some different users, then verify that gamification is doing its job. Doing this manually is a lot of work, and we're not even covering all different use cases. We need end-to-end tests, which are covered in the next chapter.

Service Discovery and Load Balancing

Service Discovery

Coming back to the current architecture as a reference, we left our gamification microservice contacting the multiplication's REST API to retrieve some data. Gamification knows where to find multiplication since it has a property pointing to `http://localhost:8080/`, and contact it to retrieve the multiplication factors, as depicted in Figure 5-4.

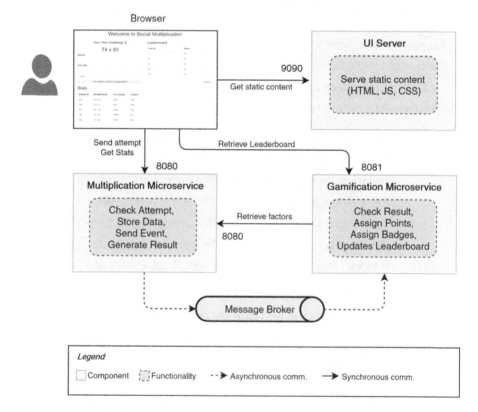

Figure 5-4. *It's almost a real microservice architecture*

As mentioned, that's a wrong design. Why should gamification know the *physical location* (IP and port number) of multiplication? In an environment with dozens of services that may be deployed everywhere, that approach is unmaintainable. It does not scale at all: what if we introduce a second instance of the multiplication microservice? Which one should we invoke from gamification?

Note that this is a similar problem to the one that we mentioned when explaining how the UI shouldn't know about our microservices architecture. The difference is that, in this case, the communication is between two microservices.

A Service Discovery tool will give us the solution we're looking for. These kinds of tools consist of several pieces:

- The Service Registry, which keeps track of all service instances and their names.

- The Register Agent, which every service should use to provide its configuration so others can find it.

- The Service Discovery Client, which contacts the registry asking for a service using its alias.

There are different service discovery tools, among others Consul and Eureka, that are nicely supported by Spring. We'll use Eureka in this book, which is part of the very popular Netflix OSS stack. Spring provides wrappers for those Netflix tools within the successful Spring Cloud project: Spring Cloud Netflix.

Keep in mind that you could follow similar instructions to the ones in this book to make the following setup work with a different implementation (for example, Consul). What's important to understand is the concept— we need to provide a mechanism to services so they can find each other's instances without hard-coding links between them. As we'll also detail later, behind each reference between services may exist one or several instances, so the load balancing aspect is closely linked to service discovery.

Now that we introduced the concept and the involved parts of it, let's see—in an evolved logical view—how they can fit into our existing architecture. Figure 5-5 is not going to be our final solution, but it's good to have a look at this state to better understand how our entire system will work, and later understand what are the differences and the synergies between service discovery and the API gateway.

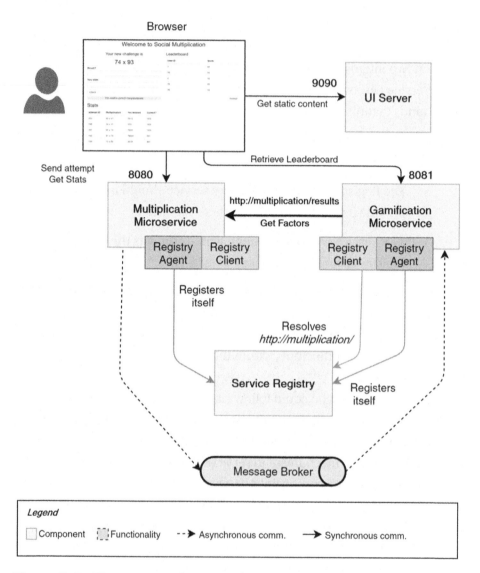

Figure 5-5. *How service discovery fits into our system*

We can see the three pieces of service discovery working together in Figure 5-5. First, there is a new separate component: *the Service Registry*. We will deploy it as a new microservice. Multiplication and gamification microservices will register themselves by contacting it when they start, using their *Registry Agents*. At that point, they will get an alias in the registry, which is by default the microservice's name (we'll see that in practice later). Now they can be found by using the `http://multiplication/` or `http://gamification/` addresses, instead of `http://[HOST]:[PORT]` URLs. However, for those addresses to work, our microservices must use their *Registry Client*, which will translate the aliases to specific URLs using the mapping located at the Service Registry. In this scenario, only Gamification's registry client would come into play, translating `http://multiplications/` into `http://localhost:8080`.

If you look at this pattern with some nostalgic vision, doesn't it look familiar to you? It's pretty similar to a *dynamic DNS*: we assign an alias to a service so it can move around locations without us needing to care about the particular place (or IP) in which the service is deployed.

Load Balancing

There is still a gap in our architecture: how does Eureka work with multiple instances of the same service? The guys at Netflix solved that challenge too: they implemented Ribbon to provide *client-side load balancing* integrated with Eureka.

If we spin up two instances of multiplication microservice, they will both register in Eureka with the same alias (since they have the same application name). Let's say we have our new instance located at `http://localhost:8082`. When the gamification microservice, as a client, wants to contact `http://multiplication/`, Eureka will return both URLs and it's up to the consumer to decide which instance should be called (using Ribbon—the load balancer—together with Eureka's registry client). By default, Ribbon would apply a simple Round-Robin strategy, but we'll see in practice how to change that later. See Figure 5-6.

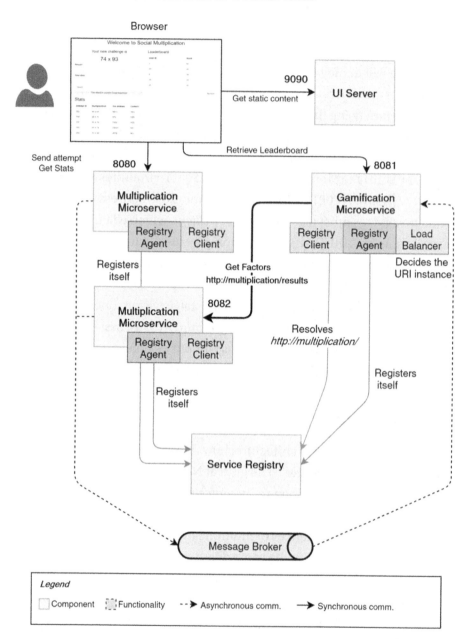

Figure 5-6. *How load balancing fits into our system*

Note that client-side load balancing is a tricky concept since it does not look natural when reading it for the first time. You might be asking yourself: why should the caller worry about the load balancing part or the number of instances of another service? You're right, it shouldn't. That's precisely why Eureka and Ribbon provide us with that functionality transparently, so we don't need to take care of that within the code. We call the service as if it were only one instance of it. But remember: *Ribbon just hides the load balancing, but it's still there, on your client.*

THE PROBLEM OF OUR LOGICAL VIEW

The last figure showed us the UI connecting directly to one of the instances of our multiplication microservice (on port 8080), which is a bad idea but it's the best we can do for now. The problem is that we can't integrate service discovery directly in the UI so, how can we solve this? The next section about routing and the API gateway pattern will provide an answer to this problem.

Polyglot Systems, Eureka, and Ribbon

There is a million-dollar question for polyglot-environment fans at this point: *what should we do if one of our microservices is not written using Spring?* How are we supposed to include Eureka and Ribbon? The answer implies, as usual, adding an extra player in our microservices ecosystem: the *Spring Cloud Sidecar* (see `https://tpd.io/spr-sidecar`). Sidecar is a project inspired by Netflix Prana and, as its name suggests, requires you to start an instance of this application appendix per non-Java application instance for which you want to use Ribbon and Eureka (which would be the motorbike's part of your sidecar, I presume).

We won't use Sidecar in our system, but you can see Figure 5-7 how that would look in the hypothetical case of having a gamification microservice written in a different language other than Java.

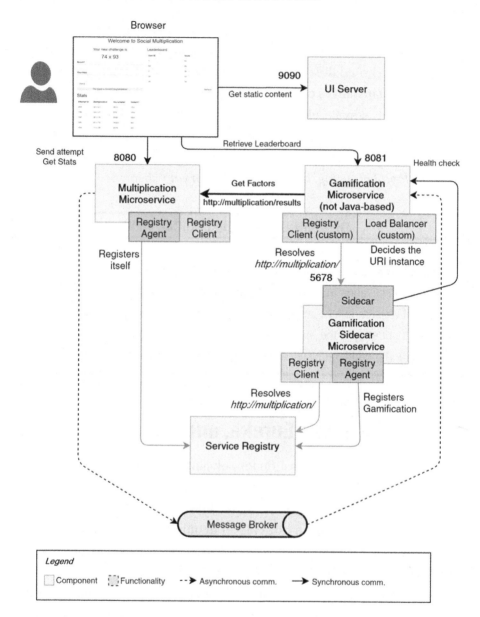

Figure 5-7. *The hypothetical case of having the gamification microservice written in a different language other than Java*

The Sidecar microservice (deployed on port 5678 following the documentation example) acts as a proxy and requires your application to expose a health endpoint so it can be discovered and monitored about its status. It uses Eureka to register (and update) the different instances of the non-Java application (via the Registry Agent) and to get the available instances of other microservices (via the Registry Client). The application attached to Sidecar can then access to the Sidecar's APIs to find instances of other services. Note that it's up to the non-Java application to do the load balancing, since it will get the list of all the available instances (not a specific one) from Sidecar.

To achieve high availability, the Sidecar microservices should be scaled and monitored as well, which introduces an extra required layer of redundancy in your system. As you can imagine, maintaining this approach with a few microservices can be fine, but having it for a big part of your system might become a nightmare. It's up to us (as team members, technical leads, or architects) to balance these kinds of drawbacks when designing our architecture and make a good choice. In this case, two valid alternatives are either going for language programming consistency across your system (coding most of your microservices in Java and Spring Boot) or exploring a different load balancing/high availability strategy for the non-Java microservices.

Routing with an API Gateway
The API Gateway Pattern

As you just saw, we can get a distributed system supported by Service Discovery and Load Balancing, which allows us to scale up our microservices without tightly coupling to our infrastructure. But there are some problems that we still need to figure out:

- *Our web client is running on a browser:* It's clear that it can't run any service discovery client nor take care of load balancing. We need an extra piece to connect it to the microservices living in the backend, without losing the load balancing capabilities.

- *Tasks like authentication, API versioning, or any request filtering in general, don't fit into our distributed scenario yet.* A centralized point of control is required for our system APIs (multiplication and gamification REST endpoints).

- *Our REST APIs are following the system's architecture, thus making our consumers dependent on it.* This problem is more difficult to see, so we'll cover it with an example.

To tackle these challenges, we'll implement an API Gateway in our system. Following our current direction, we choose Zuul since it's also part of Spring Cloud Netflix and integrates easily with the rest of the tools included in that framework. In a similar way to the service registry, Zuul will work in our architecture as an extra microservice that we need to connect to the others.

Let's see step by step how the API gateway works so we can understand how it solves our problems.

First, let's park the *UI load balancing issue* assuming there is a dedicated one per microservice and analyze our third challenge: having our consumers aware of our microservices architecture. To better understand why this is not a good idea, consider the hypothetical scenario depicted in Figure 5-8: we want to extract the Statistics functionality to a new microservice so we want to move the /stats/ endpoint there. Since the consumer (in this case our web client) is aware of the microservices structure, it needs to be updated as well to point to the new URL (something like http://statsmanager/stats). This annoying side-effect becomes even worse if we offer our REST APIs to external parties, which should adapt their applications to every microservice refactoring work we make. Instead of going that way, we want to create a REST API that doesn't reveal our inner structure to our consumers. That will give us total flexibility to later change parts of it without impacting others. What we want to achieve is having URLs like `http://application/leaders` and `http://application/results` (architecture-agnostic), instead of having `http://gamification/leaders` and `http://multiplication/results`.

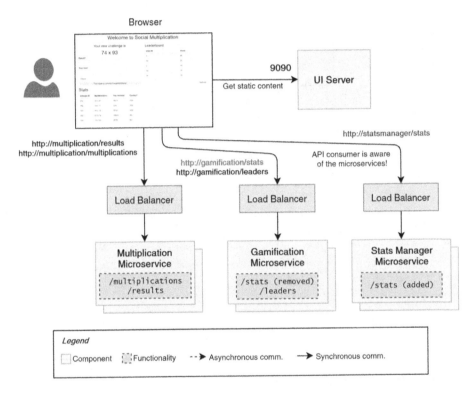

Figure 5-8. *The hypothetical case of splitting /stats to a new microservice*

The API gateway pattern will give us the solution to this problem. Our chosen tool, Zuul, will handle the routing of requests to the proper service once we configure some URL patterns, keeping the consumers totally unaware of the internal structure. With that solution in place, we have total flexibility to move our functionality around the system: we just need to change the *routing table,* as shown in Figure 5-9.

211

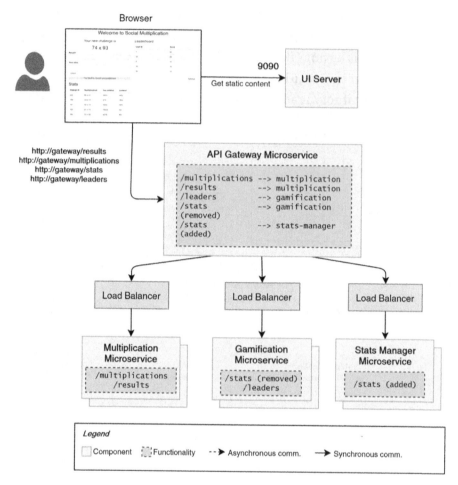

Figure 5-9. The introduction of an API Gateway and a Routing table

Note that introducing an API gateway in our system aligns nicely with the monolith-first approach. Remember that we said it's preferable to start with big chunks of functionality in small monoliths, and then start splitting them once the domain boundaries are clear and the system is evolving. With an API gateway in front of our system, our API consumers will see a monolith all the time, while we can evolve it transparently to have a distributed, scalable architecture behind it. For the same reason, including this pattern in an existing monolith is a perfect way of splitting it and evolving it to a microservices architecture step by step.

With the API gateway, we could also integrate into a central place features like Authentication since all the requests will go through that service. We could use Spring Security for example, and integrate it with Zuul with a custom Zuul filter. You can look at the API Gateway Pattern Tutorial on Spring's web site if you want to learn more about how to make that solution work (see *https://tpd.io/apigwsec*). As an alternative, we could also integrate within our Zuul microservice a third-party Authentication and Authorization provider, such as Auth0 or Okta Single Sign-On.

Keep in mind that these benefits of the API gateway pattern— abstracting our inner structure and centralizing the API access to our system—don't require service discovery or load balancing. We could also set up a routing table, which points directly to the microservice instances, based on some URI patterns in Zuul (that's actually how we'll start evolving our code within the next section). However, we already learned that we need those capabilities in our system to provide high availability and be able to keep the system working even if some microservices are down.

Now we're close to understanding how everything combines. In Figure 5-9, we simplified our logical view and placed a load balancer in front of every group of microservice instances. However, now that we have an API gateway microservice that lives in our backend, what if we make it responsible for the load balancing functionality for frontend requests? By doing that, we solve the problem we haven't tackled yet: not being able to provide load balancing on the web client side. In the next subsection, we'll cover the integration of Zuul, Eureka, and Ribbon to fully understand how these different tools (and architecture patterns) work together in the world of microservices.

PRODUCTION READINESS: EDGE SERVICES

Many people often get scared when conversations arise about having centralized parts in a microservices architecture. Parts that are critical, like routing and filtering, may become a single point of failure. This API gateway service in particular, as the gate to our microservices, is also known as an *edge service*.

The key to making this kind of services work in a microservices infrastructure is to apply proper load balancing to them. To do that, we usually need to go a level deep, and use solutions such as an infrastructure DNS load balancer, in which for example our gateway located at `http://gateway.ourwebapp.com` is backed by three different server instances. Most cloud providers offer these services out of the box, and we can also implement it by ourselves with tools like Nginx. If you want to know more about edge services with a practical example from Netflix, see `https://tpd.io/lb-ms`.

Zuul, Eureka, and Ribbon Working Together

Let's focus now on how we can leverage our system by including service discovery and load balancing in our API gateway. In other words, let's learn how Zuul, Eureka, and Ribbon work together to give us the full solution we're looking for.

Figure 5-10 represents our system with the introduction of the API gateway microservice, which relies on service discovery and load balancing to find others and to allow others to find it.

Look first at the upper side of the figure: the web client is no longer connected directly to the microservices but to the gateway instead, sending all the requests through it (we'll make it available on port 8000 within our system).

The gateway microservice, which will be implemented with Zuul and Spring Boot, contains a routing table that points to microservice aliases registered in Eureka, instead of physical addresses. This is where the integration between Zuul, Eureka, and Ribbon combines perfectly to give us a full solution based on an API gateway, service discovery, and load balancing. When Zuul receives a request, it decomposes the URL and locates the pattern in the routing table. Every pattern is mapped to a microservice alias so Zuul uses Eureka to go to the registry and find the available instances. Then Ribbon comes into play and picks one of the instances based on the load balancing strategy (Round-Robin by default). Finally, Zuul redirects the original request to the corresponding microservice instance.

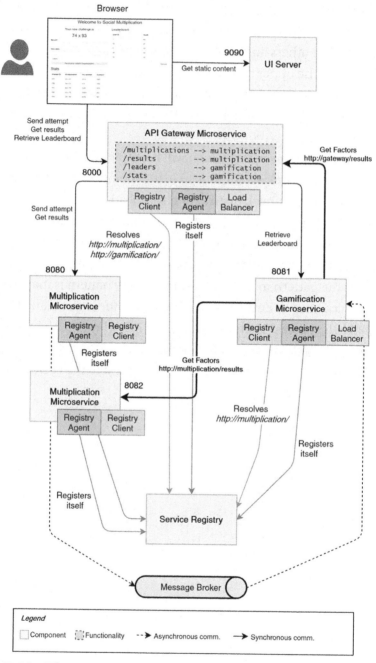

Figure 5-10. *The system with the introduction of the API gateway microservice*

Now, if we focus on the side of the figure below the gateway, we can see how our gamification microservice has two options to retrieve the results from the multiplication microservice. It can go like before and use its own connection to the service registry, but it can also use the new API gateway service to achieve its goal. Here we are facing one of the most controversial topics in microservices: *should the services use the gateway to call each other or should they keep using Eureka/Ribbon for the internal communication?* There is no right or wrong answer here: it depends on your scenario and, more specifically, on how your infrastructure is set up. However, keeping the routing and load balancing capabilities centralized can bring some advantages:

- We can keep microservices unaware of the *location of a given functionality.* No matter if we're splitting a monolith or we decide to move some functionality to a different microservice, we can have all the other microservices working without any impact if they always pass through the API gateway. We get even looser coupling between our microservices.

- Load balancing is frequently a critical topic in our infrastructure. Configuring it properly is complicated: it may depend on geographical areas, network latency, microservice load, etc. Normally, those policies are better kept centralized and that means that we shouldn't rely on the implementation of every service. Client-side load balancing is not a good approach for backend services in these situations since every service has a *local view* of the possible infrastructure issues, but a global perspective may be required instead.

On the other hand, if you take the decision of using the API gateway to process all your requests within the system, take into account that it becomes an even more critical *edge service* and you need to support it with a good redundancy strategy to keep it highly available—internally and externally.

For this application, we'll use the API gateway microservice as the only responsible for routing the requests, so we keep gamification and multiplication microservices unaware of each other. If we translate that to our last figure, it means that gamification and multiplication will use Eureka and Ribbon only to locate the gateway, which could be itself replicated in several instances. Since this is getting too theoretical, let's jump to the next section in which we'll evolve our system step by step to make this last logical view a reality.

Hands-On Code

Finally! Now that we understood the concepts, we can apply these patterns to our microservices architecture and include Zuul, Eureka and Ribbon in our Spring Boot applications. Instead of doing that in a single step, we'll introduce these tools in two phases. The first one will be Zuul, our API gateway service.

Implementing the API Gateway with Zuul

> **SOURCE CODE AVAILABLE WITH THE BOOK: V7**
>
> You can find the new version of the code with the Gateway routing the requests inside the v7 repository on GitHub: `https://github.com/microservices-practical`.

To add a gateway service with Zuul, we need to create a new Spring Boot application. We can navigate again to the Spring Initialzr (http://start. spring.io) and fill in our data, selecting Zuul as a dependency we want to use. Our project name will be gateway and the package name will be microservices.book.gateway, as shown in Figure 5-11.

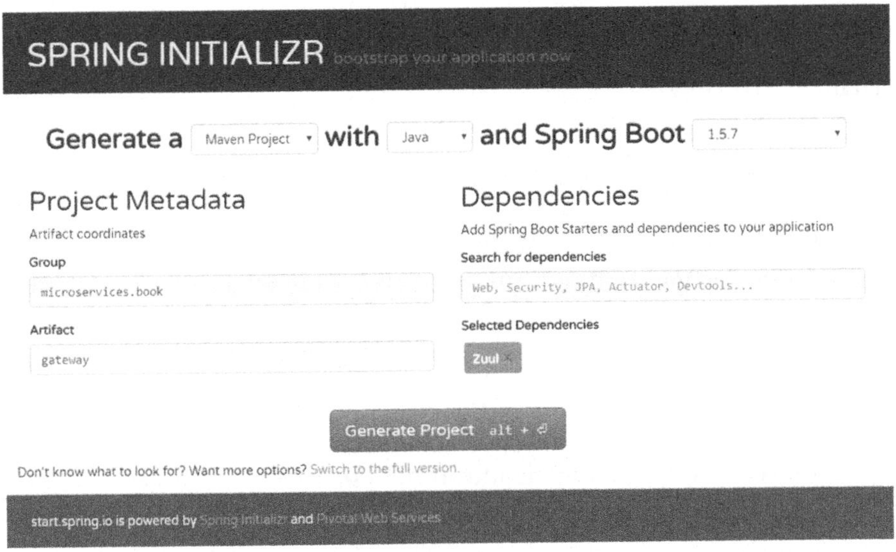

Figure 5-11. *Use Spring Initialzr to create the gateway microservice*

Then we extract it, import it into our preferred IDE, and navigate directly to our application.properties file (located under src/main/resources). We'll rename it to application.yml since, in this case, the YAML format will make our configuration more readable.

To make our Spring Boot application behave as a Zuul gateway, we just need to add an annotation to our main class: @EnableZuulProxy. See Listing 5-7.

Listing 5-7. GatewayApplication.java (gateway v7)

```java
package microservices.book.gateway;

import org.springframework.boot.SpringApplication;
import org.springframework.boot.autoconfigure.
    SpringBootApplication;
import org.springframework.cloud.netflix.zuul.EnableZuulProxy;

@EnableZuulProxy
@SpringBootApplication
public class GatewayApplication {

    public static void main(String[] args) {
        SpringApplication.run(GatewayApplication.class, args);
    }
}
```

Zuul allows you to configure routing directly in the properties file, which makes it very convenient and straightforward. In this case, we can start with this configuration, as shown in Listing 5-8.

Listing 5-8. application.yml (gateway v7)

```yaml
server:
  port: 8000

zuul:
  prefix: /api
  routes:
    multiplications:
      path: /multiplications/**
      url: http://localhost:8080/multiplications
    results:
```

```
    path: /results/**
    url: http://localhost:8080/results
  leaders:
    path: /leaders/**
    url: http://localhost:8081/leaders
  stats:
    path: /stats/**
    url: http://localhost:8081/stats

endpoints:
  trace:
    sensitive: false

ribbon:
  eureka:
    enabled: false
```

Let's look at what we're configuring within this file:

- The Gateway's server port is changed to 8000.
  Remember: that will be our entry point for all our REST
  API consumers.

- The last part is setting the `ribbon.eureka.enabled`
  property to `false` since we decided not to introduce
  Eureka and Ribbon yet so we can evolve our
  application in small increments.

- We also set Zuul's `/trace` endpoint as not sensitive (not
  requiring authentication). We'll use it later to see Zuul
  in action.

- The rest of the configuration (under `zuul`) is there to set
  up routing.

- We set a prefix for all our requests. All the requests coming in need to have that part in the URL, which will be removed by Zuul when redirecting the request. In our example, the expected URL is http://localhost:8000/api/multiplications and it will be redirected to http://localhost:8080/ multiplications (the /api prefix is removed). It's a handy way to group routes and apply different policies. We could also have two gateway configurations to handle /internal and /public prefixes, for instance.

- For every different URL pattern, we configure the routing to the proper service (hard-coding physical addresses by now). Note that we have two patterns pointing to the same service since, for instance, both the /multiplications and /results entities are being managed by the multiplication microservice.

The resulting mapping will be the following:

Request Pattern	Target
http://localhost:8000/api/ multiplications/**	http://localhost:8080/ multiplications/**
http://localhost:8000/api/ results/**	http://localhost:8080/ results/**
http://localhost:8000/api/ leaders/**	http://localhost:8081/ leaders/**
http://localhost:8000/api/ stats/**	http://localhost:8081/ stats/**

If we look at the request patterns, we notice how we managed to achieve our first goal: now it's possible to make requests to our application to a central place. API consumers don't know anything about our microservices: they all go through `http://localhost:8000`.

The next step is to include a `WebConfiguration` class enabling CORS for the gateway project too (as we did for the multiplication and gamification microservices). This is needed here as well for the same reason: the frontend, gateway, and microservices are located at different origins (port numbers in our case).

Now we need to link everything. To apply the changes to our frontend, we just modify our gamification and multiplication JavaScript clients to point to the gateway service at `http://localhost:8000/`. Note that we also need to append the prefix `api/` to all our requests. Make sure to use this new variable in all the API calls spread in both files. See Listing 5-9.

Listing 5-9. gamification-client.js/multiplication-client.js Changing Server URL (ui v7)

```
var SERVER_URL = "http://localhost:8000/api";
```

On the backend side, we need to update gamification to call multiplication using the API gateway instead of doing so directly. To do that, we need to update the property that we included in its `application.properties` file, as shown in Listing 5-10.

Listing 5-10. application.properties Changing Server URL (gamification v7)

```
# REST client settings
multiplicationHost=http://localhost:8000/api
```

It looks like we got everything set up. Since the gateway is a microservice itself, now we just need to start it together with the rest of our existing services. Let's summarize the steps to make our system work once more:

1. Run the RabbitMQ server (if it's not yet running in the background).

2. Run the gateway microservice.

3. Run the multiplication microservice.

4. Run the gamification microservice.

5. Run the Jetty web server from the `ui` root folder.

Remember that you can run microservices directly from your IDE, using `mvnw spring-boot:run` from the project's root folder or by packaging them (`mvnw package`) and using the `java -jar [resulting-artifact-name.jar]`) command in the console. Also note that the order of those steps is not important apart from the first one, which is required for multiplication and gamification to work properly. You can run Steps 2-5 in any order you prefer.

If we navigate to `http://localhost:9090/ui/index.html`, we should see our application up and running. This time when we post new multiplications and retrieve the leaderboard, we're contacting the API gateway instead of the microservice instances.

We can verify how Zuul works if, after some requests from the UI, we navigate to `http://localhost:8000/trace`. There we'll see all the requests being handled by Zuul and their corresponding responses, including the time taken to process them. If you do that from your browser, the JSON response might be difficult to read, but you can copy/paste it into an online formatter such as *https://jsonformatter.org*.

Figure 5-12 represents the current status of our system, with the gateway routing the requests to the corresponding services. Note that there is no service discovery in place yet, which is what we'll do next.

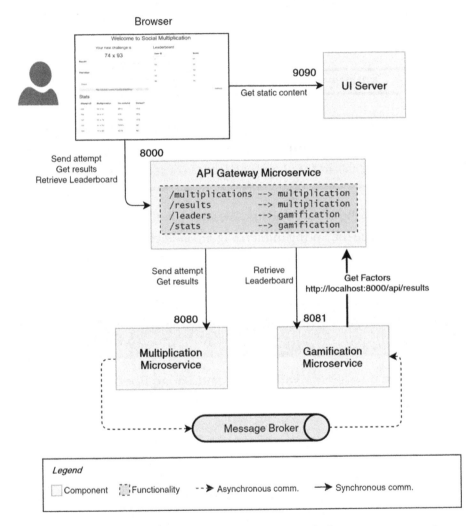

Figure 5-12. *Current status of the system, with the gateway routing the requests to the corresponding services*

Implementing Service Discovery

Following our plan defined during the first part of the chapter, we'll add service discovery and load balancing to all our microservices, including our new gateway service. Doing that, we'll be able to safely scale and distribute our services, since we won't be bound anymore to specific host/port configurations.

SOURCE CODE AVAILABLE WITH THE BOOK: V8

You can find the new version of the code with service discovery (Eureka) and load balancing (Ribbon), together with the API gateway service inside the v8 repository on GitHub: `https://github.com/microservices-practical`.

First, we'll create the service registry. We could do that manually but for simplicity let's use the Spring Initializr again, at `http://start.spring.io`. This time we only need to select the Eureka Server as a dependency. Name the project `service-registry` and keep the package name as the default of `microservices.book.serviceregistry`. See Figure 5-13.

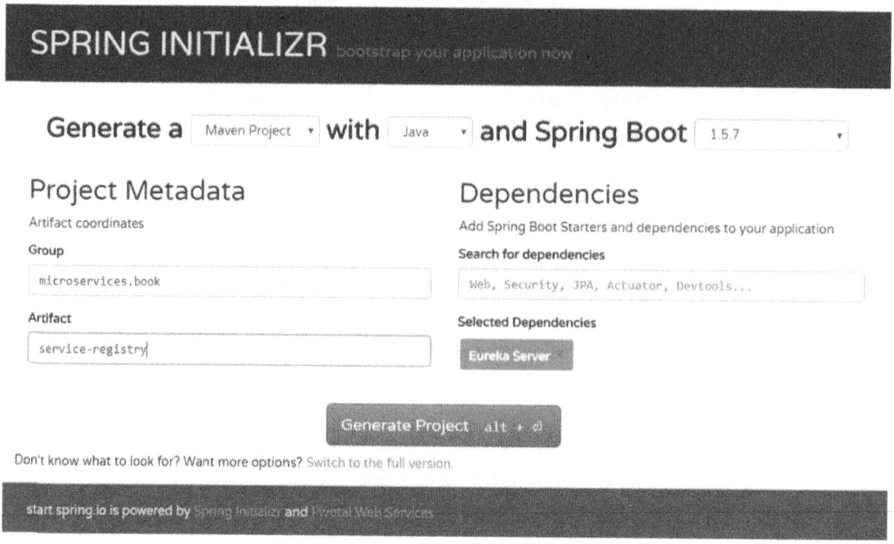

Figure 5-13. *Use the Spring Initializr to create the service registry*

As usual, we take the contents of the downloaded ZIP file and place it together with the other services in our project structure and import it into our IDE. The Spring assistant is only helping you create an empty project with the right dependencies; it's not configuring your service registry. Let's do that.

To convert our service into a Eureka Registry server, we also use an annotation (as in the Gateway) in the application class: @EnableEurekaServer. See Listing 5-11.

Listing 5-11. ServiceRegistryApplication.java (service-registry v8)

```
package microservices.book.serviceregistry;

import org.springframework.boot.SpringApplication;
import org.springframework.boot.autoconfigure.
SpringBootApplication;
import org.springframework.cloud.netflix.eureka.server.
EnableEurekaServer;

@EnableEurekaServer
@SpringBootApplication
public class ServiceRegistryApplication {

    public static void main(String[] args) {
        SpringApplication.run(ServiceRegistryApplication.class,
        args);
    }
})
```

We also need to change the default server port of Spring Boot, 8080, to the default port expected by Eureka Clients, which is 8761. We could set it to any other port number but, in that case, we would need extra configuration in all our microservices to override the default port. An extra curious thing is that the Eureka registry will try to register itself using also the port 8761, so if you don't change this port or disable the Eureka feature for registering the own instance (eureka.client.register-with-eureka=false), the application will fail when we start it because it's not able to find itself. We'll just change the port to the default one since having the server registering itself is a good practice so it can be later scaled up. See Listing 5-12.

Listing 5-12. application.properties (service-registry v8)

```
server.port=8761
```

That's all we require to have a service registry with Eureka. We could now run this *skinny* microservice as any other Spring Boot application, but it's not yet connected to anything else in our architecture.

It's time to configure the rest of the services (social-multiplication, gamification, and gateway) so they can include the Eureka client and send their information to our new Eureka Server. To accomplish this, we first must add the proper dependency to each service's pom.xml file. The changes we'll introduce are:

1. A dependency management block to resolve the Spring Cloud's dependencies.

2. A new property to reference the Spring Cloud's version.

3. Our new dependency to use the service discovery, spring-cloud-starter-eureka.

4. An extra dependency to expose the status of our microservices, spring-boot-starter-actuator.

Usually, we'd just need to include the new dependencies (Steps 3 and 4) but, in case of gamification and multiplication microservices, the first and second tasks are required because it's the first time we use Spring Cloud dependencies there. Let's look at the pom.xml file for gamification, where you can spot the main differences (see Listing 5-13). Make sure to apply the same changes to multiplication and to the API gateway, which in this case already included the Spring Cloud configuration since we created it with Zuul.

Listing 5-13. pom.xml (gamification v8)

```xml
<?xml version="1.0" encoding="UTF-8"?>
<project xmlns="http://maven.apache.org/POM/4.0.0"
xmlns:xsi="http://www.w3.org/2001/XMLSchema-instance"
    xsi:schemaLocation="http://maven.apache.org/POM/4.0.0
    http://maven.apache.org/xsd/maven-4.0.0.xsd">
    <modelVersion>4.0.0</modelVersion>

    <groupId>microservices.book</groupId>
    <artifactId>gamification-v8</artifactId>
    <version>0.8.0-SNAPSHOT</version>
    <packaging>jar</packaging>

    <name>gamification-v8</name>
    <description>Social Multiplication App - Gamification
    (Microservices - the Practical Way book)</description>

    <parent>
        <groupId>org.springframework.boot</groupId>
        <artifactId>spring-boot-starter-parent</artifactId>
        <version>1.5.7.RELEASE</version>
        <relativePath/> <!-- lookup parent from repository -->
    </parent>

    <properties>
        <project.build.sourceEncoding>UTF-8</project.build.
        sourceEncoding>
```

```
<project.reporting.outputEncoding>UTF-8</project.
reporting.outputEncoding>
<java.version>1.8</java.version>
<spring-cloud.version>Dalston.SR1</spring-cloud.
version>
</properties>

<dependencyManagement>
    <dependencies>
        <dependency>)

                <groupId>org.springframework.cloud</groupId>
                <artifactId>spring-cloud-dependencies</
                artifactId>
                <version>${spring-cloud.version}</version>
                <type>pom</type>
                <scope>import</scope>
        </dependency>
    </dependencies>
</dependencyManagement>

<dependencies>
    <dependency>
        <groupId>org.springframework.boot</groupId>
        <artifactId>spring-boot-starter-web</artifactId>
    </dependency>

    <dependency>
    <groupId>org.springframework.boot</groupId>
    <artifactId>spring-boot-starter-amqp</artifactId>
</dependency>

    <dependency>
        <groupId>org.springframework.cloud</groupId>
```

```xml
        <artifactId>spring-cloud-starter-eureka
        </artifactId>
    </dependency>)

    <dependency>
        <groupId>org.springframework.boot</groupId>
        <artifactId>spring-boot-starter-actuator
        </artifactId>
    </dependency>

    <!-- ... rest of dependencies -->
</dependencies>

<build>
    <plugins>
        <plugin>
            <groupId>org.springframework.boot</groupId>
            <artifactId>spring-boot-maven-plugin
            </artifactId>
        </plugin>
    </plugins>
</build>
</project>)
```

The extra dependency we added to our services is the *Spring Boot Actuator*. Once we add this to a Spring Boot application, it will automatically make available some endpoints that are very useful for monitoring: metrics, mappings, health, loggers, etc. Our service discovery and load balancer configuration will use the /health endpoint to check if the service is up or not. Note that we won't route these endpoints through our API gateway since we don't want external consumers accessing them (and, obviously, our infrastructure should deny public direct access to our microservices in production).

After configuring our registry clients' POMs, there are some more changes we need to perform for each Spring Boot application that wants to use the service registry (see Listings 5-14) through 5-16:

- We add the @EnableEurekaClient annotation to the main application class, which will activate the service discovery agent.

- We add some configuration to our application. properties file, telling Eureka where to find the service registry.

- To make our application name configurable and not automatically created, we include a bootstrap. properties file (in the same folder as application. properties) in which we set up the service name. That way we make sure that future changes of the project name will not impact our infrastructure. Note that we need to include it in that new file and not in application.properties since the service registration happens during application bootstrap and, during that phase, the application properties are not loaded yet.

Listing 5-14. GamificationApplication.java (gamification v8)

```
package microservices.book;

import org.springframework.boot.SpringApplication;
import org.springframework.boot.autoconfigure.
SpringBootApplication;
import org.springframework.cloud.netflix.eureka.
EnableEurekaClient;

@EnableEurekaClient
@SpringBootApplication
```

```
public class GamificationApplication {

    public static void main(String[] args) {
        SpringApplication.run(GamificationApplication.class, args);
    }

}
```

Listing 5-15. application.properties (gamification v8)

```
# Service Discovery configuration
eureka.client.service-url.default-zone=http://localhost:8761/
eureka/
```

Listing 5-16. bootstrap.properties (added) (gamification v8)

```
spring.application.name=gamification
```

Remember to add the annotation and those two new properties to multiplication (application name `multiplication`) and gateway (application name `gateway`) as well. We also add a `bootstrap.properties` file to our new service registry microservice to make sure that the application name is consistent (see Listing 5-17).

Listing 5-17. bootstrap.properties (added) (service-registry v8)

```
spring.application.name=service-registry
```

Three simple steps, small code changes, and including some new dependencies. That's all we need to make our existing services work with a service discovery tool.

The last task we need to do to finalize our service discovery setup for the entire system is change the routing configuration in our API gateway service (Zuul). Remember that we left direct links there, but now we can connect Zuul with Eureka server since the gateway is also using the discovery client to find the registry and map service names to specific addresses. The current configuration is shown in Listing 5-18.

Listing 5-18. application.yml (gateway v8)

```
server:
  port: 8000

zuul:
  ignoredServices: '*'
  prefix: /api
  routes:
    multiplications:
      path: /multiplications/**
      serviceId: multiplication
      strip-prefix: false
    results:
      path: /results/**
      serviceId: multiplication
      strip-prefix: false
    leaders:
      path: /leaders/**
      serviceId: gamification
      strip-prefix: false

eureka:
  client:
    service-url:
      default-zone: http://localhost:8761/eureka/

endpoints:
  routes:
    sensitive: false
```

- The main difference is that every route has the serviceId property instead of url. This is the most important change and the one that gives us the flexibility of having services that can change their locations dynamically and can scale up with multiple instances. That property value should be equal to the service name, which we configured in each bootstrap.properties file.

- We set strip-prefix to false since we're using explicit routes, so we don't need to remove anything from the specified path. This property is set to true by default for the dynamic routes to strip the service name from the URL.

- With the ignoredServices property we tell Zuul not to dynamically register routes for services registered with Eureka. We still want to decide our routing by ourselves.

- Eureka client is configured in the gateway too, so it can find the registry.

- We removed the part of the configuration that disables Ribbon, the load balancer. We'll see it in action later in this chapter.

CHEATING OURSELVES WITH SERVICE DISCOVERY AND THE GATEWAY

The default behavior in Zuul to automatically add routes for services in the registry is risky if not used properly. As mentioned, if we don't add the zuul.ignoredServices property, we'll get the following routing configuration *for free*, without needing to add anything to our properties file:

- /multiplication/multiplications/** –> multiplication microservice + /multiplications/**

- /multiplication/results/** –> multiplication microservice + /results/**

- `/gamification/leaders/**` –> gamification microservice + `/leaders/**`

- `/gamification/stats/**` –> gamification microservice + `/stats/**`

However, if we work with those URLs, we can no longer say that our consumers are microservice-agnostic: they would be pointing again to our inner structure. We lose one of the main benefits of the API gateway.

But some people know how to play that game and make it work. If we model our microservices to provide functionality around one single business entity, we can use the dynamic routing. Think of this situation for a moment: we split the functionality inside the multiplication microservice and extract the `/results` endpoint to a new microservice, `results-manager`. After that, we refactor the code in our controllers to move the functionality to the root (e.g., `@RequestMapping("/multiplications")` would become plainly `@RequestMapping("/")`). Then, to make everything work transparently, we change the application name of our multiplication microservice to `multiplications` (nasty), and the name of that fictional results manager to `results`. Since the `strip-prefix` property is true by default, the service name is removed from the URL when it goes through the gateway. Since your head might be about to explode, let's detail the result in three simple steps:

1. The client requests GET `http://localhost:8000/api/multiplications/1`.

2. Zuul has a dynamically-added route from the registry, mapping `/multiplications` (service name) to the multiplications service. Since `strip-prefix` is true, it maps it to GET `http://localhost:8080/1`.

3. We refactored our controller to accept root requests, so the multiplication with ID 1 is returned. This works because now the microservice only handles multiplication entities.

The same would apply to the /results endpoint. Going even further, we could also split the gamification microservice, and then we would end up with a system in which the routes are magically set. This way of working with the gateway and service discovery is sadly spread across many quick guides over the Internet, confusing people about the real purpose of service discovery. In the real world, microservices do not necessarily map with a single business entity. On the contrary, the API gateway pattern is there for us to be in full control of where and how we redirect requests to microservices; and service discovery is not about automagically discovering functionality, but about providing an efficient way to find and load-balance between one or several instances of the same microservice.

If you don't like to specify explicit routes (which is fair when your system has dozens of microservices), there are ways to load them dynamically by creating your own implementation of the RouteLocator interface or use any of the existing ones.

Playing with Service Discovery

With the extra added microservice (service-registry) and the changes we made to the others to use it, we can now play with our system and see how service discovery works in combination with the API gateway. When a new request is coming in, Zuul uses the discovery client to find a proper URL for the given serviceId and then redirects the request there. No physical addresses are specified, so we get flexibility to move or refactor services across our system, deploy several instances, etc. With the introduction of the API gateway and service discovery microservices, we finally got the benefits we want.

To start the system, we need to follow the steps we already know, adding an extra one to execute the service registry.

1.   Run the RabbitMQ server (if not yet running).

2.   Run the service registry microservice.

3. Run the gateway microservice.

4. Run the multiplication microservice.

5. Run the gamification microservice.

6. Run the Jetty server from the `ui` root folder.

Same as before, the only one for which the order is important is the first. Note that it's only convenient, but not required, that we start the service registry before the microservices. If we don't do that, our microservices will work anyway, since they retry the registering process until the registry becomes available.

You may experiment in some occasions that the interaction between the gateway and the service registry takes some time be effective, thus potentially getting some server errors (HTTP status code 500) from the gateway if you play with the application within the first minute after booting all the microservices. just need to give the service registry some more time to do its job. Later in this chapter, we'll cover how to deal with these errors in a better way using the Circuit Breaker pattern.

The service discovery feature is noticeable in different ways. First, when we start the microservices, we see a set of messages in the console output, as shown in Listing 5-19.

Listing 5-19. Console Output Multiplication (multiplication v8)

```
2017-09-27 15:41:45.238  INFO 656 --- [            main] com.
netflix.discovery.DiscoveryClient   : Getting all instance
registry info from the eureka server
2017-09-27 15:41:45.471  INFO 656 --- [            main] com.
netflix.discovery.DiscoveryClient   : The response status is
200
2017-09-27 15:41:45.472  INFO 656 --- [            main] com.
netflix.discovery.DiscoveryClient   : Starting heartbeat
executor: renew interval is: 30
```

```
2017-09-27 15:41:45.474  INFO 656 ---
[          main] c.n.discovery.InstanceInfoReplicator     :
InstanceInfoReplicator onDemand update allowed rate per min is 4
2017-09-27 15:41:45.477  INFO 656 --- [          main] com.
netflix.discovery.DiscoveryClient    : Discovery Client
initialized at timestamp 1506519705477 with initial instances
count: 3
2017-09-27 15:41:45.503  INFO 656 --- [          main] o.s.c
.n.e.s.EurekaServiceRegistry         : Registering application
multiplication with eureka with status UP
2017-09-27 15:41:45.504  INFO 656 --- [          main] com.
netflix.discovery.DiscoveryClient    : Saw local status change
event StatusChangeEvent [timestamp=1506519705504, current=UP,
previous=STARTING]
2017-09-27 15:41:45.505  INFO 656 --- [nfoReplicator-0] com.
netflix.discovery.DiscoveryClient    : DiscoveryClient_
MULTIPLICATION/localhost:multiplication:8080: registering
service...
2017-09-27 15:41:45.540  INFO 656 --- [nfoReplicator-0] com.
netflix.discovery.DiscoveryClient    : DiscoveryClient_
MULTIPLICATION/localhost:multiplication:8080 - registration
status: 204)
```

As we can see, Eureka is registering the service successfully after verifying that the registry is alive. We can also verify the status of the different services from our browser. The web interface of our Eureka server (the Eureka Server Dashboard) is located at http://localhost:8761/. There we can find a web page displaying information about which services are registered and their status, together with some details about the registry itself, as shown in Figure 5-14.

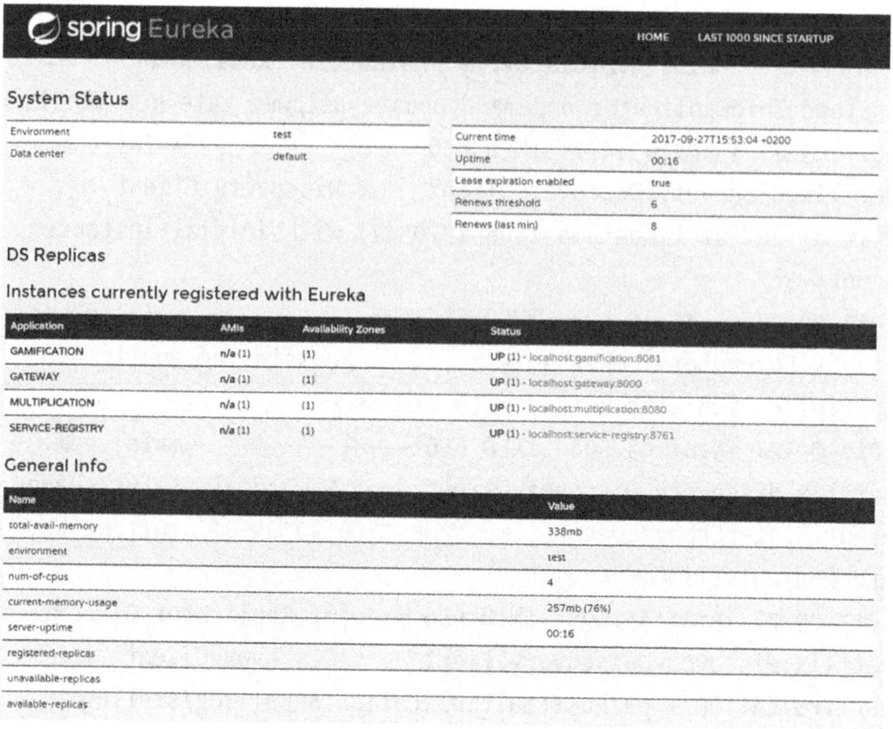

Figure 5-14. *Eureka Dashboard displaying information about services*

From the user's point of view, there are not many changes. We can still send attempts and refresh the leaderboard. The big changes are behind the scenes: requests are going through the API gateway, which uses the registry to find the instances and redirect them to the proper microservice. Our system is evolving nicely to a proper microservices architecture.

Note that we left behind the coolest part about service discovery: scaling up our system by starting multiple instances of the same microservice. We'll see how Ribbon solves that for us but, before that, we need to verify if our microservices are prepared for it.

Are Our Microservices Ready to Scale?

Before continuing our way through all these tools, let's stop for a moment to analyze what we're going to do. We want to start multiple instances of our services, and let Zuul—the API gateway—decide to which instance to redirect each request, supported by Eureka and the service registry. But, can we really do that? Is that going to work with our current microservice implementations?

One of the most critical things when we start working with scalable systems is that we need to be aware of some important basic concepts when designing our microservices. We can't just add tools to provide service discovery and routing and hope that everything will work out-of-the-box. We need to be aware of where are we heading and prepare for it. Let's analyze if our data strategy and our communication interfaces are aligned with our objectives.

Databases and Stateless Services

First, our services need to be stateless, meaning that they shouldn't keep any data or state in memory. Otherwise, we need to have *session affinity*: all requests from the same user should end up in the same microservice instance, because it's keeping some context information. To avoid overcomplicating our applications, it's better if we always design stateless microservices.

In our system, the databases are embedded in the services, thus preventing us from scaling up correctly. Every instance of our service shouldn't have its own database since that would cause retrieving different data per request. All instances need to keep their data in the same place, in the same, shared database server.

The H2 database can work in server mode too. We only need to enable an option to make this work for our databases: the *automatic mixed mode*. We just need to add the suffix AUTO_SERVER=TRUE to all our JDBC URLs. Remember to add it to both the multiplication and gamification JDBC URLs. See Listing 5-20.

Listing 5-20. application.properties: Modifying JDBC URL (gamification v8)

```
# ...
# Creates the database in a file
spring.datasource.url=jdbc:h2:file:~/gamification;DB_CLOSE_ON_
EXIT=FALSE;AUTO_SERVER=TRUE
```

Keep in mind that, as a result of our new data strategy, the microservice logic can scale nicely but we can't say the same of the database: it would be only one shared instance. To solve that part in a production system, we would need to choose a database engine that scales and create a cluster at our database tier. Depending on the DB engine we choose, the approach might be different. For example, H2 has a simple clustering mode that is based on data replication and MariaDB uses Galera, which provides load balancing as well. The good news is that, from the code point of view, we can handle a database cluster as a simple JDBC URL, keeping all the database tier logic aside of our project.

Event-Driven Architecture and Load Balancing

From the REST communication point of view, we can conclude that the system works properly thanks to the shared database engine. No matter which instance handles our request, the result of posting an attempt or retrieving data will be consistent. But, what happens with the process spanning both microservices?

Our system handles the business process *attempt-to-points* based on an event triggered from the multiplication microservice and consumed from the gamification microservice. The question now is, how does that work if we start more than one gamification instance?

In this case, everything will work *fine enough* without any modification. Every gamification instance will act as a *worker* that connects to a shared queue in RabbitMQ. Only one instance consumes each event, processes it, and stores the result in the shared database. Anyway, in a system that goes to production, we would normally need to adjust the current set up to minimize the impact if the same event is received twice, and also try to prevent events being lost because of one microservice dying unexpectedly. The RabbitMQ Reliability Guide (see `https://www.rabbitmq.com/reliability.html`) is a good starting point if you want to learn more about what you can do to prevent or react to some different issues that might happen in your system.

Last but not least, RabbitMQ can also work in clusters. In a production environment we need to configure our infrastructure in that way so the system keeps working even if one of the RabbitMQ server instances goes down. Similarly to the single database URL for a cluster, from our code's point of view nothing changes: we would connect to RabbitMQ as if there is only one instance. See Figure 5-15.

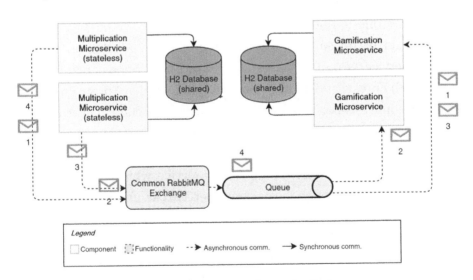

Figure 5-15. *The system working with multiple instances*

Load Balancing with Ribbon

Time for some cool stuff! Now that we know that our microservices can scale, our goal is to put that in practice with one of our services and use load balancing to redirect requests to the multiple instances. Providing high availability (or *resilience*) is one of the most important features that you need to have in your distributed system—services may fail, one of the geographical areas in which your service is deployed might be not responding well, the service could be saturated with traffic, etc.

As introduced previously, Spring Cloud Netflix Ribbon is a good choice for implementing load balancing with Spring Boot. It comes with Eureka so it combines nicely with Zuul. Take into account that, even though we're covering them separately, using Eureka without Ribbon (or service discovery without load balancing) is not a typical scenario, since in that case you only benefit from mapping a physical location (IP and port) to a service alias (one-to-one).

That said, it's not surprising to find out that to include Ribbon in our Gateway service we don't have to do anything else. Ribbon comes by default with Eureka, and it's automatically configured by Spring Boot. We'll add some extra configuration later in this subsection to override the defaults but, for now, let's play a little bit with the standard configuration.

To quickly verify that load balancing works, we'll add some logging to our /random endpoint in the multiplication service, which will print a line in the service log indicating the port number. We can use Lombok's @Slf4j annotation, which will offer an initialized log with which we can print a message in console containing the injected property server.port. Keep in mind that we need to explicitly add server.port to our application. properties (and set it to 8080); otherwise the property won't be found. See Listing 5-21.

Listing 5-21. MultiplicationController.java Adding Logs
(multiplication v8)

```
@Slf4j
@RestController
@RequestMapping("/multiplications")
final class MultiplicationController {

    private final MultiplicationService multiplicationService;

    private final int serverPort;

    @Autowired
    public MultiplicationController(final MultiplicationService
    multiplicationService, @Value("${server.port}") int
    serverPort) {
        this.multiplicationService = multiplicationService;
        this.serverPort = serverPort;
    }

    @GetMapping("/random")
    Multiplication getRandomMultiplication() {
        log.info("Generating a random multiplication from
        server @ {}", serverPort);
        return multiplicationService.createRandom
        Multiplication();
    }

}
```

```
                         EXERCISE
```

We would like to print a line in the log also when the results endpoint is
called. That means that you need to implement a similar solution in the
`MultiplicationResultAttemptController` class. In this case, you
invoke the log with this command:

```
log.info("Retrieving result {} from server @ {}",
resultId, serverPort);
```

Playing with Load Balancing

Now we can start all the services of our distributed system again, as we did
in the previous subsection. After we have everything up and running, we
want to start a second instance of our multiplication microservice.

This service instance is linked to a port number. To start a new instance
of a given service, we need to change that port number (`server.port`)
to avoid clashing, which is very easy to achieve because we have several
ways to override Spring Boot properties. To start a second instance of our
multiplication service using Maven, we can run any of the two commands
shown in Listing 5-22 (note that to be able to run the second command,
you first need to package your Spring Boot application into a JAR file).

Listing 5-22. Console: Running a Second Instance of Multiplication
(multiplication v8)

```
~/book/code/v8/social-multiplication$ ./mvnw spring-boot:run
-Drun.arguments="--server.port=8180"
~/book/code/v8/social-multiplication/target$ java -jar social-
multiplication-v8-0.8.0-SNAPSHOT.jar --server.port=8180
```

As you can see, changing the server port is simple. We pass an argument that overrides the `server.port` property to use the port 8180 instead of the default 8080. Now, we should have two instances of our multiplication service running at the same time on both ports and sharing the same database (which is initialized by the first running instance).

If we go to the Eureka Server Dashboard (`http://localhost:8761/`), we should see the two instances of our multiplication microservice registered in Eureka, as shown in Figure 5-16.

Instances currently registered with Eureka

Application	AMIs	Availability Zones	Status
GAMIFICATION	n/a (1)	(1)	UP (1) - localhost:gamification:8081
GATEWAY	n/a (1)	(1)	UP (1) - localhost:gateway:8000
MULTIPLICATION	n/a (2)	(2)	UP (2) - localhost:multiplication:8080 , localhost:multiplication:8180
SERVICE-REGISTRY	n/a (1)	(1)	UP (1) - localhost:service-registry:8761

Figure 5-16. *The Eureka Server Dashboard shows two instances of our multiplication microservice are registered*

Let's now see both instances working. Navigate to the UI client as usual (`http://localhost:9090/ui/index.html`) and refresh the page several times (thus calling the `/random` endpoint). Then check the logs for your multiplication service instances at ports 8080 and 8180. You'll see the log lines there, so you can verify how Ribbon is doing a simple round-robin strategy and redirecting each request to a different service each time.[2] We'll see how to change this load balancing strategy later.

To make it more interesting, let's kill one of the multiplication instances (e.g., by closing the terminal window or pressing Ctrl+C). In theory, that instance should be removed immediately from the registry, and all traffic would be redirected to the only instance still alive. In practice, you may find out that one out of every two times that you refresh the page you get ugly errors in the Gateway's log output, as shown in Listing 5-23.

---

[2]Note that it might take some seconds before both instances are registered in Eureka and the load balancer initiates the round-robin strategy. Be patient!

Listing 5-23. Gateway's Log Output After Killing One Instance (multiplication v8)

```
2017-09-27 18:30:55.798  WARN 14012 --- [nio-8000-exec-7]
o.s.c.n.z.filters.post.SendErrorFilter   : Error during
filtering
com.netflix.zuul.exception.ZuulException: Forwarding error
    at org.springframework.cloud.netflix.zuul.filters.
route.RibbonRoutingFilter.handleException(RibbonRoutingFi
lter.java:183) ~[spring-cloud-netflix-core-1.3.1.RELEASE.
jar:1.3.1.RELEASE]
    ...
Caused by: com.netflix.hystrix.exception.
HystrixRuntimeException: multiplication timed-out and no
fallback available.
    at com.netflix.hystrix.AbstractCommand$22.
call(AbstractCommand.java:819) ~[hystrix-core-1.5.12.
jar:1.5.12]
    ...
Caused by: java.util.concurrent.TimeoutException: null
    at com.netflix.hystrix.AbstractCommand.handleTimeoutVi
aFallback(AbstractCommand.java:997) ~[hystrix-core-1.5.12.
jar:1.5.12]
```

After two or three minutes, you can try again to send multiple requests. By that time it should work as expected: all requests will be redirected to the only available instance. Within that period, you can verify on the Eureka's dashboard how it takes that time to notice that the instance is no longer alive. We'll see next how we can improve this behavior by fine-tuning our tools.

WE DID IT! THE API GATEWAY, SERVICE DISCOVERY, AND LOAD BALANCER ARE NOW IMPLEMENTED!

We evolved our distributed system to a proper microservices architecture! We split the UI and added the gateway, service discovery and load balancing. We implemented a nice solution for the requirements of User Story 3. There are still some parts that should be improved, but we can celebrate our success!

Production Readiness: Scaling Up the Service Registry

Bear in mind that, if you implement a system like this in production, you also need to provide high availability for the registry. This feature is coming out-of-the-box with Eureka Server, and you can see from the documentation (in the "Peer Awareness" section at `http://projects.spring.io/spring-cloud/spring-cloud.html#_peer_awareness`) how easy is to configure it, just by creating a profile per instance you want to make available.

Fine-Tuning the Load Balancing Strategy

As we just saw, Spring Boot configures Ribbon by default with a round-robin strategy for load balancing. It also sets the status-check mechanism to *none* (by injecting the NoOpPing implementation of the IPing interface, see `https://tpd.io/cust-rb` for further details). That implies that the load balancer will not verify if the services are alive (NoOpPing simply returns true for the isAlive method). It makes sense from a conceptual point of view since it should be our service registry, Eureka, the one that registers and deregisters instances.

However, Eureka is very slow at noticing that a service went down unexpectedly (in my experience, it takes an average of three minutes). It's not pinging them but checking *leases*: every instance needs to contact the registry after some time (30 seconds by default) to *renew the lease* (we can picture it as the instance saying "I'm alive!"). After a longer time (90 seconds by default), the service registry will de-register instances that didn't renew the lease in that time window. Changing the leaseRenewalIntervalInSeconds parameter might look like a good idea but it's actually discouraged by the official docs.[3] As a result, instances going down unexpectedly will not be removed from the registry immediately, but after a period of minutes, and during that time our application will fail.

We can solve this problem using a Ribbon functionality to ping services and apply load balancing depending on the result (thus having some logic on the client side to detect if the instances are down). To get that working, we need to configure two Spring beans: an IPing to override the default check-status mechanism and an IRule to change the default load balancing strategy. Besides, we need to annotate our main class GatewayApplication to point to this configuration class. See Listings 5-24 and 5-25.

Listing 5-24. RibbonConfiguration.java (gateway v8)

```
package microservices.book.gateway.configuration;

import com.netflix.client.config.IClientConfig;
import com.netflix.loadbalancer.*;
import org.springframework.context.annotation.Bean;

public class RibbonConfiguration {

    @Bean
    public IPing ribbonPing(final IClientConfig config) {
        return new PingUrl(false,"/health");
    }
}
```

---

[3]https://tpd.io/ek-rnew

```
@Bean
public IRule ribbonRule(final IClientConfig config) {
    return new AvailabilityFilteringRule();
}
```

})

Listing 5-25. GatewayApplication.java (gateway v8)

```
@EnableZuulProxy
@EnableEurekaClient
@RibbonClients(defaultConfiguration = RibbonConfiguration.
class)
@SpringBootApplication
public class GatewayApplication {

    public static void main(String[] args) {
        SpringApplication.run(GatewayApplication.class, args);
    }
}
```

- Note that `RibbonConfiguration` is not annotated with `@Configuration`. It's injected in a different way. We need to reference it from a new annotation added to the main application class called `@RibbonClients`. The reason is that we could optionally have multiple ribbon clients with different load balancing configuration.

- The `PingUrl` implementation will check if services are alive. We change the default URL and point it to /health since we know that endpoint exists (it's included by Spring Actuator). The `false` flag is just to indicate that the endpoint is not secured.

- The `AvailabilityFilteringRule` is an alternative to the default `RoundRobinRule`. It also cycles through the instances but, besides that, it takes into account the availability being checked by our new pings to skip some instances in case they don't respond.

If we now test the scenario where multiple instances are registered and kill one of them, we'll notice that the reaction time to redirect all the traffic to the only instance alive is much lower. Keep in mind that the status of Eureka's Service Registry within that time will be exactly the same as before: it still takes its time to deregister the instance. The improvement is *on the client side (the load balancer)*: the gateway checks that the instance doesn't really work and picks another one.

This configuration is just an example. You can find some other options for load balancing strategies on the official repository.[4] There are implementations that allow us to balance load depending on response time, geographical affinity, etc. The best idea for a proper production environment is to design our plan, test it (putting some load into your system and monitoring the results), and then adjust it based on the results.

Figure 5-17 shows our updated logical view, with service discovery and load balancing in place. We introduced a similar view when explaining the concepts, but now we made it a reality in our source code.

---

[4]https://tpd.io/lb-opts

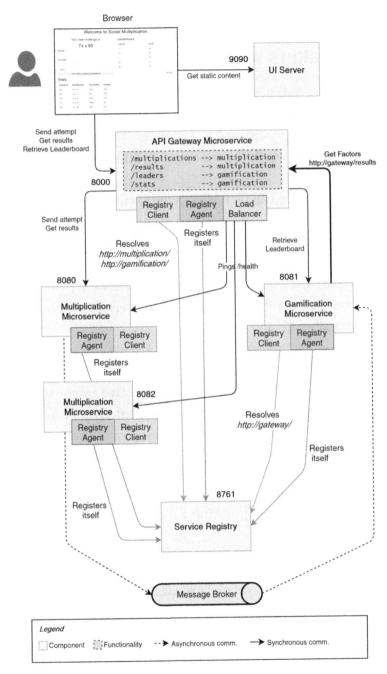

Figure 5-17. *Updated logical view, with service discovery and load balancing in place*

Circuit Breakers and REST Clients
Circuit Breakers with Hystrix

In the real world, errors happen. Services can be unreachable or not respond on time. Our distributed system shouldn't fail as a whole because one of the parts failed to answer. The circuit breaker pattern is the solution for those scenarios in which our entire system is likely to fail if one of the parts does not respond.

This pattern is based on two states. If the circuit is closed, that means the request can reach its destination and the response is received. Everything is working fine. If there are errors or a timeout expires, the connection point is down, and the circuit gets open. That implies calling to a *different part of the system,* which will act as a backup player, giving a default response for a failure. The result is a manageable response that the system can handle without further errors.

Spring Cloud Netflix also contains a well-known implementation of this pattern, called *Hystrix.* In our project, one of the places where we can connect it is to the gateway, so it can provide a default response when a service fails to respond. Actually, if we review the stack trace that we got when playing with load balancing and killing one of the multiplication instances, we can see that it is giving us a hint about what to do, as shown in Listing 5-26.

Listing 5-26. Console Output After Killing One Multiplication Instance (gateway v8)

```
...
Caused by: com.netflix.hystrix.exception.
HystrixRuntimeException: multiplication timed-out and no
fallback available.
    ...
```

Hystrix and Zuul

To connect Zuul with Hystrix, we can use the `ZuulFallbackProvider`
interface. If we inject a bean implementing this interface in our Spring
Boot context, we'll be able to provide *Hystrix fallbacks* (predefined
HTTP responses) when a service is not reachable by the API gateway.
When Zuul fails to redirect the request, it will check if there is a fallback
for that specific service (using the `getRoute()` methods of available
`ZuulFallbackProviders`). If there is one, it will construct and return a
default response (using the `fallbackResponse()` method).

Let's use it for multiplication, as an example (in real life we should do
that for all the routes for which we can provide a fallback). We'll send an
error message embedded in `factorA` when `/random` gets called and the
service is not available, so it'll be shown instead of the multiplication to
solve. See Listing 5-27.

Listing 5-27. HystrixFallbackConfiguration.java (gateway v8)

```
@Configuration
public class HystrixFallbackConfiguration {

    @Bean
    public ZuulFallbackProvider zuulFallbackProvider() {
        return new ZuulFallbackProvider() {

            @Override
            public String getRoute() {
                // Might be confusing: it's the serviceId
                property and not the route
                return "multiplication";
            }

            @Override
            public ClientHttpResponse fallbackResponse() {
```

255

```
return new ClientHttpResponse() {

    @Override
    public HttpStatus getStatusCode() throws
    IOException {
        return HttpStatus.OK;
    }

    @Override
    public int getRawStatusCode() throws
    IOException {
        return HttpStatus.OK.value();
    }

    @Override
    public String getStatusText() throws
    IOException {
        return HttpStatus.OK.toString();
    }

    @Override
    public void close() {}

    @Override
    public InputStream getBody() throws
    IOException {
        return new ByteArrayInputStream("{\"
        factorA\":\"Sorry, Service is Down!
        \",\"factorB\":\"?\",\"id\":null}".
        getBytes());
    }

    @Override
    public HttpHeaders getHeaders() {
```

```
                    HttpHeaders headers = new
                    HttpHeaders();
                    headers.setContentType(MediaType.
                    APPLICATION_JSON);
                    headers.setAccessControlAllowCredential
                    s(true);
                    headers.setAccessControl
                    AllowOrigin("*");
                    return headers;
                }
            };
        }
    };
  }
}
```

It's not a very friendly interface, but it's what they provide. In our case, we just adapt the body to the expected format for /random (a Multiplication object in JSON) but insert our message instead of the real factors. Note that we also needed to add the CORS headers to the response, since this one is not processed automatically by our WebConfiguration.

To test our new fallback, we can repeat our last experiment. We start every microservice as usual and a second instance of multiplication. After some time in which we verify that load balancing is working fine, we kill one of the multiplication instances. We'll see our fallback in action returning the predefined response, which will be displayed in our UI. Note that it's not a perfect solution, but at least we give some information to the user about what happened instead of leaving the multiplication factors empty. See Figure 5-18.

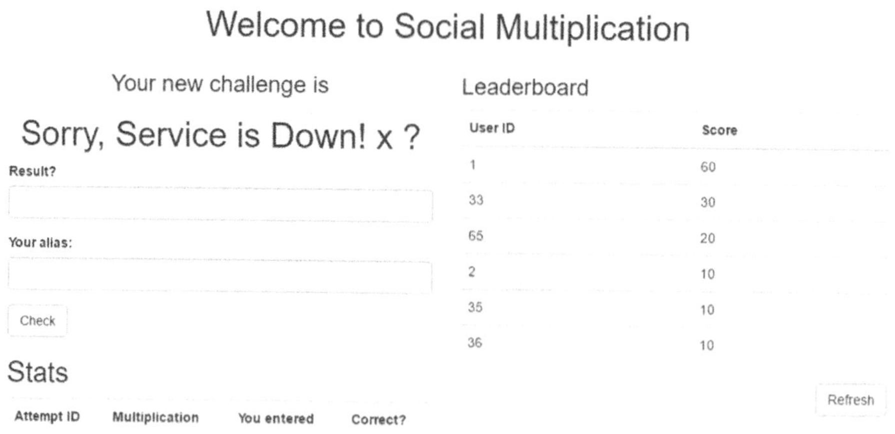

Welcome to Social Multiplication

Your new challenge is

Sorry, Service is Down! x ?

Result?

Your alias:

Check

Stats

Attempt ID   Multiplication   You entered   Correct?

Leaderboard

User ID	Score
1	60
33	30
65	20
2	10
35	10
36	10

Refresh

Figure 5-18. *UI showing that the service is down*

Hystrix provides much more functionality than its integration with Zuul. You can use it from any REST consumer you develop by just adding annotations like @HystrixCommand and @EnableCircuitBreaker, and then configuring the fallbacks. We first covered the particular case of integration with Zuul since it's one of the trickiest ones; now let's see how to make it work with a standard REST client.

Hystrix from a REST Client

We have another point in our system where a circuit breaker fits perfectly: the REST API call from gamification to multiplication to check if one of the factors is the lucky number. Our business process shouldn't fail if it doesn't have access to the service at that given point of time. We have two options for the fallback response—to include the lucky number or not. Let's be greedy this time: the user won't receive that badge if the service is down.

First, let's add Hystrix to the gamification microservice. To do that, we need to include a new dependency in the pom.xml file, as shown in Listing 5-28.

Listing 5-28. pom.xml Adding Hystrix (gamification v8)

```
<dependency>
  <groupId>org.springframework.cloud</groupId>
  <artifactId>spring-cloud-starter-hystrix</artifactId>
</dependency>
```

Now we go to our REST client implementation,
MultiplicationResultAttemptClientImpl, and annotate the method
using RestTemplate with HystrixCommand. Apart from that, we create our
method to return the default response, defaultResult, which returns two
factors that are not the lucky number. See Listing 5-29.

Listing 5-29. MultiplicationResultAttemptClientImpl.java Adding
Hystrix (gamification v8)

```
@Component
class MultiplicationResultAttemptClientImpl implements
MultiplicationResultAttemptClient {

    private final RestTemplate restTemplate;
    private final String multiplicationHost;

    @Autowired
    public MultiplicationResultAttemptClientImpl(final
    RestTemplate restTemplate,

@Value("${multiplicationHost}") final String multiplicationHost) {
        this.restTemplate = restTemplate;
        this.multiplicationHost = multiplicationHost;
    }
```

```
@HystrixCommand(fallbackMethod = "defaultResult")
@Override
public MultiplicationResultAttempt retrieveMultiplicationRe
sultAttemptbyId(final Long multiplicationResultAttemptId) {
    return restTemplate.getForObject(
            multiplicationHost + "/results/" +
            multiplicationResultAttemptId,
            MultiplicationResultAttempt.class);
}

private MultiplicationResultAttempt defaultResult(final
Long multiplicationResultAttemptId) {
    return new MultiplicationResultAttempt("fakeAlias",
            10, 10, 100, true);
}
}
```

The last change we need to make in gamification is to add the @EnableCircuitBreaker annotation to our main class, as shown in Listing 5-30.

Listing 5-30. GamificationApplication.java Adding Hystrix (gamification v8)

```
package microservices.book;

import org.springframework.boot.SpringApplication;
import org.springframework.boot.autoconfigure.
SpringBootApplication;
import org.springframework.cloud.client.circuitbreaker.
EnableCircuitBreaker;
import org.springframework.cloud.netflix.eureka.
EnableEurekaClient;
```

```
@EnableEurekaClient
@EnableCircuitBreaker
@SpringBootApplication
public class GamificationApplication {

    public static void main(String[] args) {
        SpringApplication.run(GamificationApplication.class,
        args);
    }

}
```

Testing that everything works as expected is not easy if we limit ourselves to a real scenario. We need to send via UI a correct attempt; that one will go through the multiplication microservice, and then we need to kill it after it sends the `MultiplicationSolvedEvent`, so gamification can't reach it. Luckily, there is a simpler solution to test the Hystrix's predefined response: we can just modify the multiplication host property inside gamification's `application.properties` file to a nonexistent URL (something like `multiplicationHost=http://localhost:8001/api`).

Now we can test it. We start again all our set of microservices (like we did before). We only need an instance of multiplication this time. With the new version of gamification pointing to a wrong multiplication URL, Hystrix will do its job and return the default response every time we post a correct attempt. If you want to double-check that Hystrix is working (as a classic skeptical developer), you can debug the gamification microservice and set a breakpoint inside the `defaultResult()` method.

REST Consumers with Feign

We can't finish this chapter without mentioning *Feign*, since it's another famous member of Spring Cloud Netflix.

Feign allows us to consume REST services as if they were part of our code. We can generate @FeignClients and map their methods to requests. The main advantage is that we can avoid handling requests directly with @RestTemplates across our code, so we can treat the external interfaces as if they were part of our codebase. You can see an example within the official documentation (see https://tpd.io/feigndoc), the StoreClient interface, in Listing 5-31.

Listing 5-31. StoreClient.java Sample from Documentation

```java
@FeignClient("stores")
public interface StoreClient {
    @RequestMapping(method = RequestMethod.GET, value = "/stores")
    List<Store> getStores();

    @RequestMapping(method = RequestMethod.POST, value =
    "/stores/{storeId}", consumes = "application/json")
    Store update(@PathVariable("storeId") Long storeId, Store store);
}
```

Feign combines well with Eureka, Ribbon, and Hystrix. The Feign client uses Eureka and Ribbon to find services and perform load balancing. Also, it uses annotations at the interface level to specify which classes contain Hystrix fallbacks.

In our system, we could use it to remove the MultiplicationResultAttemptClientImpl class and use just the interface with some annotations. We also need to move in that case the Hystrix fallback method to a separate class.

We won't use it in the book since the benefits of using Feign are not so valuable for us: it's oriented to the case in which services are calling each other directly, without using the API gateway. It takes time to configure it and make it work with the rest of the tools and, in our case, we can achieve the same goal with a few lines of code using RestTemplate.

Microservices Patterns and PaaS

Over the previous sections we covered some important patterns that we should apply to a microservices architecture: service discovery, load balancing, API gateway, and circuit breakers. We saw that there are tools to implement them, Spring Cloud Netflix being the de-facto solution for Spring Boot. Along the way, we introduced a new service registry microservice and an API gateway microservice, which are now part of our ecosystem.

Now that you understand all these patterns and how they work, you might be asking yourself: do I need to take care of all this plumbing every time I want to set up a microservices architecture? Isn't there any kind of framework that includes all of this for me, from a higher abstraction level than Spring? Couldn't I just focus on writing my Spring Boot application and put it *somewhere* so it works directly?

The common answer to these questions is that you can abstract many of these patterns by using a Platform as a Service (PaaS) solution. These platforms contain not only service discovery, load balancing, routing (API gateway), and Circuit Breaker patterns, but also centralized logging and integrated authentication, among other functionalities. These platforms usually reside in the cloud, and their providers offer you plans to subscribe and use not only those patterns but also their storage, CPU, network, etc.

There are many different PaaS from many different providers: Amazon AWS, Google App Engine, Pivotal's CloudFoundry, Microsoft Azure, etc. All of them offer similar services. The first thing you do is to "package" your microservices (e.g., using a *buildpack*) and deploy them directly to the platform, where they are automatically discovered after some basic configuration. You don't need to deploy a service registry or a gateway because they are part of the platform: you just configure some routing rules and load balancing policies. Databases and message brokers are offered as elastic services that scale transparently on demand. You create them by using a wizard and then you get the URLs to use them directly in your applications.

263

If you want to see an example of how easy deploying a Spring Boot application is in one of these platforms, you can have a look at the CloudFoundry Guide to deploy a Spring application (see *https://tpd.io/ cf-gs*). Within the same documentation site, you can also check how easy is to scale the services (just running a command `cf scale myApp -i 5` to get five instances) and how routing works by assigning multiple instances to the same hostname. It's not surprising to find out that Pivotal offers a circuit breaker as a service (based on Hystrix).

The advantage we have at this point is that we know what we need when we're designing our microservices architecture. We can balance all these options and decide where and how we want to implement the patterns. Depending on our needs, time, and budget, we can choose a solution based on implementing everything ourselves or rely on some platforms or frameworks.

Summary

In this chapter, we learned some of the most important concepts surrounding microservices: service discovery, load balancing, API gateway, and circuit breakers. We used the tools available in Spring Cloud Netflix to implement these patterns (Eureka, Ribbon, Zuul, and Hystrix), and we got our services nicely connected between them, supporting high availability through scaling.

We went through several steps, illustrated with diagrams, that helped us understand why we need these tools. Then, in the second part of the chapter, we included them in our codebase using an incremental approach and we experimented with our system's load balancing and circuit breaker features.

This book, yet being practical, teaches you the ideas behind the patterns. By this time you can design your microservices architecture using the tools shown in this book or explore some other alternatives to get the same result. As an example, we saw how PaaS solutions implement these patterns and can speed up your project's development time if it fits your requirements and your budget.

We've finished our system by implementing all the requirements we had and evolving it until reaching a good microservices architecture with Spring Boot. The next chapter (the last one) focuses on solving an extra challenge in the world of microservices: end-to-end integration testing.

CHAPTER 6

Testing the Distributed System

Introduction

In previous chapters, we built a complex, distributed system, composed of three *functional microservices* (UI, multiplication, gamification) and two *supporting microservices* (the API gateway built with Zuul and the service registry implemented with Eureka). Besides, our system uses an event-driven approach to fulfill the business processes that span multiple microservices (in this case, only *attempt-to-points*).

When you have an environment like this, composed of many pieces, it's very likely that one of them fails. It also happens with a monolithic system: you may have modules, or components, that need to be glued together. But, in a microservices architecture, it is even more critical to verify that all the components—the microservices—work together, given that these parts can be built and deployed independently.

They can evolve in different ways: we could, for instance, introduce a change in Multiplication's REST API to rename `factorA` and `factorB` to `factor1` and `factor2`. We could change our unit tests and make the build pass successfully for that specific microservice. However, with that change

© Moises Macero 2017
M. Macero, *Learn Microservices with Spring Boot*,
https://doi.org/10.1007/978-1-4842-3165-4_6

we would be breaking the overall functionality: Gamification is using that REST API to perform its logic (by checking the factors for the lucky number). We would have a similar issue if we change something in the `MultiplicationSolvedEvent`.

Having test suites that verify microservices independently is not enough: we need a good strategy to verify that the entire end-to-end use cases are working after changes.

Unit tests, integration tests, component tests, contract tests, and end-to-end tests—you should rely on all of them when building microservices. If you're not very familiar with these different types of tests, you may now pause your reading for a moment to watch this presentation about microservice testing at `https://martinfowler.com/articles/microservice-testing/`.

Among all kinds of tests, end-to-end tests are on the top of the pyramid: there shouldn't be many in your system since they're difficult to maintain. But, on the other hand, they are the ones guarding your business processes with the integration of all your microservices together, so having less does not mean that they're less important.

In this chapter, we'll focus on end-to-end tests for a microservices architecture (our system). The reason is that they are usually the most difficult ones to implement and maintain, so it's worthy to dedicate a chapter in this book. We'll cover some good practices with the Cucumber framework, to keep them simple and focused on the business.

We started coding our application using a TDD approach. Now we'll follow a similar strategy with these end-to-end tests, focusing first on the complete scenarios and then implementing the logic to verify that everything works.

Setting the Scene

Let's establish a reasonable objective. To verify that everything is working in our application, we should cover at least a couple of functionalities:

1. When users send requests to the application, they should receive the corresponding response and, based on whether the attempt is right or not, they will get some points.

2. The leaderboard should reflect the ranking of users correctly.

Now, we should also decide at which level we want to implement our end-to-end cases. Since our system exposes all the functionality through REST APIs, we'll go for *end-to-end service testing*. They're much easier to maintain than end-to-end UI testing (which can be implemented for example with Selenium[1]), since they depend on an extra layer of our system and are very sensitive to changes (as the Cucumber documentation states, "Validating a business rule through a UI is slow, and when there is a failure, it is difficult to pinpoint where the error is"[2]).

Finally, we must choose the approach and the technology we'll use for our end-to-end scenarios. We use Cucumber (`https://cucumber.io/`), a very powerful tool that's focused on behavior. You write your test specifications in human language, and they will be the script of your test execution and used to output reports.

Note that Cucumber can be used for *behavior-driven development* (BDD) too: we could implement the end-to-end scenarios before any other part of our code and start from there, building functionality until we make them pass. We can't go full BDD at this point since we already have our code in place. It would have been also a bad idea for this book to start

---

[1]`http://www.seleniumhq.org/`
[2]`https://cucumber.io/docs/reference`

with these end-to-end test scenarios since you would get many questions in your head from the beginning. However, you can try to follow BDD in your projects: it's a nice way to make sure that requirements are clear and documented from an early stage.

In any case, we will start coding our scenarios first and building all the rest of the test implementation afterward, so we don't lose the focus on the business.

It's much better to see Cucumber in practice to understand how it works, so Listing 6-1 shows a quick look at one of the test scenarios.

Listing 6-1. multiplication.feature (e2e-tests v9)

```
Feature: Users are able to send their multiplication
  attempts, which may be correct or not. When users
  send a correct attempt, they get a response indicating
  that the result is the right one. Also, they get points
  and potentially some badges when they are right, so they
  get motivation to come back and keep playing. Badges are
  won for the first right attempt and when the user gets 100,
  500 and 999 points respectively. If users send a wrong
  attempt, they don't get any point or badge.

  Scenario: The user sends a first right attempt and gets a badge
    When the user john_snow sends 1 right attempts
    Then the user gets a response indicating the attempt is right
    And the user gets 10 points for the attempt
    And the user gets the FIRST_WON badge

  Scenario: The user sends a second right attempt and gets
  points only
    Given the user john_snow sends 1 right attempts
    And the user gets the FIRST_WON badge
    When the user john_snow sends 1 right attempts
    Then the user gets a response indicating the attempt is right
```

```
And the user gets 10 points for the attempt
And the user does not get any badge
```

Perfectly readable. It's human-friendly and specifies what we want to do. The best part of it: this is the definition of our test that will be used by code and it can be executed by Cucumber. This language is Gherkin, and you can find the full specification on the official page at `https://tpd.io/gherkin-doc`. We'll also cover the basics in a nutshell in the following section.

Cucumber has a lot of advantages, among others is the fact that business users can read and modify the test scenarios directly and determine if they work. That's the great superpower of Cucumber, since it eliminates the gaps between development and business requirements. If they're written in Gherkin, they can't be misunderstood: they are the executables. Besides, these Gherkin files can serve as use case documentation. We know they'll be maintained for sure when functionalities change because those changes would otherwise break the tests.

How Cucumber Works

Cucumber implementations are available for multiple languages and frameworks. They all share the same functionalities, which are described on the official Reference Documentation page at `https://cucumber.io/docs/reference`.

The idea is that we organize our features into multiple `.feature` files. In each of them, we include the description of the feature on the top. That description is going to be ignored by the engine. Every feature consists of multiple scenarios, which technically are your different test case definitions. Finally, each scenario is defined by multiple steps, using the BDD keywords: *Given, When,* and *Then* (plus *And* and *But*).

Each scenario in a feature (or test case definition) will be executed within the same cached objects. This concept is very important to understand to implement our tests correctly: we can share the state between steps of the same scenario, but not across scenarios. That means that we can hold some data in memory (i.e., use some class fields) to execute several steps, even if they belong to multiple classes. Sometimes this may be confusing for Java developers since, in a JUnit test, the classes are instantiated per test method (unless we use static fields and @BeforeClass, which is usually not a good idea).

The steps can be parameterized using *arguments*, so we can reuse the same step definition in multiple scenarios with different values. We can also pass a data table to the same scenario (whose rows are called *Examples*). The scenario will then be executed once per data row.

Let's use this step to understand how arguments work. See Listing 6-2.

Listing 6-2. multiplication.feature (e2e-tests v9)

```
When the user john_snow sends 1 right attempts
```

In principle, Gherkin itself does not know which of our words are arguments. We define that at the code level. In this case, we'd like to pass to our step the *user alias*, the *number of attempts* and if they are *right* or *wrong*. Listing 6-3 shows how this step needs to be implemented in Java to support it.

Listing 6-3. MultiplicationFeatureSteps.java (e2e-tests v9)

```java
@Given("^the user ([^\\s]+) sends (\\d+) ([^\\s]+) attempts")
public void the_user_sends_attempts(final String userAlias,
final int attempts, final String rightOrWrong) throws Throwable
{
    // Implements the logic
}
```

We'll look at the coding details in the following section, but as you can see, it's just a matter of configuring the step with some regular expressions, which will match the words in the sentence. Two word-expressions and a numeric one will do the trick in this particular case.

Note that, if we change words in the sentence (the ones that are not arguments), we need to update the method's expression as well. The good news is that most IDEs can integrate with Cucumber via plugins, which will warn us if the sentences don't have a valid matching pattern in code.

The results of the execution of our features, with details about scenarios and steps, can be output in multiple formats for reporting. Those include the Cucumber specific ones (colored Gherkin) but also the standard JUnit reports, which can be used by continuous integration frameworks.

That's all in a nutshell. Let's now go practical and write some code to make it work for our application.

Hands-On Code

We'll create two features, as defined at the beginning of this chapter—the first one focuses on testing the interactions through attempts and the second one checks the functionalities of the leaderboard.

SOURCE CODE AVAILABLE WITH THE BOOK: V9

You can find the new version of the code with the new end-to-end tests project (the `tests_e2e` folder) and the modifications to make the system *testable* in the v9 repository on GitHub: `https://github.com/microservices-practical`.

Creating an Empty Project and Choosing the Tools

Since we want to interact with the system as an external agent, we'll create a new project with the code needed to do that. In this case, we're not creating a new microservice so we can change the set of tools to use.

To keep it simple, we'll start with plain Java 8 code and some libraries and frameworks to achieve a robust end-to-end test strategy:

- *Cucumber*: More specifically *cucumber-jvm*, the Java implementation of this tool.

- *Cucumber JUnit:* It will give us the integration with JUnit.

- *Cucumber Picocontainer:* We'll use it for the `leaderboard` feature, to use dependency injection in our tests.

- *JUnit:* We add this dependency to get the core support for testing in Java.

- *AssertJ:* Provides a natural way to do assertions.

- *Apache Fluent HttpClient:* We'll use it to connect to the application's REST API.

- *Jackson 2:* It allows us to deserialize JSON without too much effort.

As you can see, we don't need Spring Boot for this. An easy way to create an empty Maven project is using one of the archetypes. We can use an installed version of Maven or we could also copy the wrapper from one of our previous projects (`.mvn` folder and executable) in an empty folder that we'll name tests_e2e. Then execute the following:

```
./mvnw archetype:generate -DgroupId=microservices.book
-DartifactId=e2e-tests-v9 -DarchetypeArtifactId=maven-
archetype-quickstart -DinteractiveMode=false
```

The next step is to open our almost-empty pom.xml and include the dependencies listed. We need three different Maven artifacts to use Jackson 2. In the example in Listing 6-4, we extracted some versions as properties to better handle upgrades from a common place.

Listing 6-4. pom.xml (e2e-tests v9)

```xml
<project xmlns="http://maven.apache.org/POM/4.0.0"
xmlns:xsi="http://www.w3.org/2001/XMLSchema-instance"
        xsi:schemaLocation="http://maven.apache.org/POM/4.0.0
http://maven.apache.org/maven-v4_0_0.xsd">
    <modelVersion>4.0.0</modelVersion>
    <groupId>microservices.book</groupId>
    <artifactId>tests-e2e-v9</artifactId>
    <packaging>jar</packaging>
    <version>0.9.0-SNAPSHOT</version>
    <build>
        <plugins>
            <plugin>
                <groupId>org.apache.maven.plugins</groupId>
                <artifactId>maven-compiler-plugin</artifactId>
                <configuration>
                    <source>1.8</source>
                    <target>1.8</target>
                </configuration>
            </plugin>
        </plugins>
    </build>
    <name>tests-e2e-v9</name>
    <description>End to End tests - Microservices - The
Practical Way (Book)</description>
```

```xml
<properties>
    <project.build.sourceEncoding>UTF-8</project.build.
    sourceEncoding>
    <project.reporting.outputEncoding>UTF-8</project.
    reporting.outputEncoding>
    <java.version>1.8</java.version>
    <jackson-2-version>2.8.9</jackson-2-version>
    <cucumber-version>1.2.5</cucumber-version>
</properties>

<url>http://maven.apache.org</url>
<dependencies>
    <dependency>
        <groupId>info.cukes</groupId>
        <artifactId>cucumber-java</artifactId>
        <version>${cucumber-version}</version>
        <scope>test</scope>
    </dependency>
    <dependency>
        <groupId>info.cukes</groupId>
        <artifactId>cucumber-junit</artifactId>
        <version>${cucumber-version}</version>
        <scope>test</scope>
    </dependency>
    <dependency>
        <groupId>info.cukes</groupId>
        <artifactId>cucumber-picocontainer</artifactId>
        <version>${cucumber-version}</version>
        <scope>test</scope>
    </dependency>
    <dependency>
        <groupId>org.apache.httpcomponents</groupId>
```

```xml
        <artifactId>fluent-hc</artifactId>
        <version>4.5.3</version>
        <scope>test</scope>
    </dependency>
    <dependency>
        <groupId>junit</groupId>
        <artifactId>junit</artifactId>
        <version>4.12</version>
        <scope>test</scope>
    </dependency>
    <dependency>
        <groupId>org.assertj</groupId>
        <artifactId>assertj-core</artifactId>
        <version>3.8.0</version>
        <scope>test</scope>
    </dependency>
    <!-- the core, which includes Streaming API, shared
low-level
     abstractions (but NOT data-binding) -->
    <dependency>
        <groupId>com.fasterxml.jackson.core</groupId>
        <artifactId>jackson-core</artifactId>
        <version>${jackson-2-version}</version>
        <scope>test</scope>
    </dependency>
    <dependency>
        <groupId>com.fasterxml.jackson.core</groupId>
        <artifactId>jackson-annotations</artifactId>
        <version>${jackson-2-version}</version>
        <scope>test</scope>
    </dependency>
```

```
<dependency>
    <groupId>com.fasterxml.jackson.core</groupId>
    <artifactId>jackson-databind</artifactId>
    <version>${jackson-2-version}</version>
    <scope>test</scope>
</dependency>
</dependencies>
</project>
```

Making the System Testable

One of the main problems with some systems is that they are not testable enough. The root problem can be different in each case, but a common one is related to a misconception of the *black-box testing* approach, which states that we just interact with the system from the outside and use *what we have available* to check that the behavior is as expected. The implementation of the system remains unknown to the tester. The main advantage of applying black-box testing for end-to-end scenarios is that we can verify that the whole system works from the user's point of view. However, we shouldn't push that idea to the limits. If we find ourselves parsing multiple logs or making complicated scripts to verify some generated outputs (like files, or even the database), we should stop and think if it wouldn't be better to offer more tools to verify the behavior of the system, or even provide test-specific interfaces in our system. We should consider if what we have available is good enough.

Building *hacker-like* assertion scripts (like those parsing logs) is even more common in companies where there is a marked separation between developers and testers. In any case, it doesn't help at all: those scripts are going to become a nightmare to maintain, especially if they are based on outputs that are not a consequence of functional requirements (like logs).

They might change without notice and break the entire suite of tests with a *false negative* (since the test would fail, but the logic still works).

Diving into our system as an example, it turns out that we don't have any API to get the resulting score for an attempt identifier. What we have is a line output in the Gamification log, `User with id {} scored {} points for attempt id {}`. But, as explained, if we use that line in our test assertions, we might end up with test failures if that line changes or is removed, which may easily happen since it's not a functional requirement.

As an alternative, we can consider including the REST API to get the score for a given attempt. We could argue that there is no functional requirement to include that into our API and therefore it should never be there. However, certainly it makes sense to have it there: it's not exposing any logic, it might be useful for the functionality in the future, and it is simply a test requirement now. This is the approach that we'll follow—avoiding to overcomplicate things, we'll build some support in our application to better support testing.

In the next paragraphs, we'll explain how we need to adapt our application to be testable: including new API interfaces, using test profiles, and taking good care of test data separately.

New API Interfaces

As mentioned, we need to get the score data by its attempt identifier. Since this is a feature that might be useful in the future, we won't include it only for test but as a new available endpoint. We need it to verify that a posted attempt has generated points for the user, so if the attempt id is 1, we can call `GET /scores/1` and get the score associated with that try. To achieve

that, we'll create a new controller in the gamification service and its
corresponding unit test. See Listing 6-5.

Listing 6-5. ScoreController.java (New) (Gamification v9)

```java
package microservices.book.gamification.controller;

import microservices.book.gamification.domain.ScoreCard;
import microservices.book.gamification.service.GameService;
import org.springframework.web.bind.annotation.GetMapping;
import org.springframework.web.bind.annotation.PathVariable;
import org.springframework.web.bind.annotation.RequestMapping;
import org.springframework.web.bind.annotation.RestController;

/**
 * This class implements a REST API for the Gamification User
Statistics service.
 */
@RestController
@RequestMapping("/scores")
class ScoreController {

    private final GameService gameService;

    public ScoreController(final GameService gameService) {
        this.gameService = gameService;
    }

    @GetMapping("/{attemptId}")
    public ScoreCard getScoreForAttempt(
            @PathVariable("attemptId") final Long attemptId) {
        return gameService.getScoreForAttempt(attemptId);
    }
}
```

We can't forget to include the new routing configuration in the gateway, as shown in Listing 6-6.

Listing 6-6. application.yml (Gateway v9)

```
zuul:
  ignoredServices: '*'
  prefix: /api
  routes:
    # ... other existing routes ...
    scores:
      path: /scores/**
      serviceId: gamification
      strip-prefix: false
```

EXERCISE

We need to expose an extra endpoint, this time inside the Multiplication microservice: */users/{userId}*. The reason is that, inside our second feature to test, the leaderboard functionality, we want to map user aliases (specified in the Gherkin file) to internal user identifiers.

This should be an easy task for you by this time. Anyway, if you need help, you'll find the UserController and the UserRepository classes in the v9 repository on GitHub.

Test Profiles

Spring Boot has profiles, which are different configurations that we can load for our system (through overriding or extending properties). We'll create a test profile for our microservices to be used in the test environment. That won't change any logic inside the system, but will help us verify the features.

We have two main objectives with the introduction of the test profiles that we'll cover in the next pages:

- We want to handle dummy data that we'll discard after the tests.

- We want to be able to clean up the system and return it to a fresh state.

Note that for our end-to-end testing strategy we can't benefit from some Spring testing features like transaction rollback at the end of our tests. Those features are really powerful for all kind of tests that are executed within the scope of a single Spring application (including integration tests within a microservice). But they're not useful here for several reasons:

- The tests are executed from a different project (because of the black-box testing approach) that interacts with other applications via REST calls. The test annotations, and in general any use we do in the test project of the Spring Test capabilities, will be ignored by our microservices.

- When following and end-to-end approach, we normally like to test how the infrastructure works as well. That includes real transactions to the database and messages flowing through RabbitMQ.

- Even if we would create a profile in our microservices that mimics the transaction rollback behavior, keep in mind that our process is not a single transaction. The *attempt-to-points* process is the result of multiplication storing the attempt in database and sending an event (one transaction), plus gamification consuming the event and calculating the new score (another transaction). If we roll back the first one after it finishes, the second one would fail.

Therefore, for our end-to-end approach, we need to take care of dummy data and clean up by ourselves. Let's see how.

Handling Test Data

We'll put some test data in our system to prove that everything works, but we don't want that data in our production environment. To avoid it, we're going to create a different database for testing purposes. We need to override the database URL property to give it a different name, for both gamification and multiplication services. As explained, we'll do that in a different Spring profile (test), which for a properties file can be defined just by naming convention (our -test suffix). See Listing 6-7.

Listing 6-7. application-test.properties (Gateway v9)

```
spring.datasource.url=jdbc:h2:file:~/gamification-test;DB_
CLOSE_ON_EXIT=FALSE;AUTO_SERVER=TRUE
```

Keep in mind that we don't need to include any other property in that profile since they will be loaded from the plain application.properties file. Spring handles these files with inheritance. If we start our application with the test profile active, we load into our application context all properties from the main properties file (the one with no suffix) plus the ones from the specific profile (that will override the main values if they have the same key).

Besides separating data, we also want to start every test case with a clean database, so we make sure that existing data (coming from previously executed tests) won't impact the result of our test execution. There are many ways to achieve this, but a simple one from the point of view of maintenance (and aligned with a DevOps vision) is to embed that cleanup functionality in our application. Since the service owns the logic to create entities, there is no one better than a developer to write and maintain a REST endpoint to delete the data and do a fresh initialization of a service. Don't worry about the potential risk of doing this: we'll expose this functionality only while running in test mode.

We create an AdminController in both the gamification and multiplication microservices. To restrict it correctly, we include the @Profile annotation, which will tell Spring to load that bean only when the profile is test. See Listing 6-8.

Listing 6-8. AdminController.java (Gamification v9)

```java
@Profile("test")
@RestController
@RequestMapping("/gamification/admin")
class AdminController {

    private final AdminService adminService;

    public AdminController(final AdminService adminService) {
        this.adminService = adminService;
    }

    @PostMapping("/delete-db")
    public ResponseEntity deleteDatabase() {
        adminService.deleteDatabaseContents();
        return ResponseEntity.ok().build();
    }
}
```

Now, every time we do a POST /[service]/admin/delete-db, it will clean the database. Given that this is a functionality we want to make sure is properly hidden, we'll also verify with unit tests that it's accessible only when the profile test is set. We accomplish that by using in our tests the annotation @ActiveProfiles and making sure that, in the case of no profile set, the endpoint returns a NOT_FOUND status. Let's implement a couple of tests inside multiplication and gamification to verify this— AdminControllerEnabledTest and AdminControllerDisabledTest—see Listings 6-9 and 6-10.

Listing 6-9. AdminControllerEnabledTest.java (Gamification v9)

```
@RunWith(SpringRunner.class)
@ActiveProfiles(profiles = "test")
@WebMvcTest(AdminController.class)
public class AdminControllerEnabledTest {

    @MockBean
    private AdminService adminService;

    @Autowired
    private MockMvc mvc;

    /**
     * This test checks that the controller is working as
     expected when
     * the profile is set to test (see annotation in class
     declaration)
     * @throws Exception if any error occurs
     */
    @Test
    public void deleteDatabaseTest() throws Exception {
        // when
        MockHttpServletResponse response = mvc.perform(
                post("/gamification/admin/delete-db")
                        .accept(MediaType.APPLICATION_JSON))
                .andReturn().getResponse();

        // then
        assertThat(response.getStatus()).isEqualTo(HttpStatus.
        OK.value());
        verify(adminService).deleteDatabaseContents();
    }
}
```

Listing 6-10. AdminControllerDisabledTest.java (Gamification v9)

```java
@RunWith(SpringRunner.class)
@WebMvcTest(AdminController.class)
public class AdminControllerDisabledTest {

    @MockBean
    private AdminService adminService;

    @Autowired
    private MockMvc mvc;

    /**
     * This test checks that the controller is NOT ACCESSIBLE
     * when profile is not set to test
     *
     * @throws Exception if any error occurs
     */
    @Test
    public void deleteDatabaseTest() throws Exception {
        // when
        MockHttpServletResponse response = mvc.perform(
                post("/gamification/admin/delete-db")
                        .accept(MediaType.APPLICATION_JSON))
                .andReturn().getResponse();

        // then
        assertThat(response.getStatus()).isEqualTo(HttpStatus.
        NOT_FOUND.value());
        verifyZeroInteractions(adminService);
    }
}
```

Lastly, to align that with our routing strategy in Zuul, we create a test profile also in the gateway service and load the appropriate routing configuration only for test mode. Note that for a YAML properties file, we have an extra way to create a profile, adding three dashes and the profile name (although you can also create an application-test.yml if you prefer). See Listing 6-11.

Listing 6-11. application.ym: Adding a Profile (Gateway v9)

```
# ... (our previous application.yml content)
---
# Adds admin routes for testing purposes
spring:
  profiles: test
zuul:
  routes:
    gamification-admin:
      path: /gamification/admin/**
      serviceId: gamification
      strip-prefix: false
    multiplication-admin:
      path: /multiplication/admin/**
      serviceId: multiplication
      strip-prefix: false
```

Writing the First Cucumber Test

After we prepared our system for the tests, let's focus back again on our end-to-end project, which we left empty. The first step is to create a feature in a Gherkin file inside src/test/resources, with some scenarios. We'll name it multiplication.feature. If you have an IDE that has an available plugin for Cucumber (like IntelliJ), it's time to install it so you can benefit from syntax coloring, compiler warnings when steps in features don't match with expressions in code, etc.

The first feature we want to create is the main functionality provided by our application: users are sending their attempts and receiving responses. If the attempt is correct, they receive points and, in some cases, badges. Let's write the full description in our feature and define our different scenarios and steps. See Listing 6-12.

Listing 6-12. Multiplication.feature (tests-e2e v9)

```
Feature: Users are able to send their multiplication
   attempts, which may be correct or not. When users
   send a correct attempt, they get a response indicating
   that the result is the right one. Also, they get points
   and potentially some badges when they are right, so they
   get motivation to come back and keep playing. Badges are
   won for the first right attempt and when the user gets 100,
   500 and 999 points respectively. If users send a wrong
   attempt, they don't get any point or badge.

   Scenario: The user sends a first right attempt and gets a badge
      When the user john_snow sends 1 right attempts
      Then the user gets a response indicating the attempt is right
      And the user gets 10 points for the attempt
      And the user gets the FIRST_WON badge

   Scenario: The user sends a second right attempt and gets points only
      Given the user john_snow sends 1 right attempts
      And the user gets the FIRST_WON badge
      When the user john_snow sends 1 right attempts
      Then the user gets a response indicating the attempt is right
      And the user gets 10 points for the attempt
      And the user does not get any badge
```

Scenario: The user sends a wrong attempt and gets nothing
  When the user john_snow sends 1 wrong attempts
  Then the user gets a response indicating the attempt is wrong
  And the user gets 0 points for the attempt
  And the user does not get any badge

Checks the Bronze, Silver and Gold badges
Scenario Outline: The user sends a right attempt after
<previous_attempts> right attempts and then gets a badge
<badge_name>
  Given the user john_snow sends <previous_attempts> right
  attempts
  When the user john_snow sends 1 right attempts
  Then the user gets a response indicating the attempt is
  right
  And the user gets 10 points for the attempt
  And the user gets the <badge_name> badge

  Examples:
    | previous_attempts | badge_name |
    | 9 | BRONZE_MULTIPLICATOR |
    | 49 | SILVER_MULTIPLICATOR |
    | 99 | GOLD_MULTIPLICATOR |

As we saw already, the good part about Gherkin is that we don't
need to describe what we want to test with that file; it's perfectly
understandable. We check the cases in which the user sends a right and
a wrong attempt, and then the different badge scenarios. For the badges
based on the number of good attempts, we can use a table with examples
since the scenario outline is exactly the same.

Note that in our Gherkin file we're reusing some of the steps, and also writing them in a way that can be easily parsed later. Sentence rewording is a skill that you learn after the first time you write scenarios. Don't worry about the wording as you write; just focus on the content, writing sentences in the most human-friendly way you can imagine, and then do a second round by identifying phrases that can be parameterized and combined using arguments. For instance, while writing this feature, I found myself writing the sentences in Listing 6-13.

Listing 6-13. Multiplication.feature: Fragment That Can Be Improved (tests-e2e v9)

```
# First example of a sentence that can be combined with another
one
And the user does not get points for the attempt
# Another example
And the user gets the badge linked to the first attempt
```

When you pay attention to the complete feature definition, you notice that the first one can be generalized to the common one to check the score (and set to 0), and the second one can be rephrased so it is generic and we can use it for any badge. See Listing 6-14.

Listing 6-14. Multiplication.feature: Improved Fragment (tests-e2e v9)

```
# First example translated to existing sentence
And the user gets 0 points for the attempt
# Second example made generic
And the user gets the FIRST_WON badge
```

In a real-life case, this is part of the process of software development: the business user will write a gherkin file without paying attention to step reusability, but then the developer can suggest light modifications to make it more efficient from a technical point of view. You may argue that that should never happen and we should keep the Gherkin file as it comes, and then implement some method references in the background. That's also feasible, but the fact is that we can find some modifications that keep our feature definitions pretty readable but at the same time nicely parameterized, so we reduce maintenance and help to write more flexible sentences (instead of ad hoc, one-time use). Keep the sentences functional and human-friendly, but generic enough to reuse them if needed. That should be your goal.

Linking a Feature to Java Code

Once we have a .feature file describing the use cases, we write our Java code to process them and perform the desired actions and assertions. First, we need to link our feature to a test class in Java. Let's create MultiplicationFeatureTest within the microservices.book package. Cucumber provides a test runner (Cucumber, which we need to pass to JUnit's @RunWith annotation) and a @CucumberOptions annotation that we can use to set up some plugins. In this case, we'd like to add some extra reports, so we configure it there. See Listing 6-15.

Listing 6-15. MultiplicationFeatureTest.java (tests-e2e v9)

```
package microservices.book;

import cucumber.api.CucumberOptions;
import cucumber.api.junit.Cucumber;
import org.junit.runner.RunWith;
```

```java
/**
 * @author moises.macero
 */
@RunWith(Cucumber.class)
@CucumberOptions(plugin = { "pretty", "html:target/cucumber",
"junit:target/junit-report.xml" },
        features = "src/test/resources/multiplication.feature")
public class MultiplicationFeatureTest {
}
```

To define the steps within that class, we could start from scratch, but we can also benefit from an interesting feature in Cucumber: the auto-generation of code for undefined steps. From the project's root folder, we execute ./mvnw test. That should run our tests but, since there are no defined steps linked to our defined .feature file, the Cucumber runner will generate very helpful content at the end of our console output, as shown in Listing 6-16.

Listing 6-16. Console Output: Auto-Generated Steps (tests-e2e v9)

```
...
You can implement missing steps with the snippets below:

@When("^the user john_snow sends (\\d+) right attempts$")
public void the_user_john_snow_sends_right_attempts(int arg1)
throws Throwable {
    // Write code here that turns the phrase above into
    concrete actions
    throw new PendingException();
}

@Then("^the user gets a response indicating the attempt is
right$")
```

```
public void the_user_gets_a_response_indicating_the_attempt_is_
right() throws Throwable {
    // Write code here that turns the phrase above into
    concrete actions
    throw new PendingException();
}

@Then("^the user gets (\\d+) points for the attempt$")
public void the_user_gets_points_for_the_attempt(int arg1)
throws Throwable {
    // Write code here that turns the phrase above into
    concrete actions
    throw new PendingException();
}

@Then("^the user gets the FIRST_WON badge$")
public void the_user_gets_the_FIRST_WON_badge() throws
Throwable {
    // Write code here that turns the phrase above into
    concrete actions
    throw new PendingException();
}

@Given("^the user john_snow sends (\\d+) right attempts$")
public void the_user_john_snow_sends_right_attempts(int arg1)
throws Throwable {
    // Write code here that turns the phrase above into
    concrete actions
    throw new PendingException();
}
...
```

That code needs some modification, but it's a good start. We copy it into a new class called `MultiplicationFeatureSteps` within the same `microservices.book` package. That class will contain the logic for all the steps included in this feature. Bear in mind that the order of the steps in your Java class is not important, but you may want to keep some order of appearance for readability when comparing it to the feature.

First, let's correct the different step definitions defined in the `Given`, `When`, and `Then` annotations. We want to use some extra words as arguments, not only numbers, which are the only ones interpreted as arguments in the autogenerated code:

- *User alias*: We'd like to pass the user alias as an argument (text), so we can reuse the same steps for different attempts of various users.

- *Correctness*: We'd like to specify if the attempt is *right* or *wrong* (text).

- *Badge name*: We want to pass the badge name (text) instead of hard-coding it in different steps.

To accomplish that, we just need to replace these words in our sentence patterns with regular expressions. We can use (`[^\s]+`) as a simple regular expression to match the word between spaces. Then, when replaced with the hard-coded word, it will do the trick. Let's apply the change to the original version, as shown in Listing 6-17.

Listing 6-17. MultiplicationFeatureSteps.java : Adding Arguments (tests-e2e v9)

```
// Original
@When("^the user john_snow sends (\\d+) right attempts$")
public void the_user_john_snow_sends_right_attempts(int arg1)
throws Throwable {
```

```
    // Write code here that turns the phrase above into
    concrete actions
    throw new PendingException();
}

// Modified with extra parameters
@Given("^the user ([^\\s]+) sends (\\d+) ([^\\s]+) attempts")
public void the_user_sends_attempts(final String userAlias,
   final int attempts, final String rightOrWrong) throws
   Throwable {
    // Write code here that turns the phrase above into
    concrete actions
    throw new PendingException();
}
```

Note that we need to add the extra arguments to the method too, which must follow the same order of appearance as in the sentence.

That's how we parameterize our steps. Now we can write sentences such as "the user john_snow sends 12 right attempts" or "the user jack_smith sends 3 wrong attempts" and both will be handled by the same step method.

We still miss the real logic of the steps. To avoid creating a huge class with a lot of logic, we'll use our object-oriented common sense and split it:

- The MultiplicationFeatureSteps class will contain the main logic of our tests, orchestrating the actions and asserting the results. We should try to keep every step below 10 lines of code.

- The MultiplicationApplication is a new class that we'll create to model the exposed services in our application: sending an attempt, getting statistics, etc.

- The ApplicationHttpUtils is a class we'll add to provide basic support to perform HTTP calls so that we can access the REST API of our application.

Listing 6-18 shows the final version of MultiplicationFeatureSteps.

Listing 6-18. MultiplicationFeatureSteps.java (tests-e2e v9)

```java
public class MultiplicationFeatureSteps {

    private MultiplicationApplication app;
    private AttemptResponse lastAttemptResponse;
    private Stats lastStatsResponse;

    public MultiplicationFeatureSteps() {
        this.app = new MultiplicationApplication();
    }

    @Before
    public void cleanUp() {
        app.deleteData();
    }

    @Given("^the user ([^\\s]+) sends (\\d+) ([^\\s]+) attempts")
    public void the_user_sends_attempts(final String userAlias,
                                        final int attempts,
                                        final String
                                        rightOrWrong)
                                                        throws
                                                        Throwable {
        int attemptsSent = IntStream.range(0, attempts)
            .mapToObj(i -> app.sendAttempt(userAlias, 10, 10,
                                "right".
                                equals(rightOrWrong) ?
                                    100 : 258))
```

```
        // store last attempt for later use
        .peek(response -> lastAttemptResponse =
        response)
        .mapToInt(response -> response.isCorrect()
        ? 1 : 0)
        .sum();
    assertThat(attemptsSent).isEqualTo("right".
    equals(rightOrWrong) ? attempts : 0)
        .withFailMessage("Error sending attempts to the
        application");
}
@Then("^the user gets a response indicating the attempt is
([^\\s]+)$")
public void the_user_gets_a_response_indicating_the_
attempt_is(
        final String rightOrWrong) throws Throwable {
    assertThat(lastAttemptResponse.isCorrect())
        .isEqualTo("right".equals(rightOrWrong))
        .withFailMessage("Expecting a response with a "
                + rightOrWrong + " attempt");
}

@Then("^the user gets (\\d+) points for the attempt$")
public void the_user_gets_points_for_the_attempt(
        final int points) throws Throwable {
    long attemptId = lastAttemptResponse.getId();
    Thread.currentThread().sleep(2000);
    int score = app.getScoreForAttempt(attemptId).
    getScore();
    assertThat(score).isEqualTo(points);
}
```

```java
@Then("^the user gets the ([^\\s]+) badge$")
public void the_user_gets_the_type_badge(
        final String badgeType) throws Throwable {
    long userId = lastAttemptResponse.getUser().getId();
    Thread.currentThread().sleep(200);
    lastStatsResponse = app.getStatsForUser(userId);
    List<String> userBadges = lastStatsResponse.
    getBadges();
    assertThat(userBadges).contains(badgeType);
}

@Then("^the user does not get any badge$")
public void the_user_does_not_get_any_badge() throws
Throwable {
    long userId = lastAttemptResponse.getUser().getId();
    Stats stats = app.getStatsForUser(userId);
    List<String> userBadges = stats.getBadges();
    if (stats.getScore() == 0) {
        assertThat(stats.getBadges()).isNullOrEmpty();
    } else {
        assertThat(userBadges).isEqualTo(lastStatsResponse.
        getBadges());
    }
}

@Given("^the user has (\\d+) points$")
public void the_user_has_points(final int points) throws
Throwable {
```

```
        long userId = lastAttemptResponse.getUser().getId();
        int statPoints = app.getStatsForUser(userId).
        getScore();
        assertThat(points).isEqualTo(statPoints);
    }

    public AttemptResponse getLastAttemptResponse() {
        return lastAttemptResponse;
    }

    public Stats getLastStatsResponse() {
        return lastStatsResponse;
    }

    public MultiplicationApplication getApp() {
        return app;
    }
}
```

Be aware that this class won't compile until we implement the MultiplicationApplication, Stats, and AttemptResponse classes. That part is pretty straightforward, so we'll cover that later in the chapter to avoid diversions from our implementation of Cucumber's feature steps.

The first important concept to understand is that this class will be instantiated per the scenario we execute, so we can keep the state across the different steps of the script. Therefore, we can use class fields to share information between steps. In this case, we need to keep a reference to our application model app, and to the last responses received for an attempt-request (lastAttemptResponse) and a stats request (lastStatsResponse).

Given the similarity with JUnit, it's not a surprise that the method annotated with @Before is going to be executed before every scenario. In this case, we invoke the application method called cleanUp(), which will call (as we'll see later in the chapter) our new API endpoints created specifically for tests: /gamification/admin/delete-db and /multiplication/admin/delete-db. We want to execute every scenario with a clean database.

Having that knowledge, the implementation of our steps is just a Java-as-usual task. We just need to use our application class MultiplicationApplication to call the REST API (supported by ApplicationHttpUtils). As you can see here, we use AssertJ to check the results in our MultiplicationFeatureSteps class. Note that Cucumber does not give us a full testing framework: it's just a tool to link feature definitions in Gherkin to Java code using a BDD approach. To be able to build our tests we need to combine it with JUnit and most likely other frameworks/libraries like AssertJ, TestNG, Mockito, etc., depending on our needs. Figure 6-1 shows an overall view of the different parts in our end-to-end project and how it connects to the existing system.

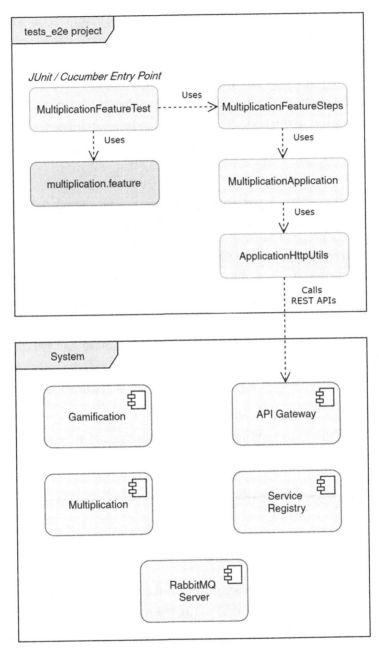

Figure 6-1. *Overall view of the end-to-end project and how it connects to the existing system*

Last but not least, it's worth it to mention that Cucumber does not distinguish between the annotations @Given, @When, and @Then to link the steps to code. You can see some examples in the feature file: the step `^the user ([^\s]+) sends (\d+) ([^\s]+) attempts` is being used in a Given and a When statement indistinctly, but the step is defined with a @ Given annotation in the code. This is useful to implement cases like these, in which the same step can be reused to set up the scenario and to assert an expected result.

PRODUCTION READINESS: SLEEP GUARDS IN CI SYSTEMS

Maybe you noticed that we're using some `sleep()` calls to wait before continuing with some steps. We need them there because our system is *eventually consistent*—the event will take some time to be consumed by the second microservice, and that one will take its time to complete the operation. The `sleep()` methods are there just to illustrate this; make sure you don't use those waits in a real CI system. They can become easily the source of many spurious errors (e.g., if you have a congested CI machine that doesn't respond in time).

Take this as an exercise and implement a retry mechanism in the system that performs the REST call several times until it gets a valid response or a timeout expires.

The Supporting Classes

As introduced earlier, Cucumber is not a full end-to-end test framework. It delivers nicely on its promises: linking feature definitions in a human-friendly language to test suites in code, with defined steps. In our system, we need to build some extra logic to fulfill our end-to-end strategy. Note that this logic is not Cucumber- nor Spring-Boot specific, so you can take this whole subsection as a challenge and implement the rest of the code yourself, using the methods you saw in the `MultiplicationFeatureSteps` class as a reference.

The `MultiplicationApplication` class, which we left pending to be implemented, will model the system behavior (see Listing 6-19). The methods represent actions that a REST consumer can perform. Note that it relies on `ApplicationHttpUtils`, which we haven't covered yet. However, as you can imagine, it performs the real *HTTP connection plumbing.*

Listing 6-19. MultiplicationApplication.java: Adding Arguments (tests-e2e v9)

```
public class MultiplicationApplication {

    private static final String APPLICATION_BASE_URL = "http://
    localhost:8000/api";
    private static final String CONTEXT_ATTEMPTS = "/results";
    private static final String CONTEXT_SCORE = "/scores/";
    private static final String CONTEXT_STATS = "/stats";
    private static final String CONTEXT_USERS = "/users/";
    private static final String CONTEXT_LEADERBOARD = "/
    leaders";
    private static final String CONTEXT_DELETE_DATA_GAM = "/
    gamification/admin/delete-db";
    private static final String CONTEXT_DELETE_DATA_MULT = "/
    multiplication/admin/delete-db";

    private ApplicationHttpUtils httpUtils;

    public MultiplicationApplication() {
        this.httpUtils = new ApplicationHttpUtils(APPLICATIO
        N_BASE_URL);
    }
```

```java
public AttemptResponse sendAttempt(String userAlias, int
factorA, int factorB, int result) {
    String attemptJson = "{\"user\":{\"alias\":\"" +
    userAlias + "\"}," +
            "\"multiplication\":{\"factorA\":\"" + factorA
            + "\",\"factorB\":\"" + factorB + "\"}," +
            "\"resultAttempt\":\"" + result + "\"}";
    String response = httpUtils.post(CONTEXT_ATTEMPTS,
    attemptJson);
    ObjectMapper objectMapper = new ObjectMapper();
    objectMapper.configure(DeserializationFeature.FAIL_ON_
    UNKNOWN_PROPERTIES, false);
    try {
        return objectMapper.readValue(response,
        AttemptResponse.class);
    } catch (IOException e) {
        throw new RuntimeException(e);
    }
}

public ScoreResponse getScoreForAttempt(long attemptId) {
    String response = httpUtils.get(CONTEXT_SCORE +
    attemptId);
    if (response.isEmpty()) {
        return new ScoreResponse(0);
    } else {
        ObjectMapper objectMapper = new ObjectMapper();
        objectMapper.configure(DeserializationFeature.FAIL_
        ON_UNKNOWN_PROPERTIES, false);
        try {
            return objectMapper.readValue(response,
            ScoreResponse.class);
```

```
        } catch (IOException e) {
            throw new RuntimeException(e);
        }
    }
}

public Stats getStatsForUser(long userId) {
    String response = httpUtils.get(CONTEXT_STATS +
    "?userId=" + userId);
    ObjectMapper objectMapper = new ObjectMapper();
    objectMapper.configure(DeserializationFeature.FAIL_ON_
    UNKNOWN_PROPERTIES, false);
    try {
        return objectMapper.readValue(response, Stats.
        class);
    } catch (IOException e) {
        throw new RuntimeException(e);
    }
}

public User getUser(long userId) {
    String response = httpUtils.get(CONTEXT_USERS +
    userId);
    ObjectMapper objectMapper = new ObjectMapper();
    objectMapper.configure(DeserializationFeature.FAIL_ON_
    UNKNOWN_PROPERTIES, false);
    try {
        return objectMapper.readValue(response,
        User.class);
    } catch (IOException e) {
        throw new RuntimeException(e);
    }
}
```

```java
public List<LeaderBoardPosition> getLeaderboard() {
    String response = httpUtils.get(CONTEXT_LEADERBOARD);
    ObjectMapper objectMapper = new ObjectMapper();
    objectMapper.configure(DeserializationFeature.FAIL_ON_
    UNKNOWN_PROPERTIES, false);
    try {
        JavaType javaType = objectMapper.getTypeFactory().
        constructCollectionType(List.class,
        LeaderBoardPosition.class);
        return objectMapper.readValue(response, javaType);
    } catch (IOException e) {
        throw new RuntimeException(e);
    }
}

public void deleteData() {
    httpUtils.post(CONTEXT_DELETE_DATA_GAM, "");
    httpUtils.post(CONTEXT_DELETE_DATA_MULT, "");
}
}
```

This class basically retrieves the JSON representations from the
REST APIs and maps them to plain objects using Jackson. We also
need to create the Stats, AttemptResponse, User, ScoreResponse, and
LeaderBoardPosition classes.

EXERCISE

Create the Stats, AttemptResponse, User, ScoreResponse, and
LeaderBoardPosition simple classes. Don't forget to either follow the
same structure as the received JSON or code the parsers yourself. To keep
it simple, the listed classes represent the same structure. For instance, you

need to reference User from AttemptResponse. If you need help, remember that you can find the complete source code inside the v9 repository on GitHub (tests_e2e folder).

The last supporting class of this little framework to connect to our system is ApplicationHttpUtils (see Listing 6-20). This one uses Apache HTTP Fluent API to execute the requests and get the responses from the API Gateway. See *https://tpd.io/fl-api* for more information about the Apache HTTP Fluent API.

Listing 6-20. ApplicationHttpUtils.java (tests-e2e v9)

```java
public class ApplicationHttpUtils {

    private final String baseUrl;

    public ApplicationHttpUtils(final String baseUrl) {
        this.baseUrl = baseUrl;
    }

    public String post(final String context, final String body) {
        try {
            HttpResponse response = Request.Post(baseUrl +
            context)
                        .bodyString(body, ContentType.APPLICATION_
                        JSON)
                        .execute().returnResponse();
            assertIs200(response);
            return EntityUtils.toString(response.getEntity());
        } catch (IOException e) {
            throw new RuntimeException(e);
        }
    }
}
```

```
public String get(final String context) {
    try {
        HttpResponse response = Request.Get(baseUrl +
        context)
                    .execute().returnResponse();
        assertIs200(response);
        return EntityUtils.toString(response.getEntity());
    } catch (IOException e) {
        throw new RuntimeException(e);
    }
}

private void assertIs200(final HttpResponse httpResponse) {
    assertThat(httpResponse.getStatusLine().
    getStatusCode()).isEqualTo(200);
}
}
```

Reusing Steps Across Features

This section introduces the second feature to test, and while coding it, you'll see how you can use steps defined before, thus saving a lot of time and code duplication.

We now cover the leaderboard functionality with some end-to-end tests. Let's test two basic scenarios:

1. From a fresh start, when the user sends more right attempts than another, and therefore becomes first in the ranking.

2. Given a situation in which a user is above another in the ranking, and the one below the user can pass to a higher ranking position by getting a higher score.

The feature file is nothing more than writing the same story in Gherkin, as shown in Listing 6-21.

Listing 6-21. leaderboard.feature (tests-e2e v9)

```
Feature: Users are listed from highest score to lowest, and
when
  they get points they can move up on the ranking.

  Scenario: A user sends a higher number of right attempts and
  it's positioned at the first place in the ranking.
    When the user john sends 2 right attempts
    And the user peter sends 1 right attempts
    Then the user john is the number 1 on the leaderboard
    And the user peter is the number 2 on the leaderboard

  Scenario: A user passes another one when gets higher score.
    Given the user john sends 3 right attempts
    And the user peter sends 2 right attempts
    And the user john is the number 1 on the leaderboard
    When the user peter sends 2 right attempts
    Then the user peter is the number 1 on the leaderboard
    And the user john is the number 2 on the leaderboard
```

As you can see, we're using the steps defined in the MultiplicationFeatureSteps class to set up the scene (sending attempts). The tricky part here is that we don't want to put our new steps together with others in the same class since we want to organize them properly and avoid having a huge class with all the steps of all our features together. We will create a new class called LeaderboardFeatureSteps. But, if we do that, how can we access to the functionality—and data—existing inside MultiplicationFeatureSteps? Remember that the "send attempt" step stores the result within its class (lastAttemptResponse), which is inaccessible from leaderboard feature's steps class. That is, unless we can pass it to our new class.

The good news is that we can solve this with standard dependency injection, which is provided by the `cucumber-picocontainer` dependency (note that we don't need Spring for it to work). Since Cucumber will instantiate a new object of every class that contains steps (one of its annotations), we can use constructor injection to tell Cucumber to inject the instance of `MultiplicationFeatureSteps` into `LeaderboardFeatureSteps`. To accomplish this, we only need to pass the step definition class as a constructor argument. The lightweight dependency injection library made ad hoc for Cucumber (Picocontainer) will do the trick for us.

Taking dependency injection into account for our new class, we can now code it and include the only new step needed to verify the functionality of the leaderboard. As you can see in Listing 6-22, we don't need any annotation whatsoever to make the dependency injection works.

Listing 6-22. LeaderboardFeatureSteps.java (tests-e2e v9)

```java
public class LeaderboardFeatureSteps {

    private MultiplicationFeatureSteps mSteps;

    public LeaderboardFeatureSteps(final MultiplicationFeature
    Steps mSteps) {
        this.mSteps = mSteps;
    }

    @Then("^the user ([^\\s]+) is the number (\\d+) on the
    leaderboard$")
    public void the_user_is_the_number_on_the_leaderboard(final
    String user, final int position) throws Throwable {
        Thread.currentThread().sleep(500);
        List<LeaderBoardPosition> leaderBoard = mSteps.
        getApp().getLeaderboard();
        assertThat(leaderBoard).isNotEmpty();
```

```
long userId = leaderBoard.get
(position - 1).getUserId();
String userAlias = mSteps.getApp().getUser(userId).
getAlias();
assertThat(userAlias).isEqualTo(user);
    }
}
```

It's a straightforward feature—we just need to check the position of the user, and the orchestration of steps made by the Cucumber scenario will do everything else. Remember that, to make it work, we also need to create the main test class LeaderboardFeatureTest with the corresponding runner and Cucumber options, as shown in Listing 6-23.

Listing 6-23. LeaderboardFeatureTest.java (tests-e2e v9)

```
@RunWith(Cucumber.class)
@CucumberOptions(plugin = { "pretty", "html:target/cucumber",
"junit:target/junit-report.xml" },
        features = "src/test/resources/leaderboard.feature")
public class LeaderboardFeatureTest {
}
```

Running Tests and Checking Reports

It's time to see it working. As usual, we need to start our set of services, but now remember that we need to activate the test profile for the gateway (to route the admin endpoints), the multiplication, and the gamification services (to use a test database and expose admin beans). To do that, just execute them with the Maven wrapper as shown in Listing 6-24 (or follow the instructions of your preferred IDE).

Listing 6-24. Command Line: Running a Specific Profile (Gamification v9)

```
mvnw spring-boot:run -Drun.profiles=test
```

Here's a summary of the steps:

1. Run the RabbitMQ server (if not yet running).

2. Run the service registry microservice (no specific profile).

3. Run the gateway microservice (`test` profile).

4. Run the multiplication microservice (`test` profile).

5. Run the gamification microservice (`test` profile).

6. Run the jetty server from the `ui` root folder (optional, since our tests don't use the UI).

When the application is up and running, simply execute the tests for the `e2e-tests` project as usual with Maven:

```
mvnw test
```

You'll see a pretty printed output in which Cucumber is telling you the status of the scenarios and steps that are executing, as shown in Figure 6-2.

```
Scenario Outline: The user sends a right attempt after <previous_attempts> right attempts and
then gets a badge <badge_name> # src/test/resources/multiplication.feature:32
    Given the user john_snow sends <previous_attempts> right attempts
    When the user john_snow sends 1 right attempts
    Then the user gets a response indicating the attempt is right
    And the user gets 10 points for the attempt
    And the user gets the <badge_name> badge

Examples:

Scenario Outline: The user sends a right attempt after 9 right attempts and then gets a badge
BRONZE_MULTIPLICATOR # src/test/resources/multiplication.feature:41
    Given the user john_snow sends 9 right attempts
                            # MultiplicationFeatureSteps.the_user_sends_attempts(String,int,String)
    When the user john_snow sends 1 right attempts
                        # MultiplicationFeatureSteps.the_user_sends_attempts(String,int,String)
    Then the user gets a response indicating the attempt is right
                            # MultiplicationFeatureSteps.the_user_gets_a_response_indicating_the_attemp
t_is(String)
    And the user gets 10 points for the attempt
                        # MultiplicationFeatureSteps.the_user_gets_points_for_the_attempt(int)
    And the user gets the BRONZE_MULTIPLICATOR badge
                        # MultiplicationFeatureSteps.the_user_gets_the_type_badge(String)

Scenario Outline: The user sends a right attempt after 49 right attempts and then gets a badge
SILVER_MULTIPLICATOR # src/test/resources/multiplication.feature:42
    Given the user john_snow sends 49 right attempts
                            # MultiplicationFeatureSteps.the_user_sends_attempts(String,int,String)
    When the user john_snow sends 1 right attempts
                        # MultiplicationFeatureSteps.the_user_sends_attempts(String,int,String)
    Then the user gets a response indicating the attempt is right
                            # MultiplicationFeatureSteps.the_user_gets_a_response_indicating_the_attem
pt_is(String)
    And the user gets 10 points for the attempt
                        # MultiplicationFeatureSteps.the_user_gets_points_for_the_attempt(int)
    And the user gets the SILVER_MULTIPLICATOR badge
                        # MultiplicationFeatureSteps.the_user_gets_the_type_badge(String)

Scenario Outline: The user sends a right attempt after 99 right attempts and then gets a badge
GOLD_MULTIPLICATOR # src/test/resources/multiplication.feature:43
    Given the user john_snow sends 99 right attempts
                            # MultiplicationFeatureSteps.the_user_sends_attempts(String,int,String)
    When the user john_snow sends 1 right attempts
                        # MultiplicationFeatureSteps.the_user_sends_attempts(String,int,String)
    Then the user gets a response indicating the attempt is right
                            # MultiplicationFeatureSteps.the_user_gets_a_response_indicating_the_attempt
_is(String)
    And the user gets 10 points for the attempt
                            # MultiplicationFeatureSteps.the_user_gets_points_for_the_attempt(int)
    And the user gets the GOLD_MULTIPLICATOR badge
                        # MultiplicationFeatureSteps.the_user_gets_the_type_badge(String)

6 Scenarios (6 passed)
29 Steps (29 passed)
0m14,862s

Tests run: 35, Failures: 0, Errors: 0, Skipped: 0, Time elapsed: 14.947 sec

Results :

Tests run: 47, Failures: 0, Errors: 0, Skipped: 0
```

Figure 6-2. *Pretty printed output of test execution in Cucumber*

Besides that, and thanks to the @CucumberOptions annotation that we used for our main test classes, you'll have a Cucumber report and JUnit (surefire) XML reports in the target folder. They can be published to the CI system so you can see the results from a centralized place.

Summary

In this chapter, you saw the importance of having good test suites in a distributed system. All the layers are important, but choosing the end-to-end approach might become a tough decision due to the maintenance and complexity that it commonly requires.

You saw how a combination of Cucumber and structuring the test project into layers can provide a simple and powerful solution to cover an end-to-end strategy. Cucumber provides a business-friendly language to design the test cases—Gherkin—and it integrates with Java, so it's a choice that combines perfectly with our use case.

Also, the chapter paid extra attention to some details that can ease development—step parameterization and reusability, understanding how Cucumber works when instantiating tests, and how to benefit from dependency injection. And, most importantly, you saw how making your code testable makes everything simpler just by adding some optional logic to your services.

What you got here is a great achievement too. You can now test the system end-to-end, not only verifying that each part works on its own, but also that the overall business cases make sense. Having a framework like this will pay off even more as the project matures, because it provides an extra layer of stability that's difficult to obtain otherwise.

APPENDIX A

Upgrading to Spring Boot 2.0

Introduction

This book uses the Spring Boot version 1.5.7 for the different microservices that are part of the evolving application. Spring Boot 2.0, which is to be released after writing this book, introduces some breaking changes to the system since it's a major update.

This appendix helps you upgrade your applications to Spring Boot 2.0 in case you want to use it.

SOURCE CODE AVAILABLE WITH THE BOOK: V10

The repository v10 on GitHub (see `https://github.com/microservices-practical`) contains the system code, working with Spring Boot 2.0. It works exactly the same way as the previous version (v9), just with the new version. All changes made to the application are tagged with a comment starting with BOOT2 so you can easily find them by performing a text search.

Note that, since there is no official version at the time of writing the book, we're using a milestone version: 2.0.0.M2.

© Moises Macero 2017
M. Macero, *Learn Microservices with Spring Boot*,
https://doi.org/10.1007/978-1-4842-3165-4

Upgrading the Dependencies

If you want to use the latest version of Spring Boot, you need to change your pom.xml files. Keep in mind that you also need to upgrade the Spring Cloud release version, but it does not follow exactly the same schedule as Spring Boot—it's a few weeks delayed.

Therefore, the plan this appendix follows is to include the Spring Boot 2.0 Milestone 2 (2.0.0.M2), since it has an equivalent working version for Spring Cloud early releases: Finchley.M2. To be able to use milestone versions in your projects, you also need to append to your pom.xml the additional Spring repositories where these versions reside.

Listing A-1 shows the file for the multiplication microservice as a reference; you need to apply these same changes to all the other Spring Boot applications (upgrading the Spring Boot and Spring Cloud versions and adding the repositories and pluginRepositories blocks).

Listing A-1. pom.xml (multiplication v10)

```xml
<?xml version="1.0" encoding="UTF-8"?>
<project xmlns="http://maven.apache.org/POM/4.0.0"
xmlns:xsi="http://www.w3.org/2001/XMLSchema-instance"
xsi:schemaLocation="http://maven.apache.org/POM/4.0.0 http://
maven.apache.org/xsd/maven-4.0.0.xsd">
    <modelVersion>4.0.0</modelVersion>

    <groupId>microservices.book</groupId>
    <artifactId>social-multiplication-v10</artifactId>
    <version>0.10.0-SNAPSHOT</version>
    <packaging>jar</packaging>

    <name>social-multiplication-v10</name>
    <description>Social Multiplication App (Learn Microservices
    with Spring Boot)</description>
```

```xml
<parent>
    <groupId>org.springframework.boot</groupId>
    <artifactId>spring-boot-starter-parent</artifactId>
    <version>2.0.0.M2</version>
</parent>

<properties>
    <project.build.sourceEncoding>UTF-8</project.build.
    sourceEncoding>
    <project.reporting.outputEncoding>UTF-8</project.
    reporting.outputEncoding>
    <java.version>1.8</java.version>
    <spring-cloud.version>Finchley.M2</spring-cloud.
    version>
</properties>

<dependencyManagement>
    <dependencies>
        <dependency>
            <groupId>org.springframework.cloud</groupId>
            <artifactId>spring-cloud-dependencies
            </artifactId>
            <version>${spring-cloud.version}</version>
            <type>pom</type>
            <scope>import</scope>
        </dependency>
    </dependencies>
</dependencyManagement>

<dependencies>
<!-- All our existing dependencies... -->
</dependencies>
```

```xml
<build>
    <plugins>
        <plugin>
            <groupId>org.springframework.boot</groupId>
            <artifactId>spring-boot-maven-plugin
            </artifactId>
        </plugin>
    </plugins>
</build>

<repositories>
    <repository>
        <id>spring-snapshots</id>
        <name>Spring Snapshots</name>
        <url>https://repo.spring.io/snapshot</url>
        <snapshots>
            <enabled>true</enabled>
        </snapshots>
    </repository>
    <repository>
        <id>spring-milestones</id>
        <name>Spring Milestones</name>
        <url>https://repo.spring.io/milestone</url>
        <snapshots>
            <enabled>false</enabled>
        </snapshots>
    </repository>
</repositories>

<pluginRepositories>
    <pluginRepository>
        <id>spring-snapshots</id>
        <name>Spring Snapshots</name>
```

```
    <url>https://repo.spring.io/snapshot</url>
    <snapshots>
        <enabled>true</enabled>
    </snapshots>
  </pluginRepository>
  <pluginRepository>
      <id>spring-milestones</id>
      <name>Spring Milestones</name>
      <url>https://repo.spring.io/milestone</url>
      <snapshots>
          <enabled>false</enabled>
      </snapshots>
  </pluginRepository>
 </pluginRepositories>

</project>
```

Fixing the Breaking Changes

The CrudRepository Interface Does Not Include findOne()

The book's code uses the findOne() method included in the CrudRepository interface to retrieve a single entity from the database using Spring Data JPA. For some reason (documentation is not available yet at the time of writing), that method has been removed in an earlier version to the one included by the Spring Boot starter, which uses the version 2.0.0.M4 of spring-data-commons (you can see it by running mvnw dependency:tree from any of the root project folders).

That doesn't have a big impact on the code, but you need to change these method references to make everything compile again. The code

uses findOne() in three classes inside the multiplication project:
MultiplicationServiceImpl, UserController, and UserControllerTest.

Follow the same strategy to replace it in those three places: changing
it to the preferred findById() method and using the returned Optional to
throw an IllegalArgumentException if the identifier does not exist in your
database. Listing A-2 shows one of the code snippets as a reference.

Listing A-2. MultiplicationServiceImpl.java (multiplication v10)

```
@Override
public MultiplicationResultAttempt getResultById(final Long
resultId) {
    // BOOT2: changed from findOne
    return attemptRepository.findById(resultId)
            .orElseThrow(() -> new IllegalArgumentException(
                    "The requested resultId [" + resultId +
                        "] does not exist."));
}
```

Actuator Endpoints Have Been Moved

We know from the release notes[1] that in Spring Boot 2.0, the actuator
endpoints have been moved under /application. That means that you
need to change the load balancing strategy configuration inside the API
gateway to point to /application/health instead of just /health. If you
don't change this, Ribbon will think all services are down and the API
Gateway won't work. See Listing A-3.

---

[1]https://tpd.io/bootm1-rn

Listing A-3. RibbonConfiguration.java (gateway v10)

```
@Bean
public IPing ribbonPing(final IClientConfig config) {
    // BOOT2: changed from /health to /application/health
    return new PingUrl(false,"/application/health");
}
```

Applying Optional Updates

The WebMvcConfigurerAdapter Class Has Been Deprecated

The current code uses the class WebMvcConfigurerAdapter to disable CORS in the multiplication, gamification, and gateway microservices. That class has been deprecated in favor of the WebMvcConfigurer interface, since starting with Java 8, interfaces can include default implementations and Spring Boot 2.0 no longer supports earlier Java versions.

This change is optional here since it's just deprecated, but it's better to adapt to the change as soon as possible. Listing A-4 shows the change in one of the classes; be sure to apply this change to all three of the classes (inside the aforementioned microservices projects).

Listing A-4. WebConfiguration.java (gateway v10)

```
@Configuration
@EnableWebMvc
//BOOT2 changed to interface WebMvcConfigurer instead of
subclass of WebMvcConfigurerAdapter
public class WebConfiguration implements WebMvcConfigurer
{ //... }
```

Working with Spring Boot 2.0

Those are all the changes you should apply to make the system work with Spring Boot 2.0. Note that I couldn't try the release version, so it might happen (though it's unlikely) that there are other breaking changes to come, not covered by this appendix. If that is the case, you can visit the Spring Boot 2.0 release notes page to check. (See `https://github.com/spring-projects/spring-boot/wiki/Spring-Boot-2.0-Release-Notes`.)

On that same page, you'll find the new features coming with Spring Boot 2.0 as well. Some of the major new functionalities are support for Java 9 and some great features in Spring 5, such as the Reactive Web framework (Spring WebFlux). Have a look at them and keep learning!

Afterword

In this book, we covered the main topics related to microservices architecture. We started with a look *inside* a Spring Boot application, traveling from an empty project to a microservice properly structured in layers. To build it, we followed a test-driven development approach.

The book tried to explain from the beginning why it's a good idea to start with a small monolith. Actually, it's an idea supported by many people very experienced with microservices—start with a single project, identify boundaries, and decide if it's worthwhile to split your functionality. What happens frequently is that it's difficult to understand the *why* if you never worked with microservices and only with monolithic applications. However, at this point in time, I'm pretty sure you understand the pain you might suffer if you go for microservices from scratch. Setting up the ecosystem without having a strong knowledge baseline will cause chaos, at the least. Service discovery, routing, load balancing, communication between services, error handling—it's important that you know what you'll face on your way *before* you start your adventure with microservices.

In this particular adventure, you built a web application to allow users to practice multiplication every day without any help, to train their brains. That was the first microservice, but the real challenge started when we introduced the second one: a service that reacts to events happening in our previous logic and calculates the score and assigns badges to make the application look like a game. At that point, the book covered some basics about *gamification* and applied it to our system using an event-driven pattern.

© Moises Macero 2017
M. Macero, *Learn Microservices with Spring Boot*,
https://doi.org/10.1007/978-1-4842-3165-4

Then we got deep into some core concepts of microservices, including how they can find each other with service discovery and apply load balancing to them when they scale up and down, how to route from the outside to the corresponding piece of the system using an API gateway, how to provide resilience using the circuit breaker pattern, etc. We made it practical, but I tried to put the focus on the concepts too. The reason is that nowadays you can find these patterns embedded in many cloud PaaS, including Cloud Foundry, Google App Engine, and Amazon AWS.

Some of those platforms will manage the microservice ecosystem for you: you just *push* your Spring Boot application to the cloud, set the number of instances and how they should be routed, and everything else is handled by the platform. *Pivotal's Cloud Foundry* even includes the same tools we used (Spring Cloud Netflix). However, you always need to understand what you're doing. Pushing your applications to the cloud without knowing what is happening behind the curtains is risky. If errors arise, it might be impossible for you to know which part of *the magic* (something that you don't understand) is not doing its job.

Finally, I stressed the importance of having a good test base in a system based on microservices. You saw how to implement end-to-end scenarios to protect your business flows using Cucumber and its human-friendly language, Gherkin.

This book doesn't cover *everything* you need to know to work with microservices. That would be impossible. There are some other important topics surrounding this type of architecture—containerization, centralized logging, continuous integration and deployment, etc. I recommend that you continue learning these topics following the same practical approach. You can keep evolving the architecture built in this book, focusing on the problems you want to solve and learning concepts incrementally, one by one.

I hope that, now that you've reached the end of the book, you have a better understanding of the topics and you can use them at work or in your personal projects. I've enjoyed writing this book a lot and, most importantly, I've learned along the way. Thanks.

Index

Microservices (*cont.*)
  concept of, 176
  domains isolation, 162–163, 165
  gamification (*see* Gamification)
  implementation, REST
    Client, 165–169
  patterns and PaaS, 263–264
  RabbitMQ (*see* RabbitMQ)
  reactive patterns and REST,
    160–161
  sending events
    business logic, 144–151
    data, 141–144
    dispatcher pattern, 128, 130,
     132–133
    gamification domain model,
     135–137, 139–140
    implementation, new
     gamification
     microservice, 134
    modeling, 125–127
    RabbitMQ configuration,
     122, 124–125
    REST API, 151, 153
  small monolith (*see* Small
    monolith approach)
  Spring AMQP, 121
Mini-monolith-first approach, 53

P, Q

Platform as a Service (PaaS),
  263–264
Polyglot systems, 207
Presentation layer, *see* REST API

R

RabbitMQ
  configuration, 122, 124–125
  defining, 120–121
  download and install, 173
  event handler, 157, 159
  RabbitMQConfiguration,
    154–157
  rabbitmq_management, 173
  and Spring AMQP, 121
  subscriber, 154
Refactoring
  multiplication-client, 68
  MultiplicationResultAttempt, 63
  MultiplicationResultAttempt
    Controller, 66–67
  MultiplicationResultAttempt
    ControllerTest, 67
  MultiplicationService
    Impl, 65–66
  MultiplicationServiceImpl
    Test, 64–65
REST API, 5, 306
  controllers, 151–153
  index.html, 54–55
  multiplication-client, 56–58
  MultiplicationController, 43, 47
  MultiplicationControllerTest, 44
  MultiplicationResultAttempt
    Controller, 49–50, 52
  MultiplicationResultAttempt
    ControllerTest, 50–52
  Spring MVC, 41
  styles, 55

Get the eBook for only $5!

Why limit yourself?

With most of our titles available in both PDF and ePUB format, you can access your content wherever and however you wish—on your PC, phone, tablet, or reader.

Since you've purchased this print book, we are happy to offer you the eBook for just $5.

To learn more, go to http://www.apress.com/companion or contact support@apress.com.

Apress®

Made in the USA
Columbia, SC
02 November 2020

23853364R00189